Praise for *Service Fanatics*

"*Service Fanatics* will become the gold standard on patient-centered care. Cleveland Clinic in all its glory, like many of the rest of us in healthcare, had lost its way with compassion and empathy. Dr. James Merlino in his role as the Clinic's Chief Experience Officer, along with CEO Toby Cosgrove and the rest of the healers at Cleveland Clinic, changed that by putting Patients First. Merlino's description of this journey is at times painful, raw, and brutally honest. *Service Fanatics* and its author exude passion, humility, integrity, and caring. It will make any organization better and is a must-read for everyone in healthcare."

—David T. Feinberg, MD, president of
UCLA Health System and
CEO of UCLA Hospital System

"Merlino gives a behind-the-scenes account of how Cleveland Clinic, traditionally known for medical excellence, transformed itself to put equal focus on the patient experience. It's a fascinating story on its own merits, but it's also the story of the future of healthcare. For all healthcare leaders who are (or those who soon will be) leading a similar transformation, this book will be an indispensable guide to the journey ahead."

—Dan Heath, coauthor of the
New York Times bestsellers
Made to Stick, Switch, and *Decisive*

"This book is a candid recounting of Cleveland Clinic's rocky, flawed journey toward creating world-class patient experience. James Merlino is painfully honest about the failures and mistakes along the way, even as he lays out a practical road map for change. This combination of candor, pragmatism, and hope is why Merlino has emerged as one of the most respected healthcare leaders in the country. *Service Fanatics* is invaluable for any hospital administrator determined to transform patient experience."

—Leah Binder, president and CEO
of The Leapfrog Group

"Driven by his experience as a family member, patient, and physician, Jim's passion has created a movement to refocus the healthcare system's design, process, and culture on the patient. With his colleagues at Cleveland Clinic, he has championed the effort to once again center care around the patient and has engaged healthcare leaders across the industry to embrace transparency in the spirit of improvement. Jim's commitment to his patients and empathy for their journey resonates on every page of this book. When we reflect on the major transformation of the industry, history will show that Jim Merlino and Cleveland Clinic were at the forefront of returning our healthcare system to the patient and helping us return to the noble cause that drew us all to careers in healthcare."

—Pat Ryan, CEO of Press Ganey

"It's an important work by the leading voice in patient experience. It's also a gripping personal narrative that changed my perspective on every doctor-patient interaction I've had in my life. . . . *Service Fanatics* is upfront about just how hard it is to change a culture so that it becomes truly customer-centric—then tells you how you can do it anyway. Merlino describes the challenges at Cleveland Clinic with an unsentimental eye, and he also provides detailed descriptions of what the leadership team did to overcome those challenges. . . . All in all, *Service Fanatics* is a great read that's also making me smarter about patient experience. If only all business books could bring those two elements together."

—Harley Manning, Forrester.com

"It is one thing for a leader to establish an organization-wide priority and quite another to achieve it. To many, Cleveland Clinic's rapid improvement in patient satisfaction scores appears nearly miraculous. Dr. Merlino's book offers a compelling and candid tale of how an already great hospital engaged its 43,000 employees to become even better. By detailing every step with candor and eloquence, this book explains precisely how the hospital achieved its gains—and, in so doing, offers invaluable lessons not only for healthcare leaders but also for anyone interested in how to achieve meaningful progress across any organization."

—Barbara R. Snyder, president of
Case Western Reserve University

"Anyone involved in healthcare will treasure Dr. Jim Merlino's book because it provides a candid, poignant look at patient care from both provider and patient perspectives. The stories and lessons around empathy and compassion are inspirational and help us think more clearly about the importance of the overall patient experience."

—Kurt Newman, MD, president and CEO
of Children's National Health System

"In this warts-and-all account, Jim Merlino describes how he and his Cleveland Clinic colleagues transformed a culture focused almost exclusively on clinical excellence into one that fully embraced the need to deliver a caring and empathic experience for people. In so doing, Merlino has created a comprehensive and methodical playbook for other healthcare organizations seeking to fulfill the same paramount objective: putting patients first."

—Susan Dentzer, senior policy adviser to
the Robert Wood Johnson Foundation

"The art and science of *caring* for others is remarkably highlighted in Dr. Merlino's splendid *Service Fanatics*. This is a must-read for all leaders or aspiring leaders in the business of delivering professional services. Dr. Merlino and his Cleveland Clinic colleagues *get it*!"

—Marc Byrnes, chairman
of Oswald Companies

"Cleveland Clinic is a great example of what healthcare should embody—full service to each and every patient. I've seen what their work and commitment have done, with a very important member of my family, my brother, and it's fantastic. Every medical venue should emulate their facilities as well as their superb and comprehensive services. Keep up the great work."

—Donald J. Trump

Service
Fanatics

Service Fanatics

HOW TO BUILD SUPERIOR PATIENT EXPERIENCE THE CLEVELAND CLINIC WAY

James Merlino, MD
Chief Experience Officer of Cleveland Clinic

New York   Chicago   San Francisco   Athens   London   Madrid
Mexico City   Milan   New Delhi   Singapore   Sydney   Toronto

1 2 3 4 5 6 7 8 9 0   DOC/DOC   1 2 0 9 8 7 6 5 4

ISBN   978-0-07-183325-7
MHID   0-07-183325-0

e-ISBN   978-0-07-183326-4
e-MHID   0-07-183326-9

McGraw-Hill Education books are available at special quantity discounts to use as premiums and sales promotions or for use in corporate training programs. To contact a representative, please visit the Contact Us pages at www.mhprofessional.com.

For my father, who showed me the other side

To Amy, for her unwavering support

To Toby and Joe, for never saying no and never doubting

Contents

Foreword

I've learned that people will forget what you said, people will forget what you did, but people will never forget how you made them feel.

—MAYA ANGELOU

n 2004, acclaimed heart surgeon Dr. Delos "Toby" M. Cosgrove became the CEO of Cleveland Clinic, an institution known for innovation and excellence in patient outcomes. As he transitioned from surgery to strategy, he was invited to speak to Harvard Business School students about the Cleveland Clinic model of care. During that address, he was challenged by a student who asked whether he taught empathy for patients at Cleveland Clinic. It is a story that Toby has shared over the years as a defining moment in his strategic thinking. Patients go home from the Clinic "well," but do they feel well cared for? The seed and the stake were planted for Patients First, Cleveland Clinic's defining purpose.

I am on the board of the Clinic, and Toby asked me to translate my business credentials in customer experience to help the Clinic with the patient experience by chairing a board-level committee on patient safety, quality, and experience and to work with the new chief experience officer, Dr. Jim Merlino. In my role as then vice chairman of community banking at KeyBank, I had embarked on a similar journey—to differentiate through the customer experience by putting the customer at the center of everything we do.

Jim Merlino is a rising star, whose passion for the patient is rooted in an experience with his ailing father, where he found himself on the "other side" of medical practices and outcomes. In the early days, Jim and I would meet to discuss ways to institutionalize the Clinic's nascent efforts in patient experience. The principles I had developed in banking on how to drive change and customer experience were relevant, but being involved in Cleveland Clinic's transformation around the patient opened my eyes and upped my game as well. And in the process of working together, Jim and I became friends.

Jim had no clear starting point and no clear definition of success. There were no playbooks or manuals on what to do. He launched a methodical internal and external process to learn best practices from a variety of industries, as well as understand and determine what success would look like for Cleveland Clinic.

It takes leadership to set the tone and to set aspirational goals for an institution. Together, Toby and Jim created the processes for organizational change and required and empowered all the employees of the Clinic—from physicians to service workers—to become caregivers. With no guidebook on how to take Patients First from aspirational goal to operational reality, the Clinic embarked on a journey of trial and error, success and failure, until the aspiration became a strategy and tactics were developed that allowed the Clinic to implement world-class patient experience. *Service Fanatics* is a testament to Jim's passion and work, but also to Toby Cosgrove and Cleveland Clinic.

A senior leader of another hospital once said, "We can't all be Cleveland Clinic." To which Jim responds, "Yes, you can."

Service Fanatics shows you how. It is the road map, rich with stories and examples, as well as tools and insights to operationalize the patient experience. Improving the patient experience is not only the right thing to do; it is an imperative in the changing world of regulation and law in American healthcare. But its message and content transcend healthcare. *Service Fanatics* provides pragmatic lessons and actionable takeaways for business professionals in many industries—mine included. In an era of content overload, it is a compelling and valuable read.

Beth E. Mooney
Chairman and CEO
KeyCorp

Preface

Dana Bernstein is a smart, energetic, beautiful 25-year-old woman out to conquer the world. She enchants everyone she meets. Dana is also an expert in understanding the world of healthcare: expert not because she's on the provider or delivery side of healthcare, but expert because she's lived on the patient side since she was three. In the past 22 years, Dana has had more interactions with doctors and nurses, more admissions to hospitals, and more procedures than most people have in a lifetime.

What gives Dana her expert credentials is a battle with Crohn's disease,[1] one of the two major bowel diseases characterized by inflammation, or in layman's terms, significant irritation and erosion of the bowel lining and walls. It's a disease in which the body's immune system essentially attacks its own organs. An estimated 1.4 million in the United States suffer from inflammatory bowel disease.[2] Not many are familiar with it, and there is no known cause or cure.

Crohn's disease represents a terrifying spectrum of possibilities. Some can live their entire lives with only very minor manifestations of it, while others develop significant, frequently recurrent, episodes involving the constant use of medications, multiple surgical procedures, and potential loss of the entire intestine, necessitating a small bowel transplant. Crohn's can affect any part of the intestinal tract and can lead to significant problems in just about every major organ system.

Dana lives at the extreme end of the spectrum. Since her diagnosis, she's had multiple operations and innumerable hospital admissions and procedures. If you sat and talked with her, you'd believe she's no different from anyone else her age. But if she shared her struggle with Crohn's, you'd learn that she has little of her intestines left, uses an ostomy, and receives daily nutritional support through a catheter threaded into her chest. Dana also struggles with managing chronic pain caused by extensive inflammation and the significant scarring from multiple surgeries. She's facing the possibility of a small bowel transplant, which is a daunting procedure. It will put her life in jeopardy, and she'll need more than just expert medical care to get through it.

By her own admission, Dana is not an undemanding patient. Aside from the complexities of her disease, she is very much the captain of her body. She and her mother, Cari Marshall, probably know as much about Crohn's disease as many of the physicians who've provided Dana's care, and Cari has dedicated her life to helping Dana fight her disease. Dana is an activated patient who's not afraid to be her own advocate. She and her mother don't just want information to make a decision; they want to be involved in how and why decisions are made.

But Dana also wants something more, and that's the reason she travels 2,000 miles for healthcare, while there may be experts who could treat her closer to home in Las Vegas. Dana wants her physician to be someone not only who is at the top of his field, but who brings compassion and humility to his work. She found that combination in Dr. Feza Remzi, chair of the Department of Colorectal Surgery at Cleveland Clinic.

In Dana's words, "I know I'm a tough patient, but I've been through a lot and know what works for me and what doesn't. I often feel when I challenge doctors, they don't want to engage and have a serious conversation with me about what's going on." She believes that Remzi cares for her as a patient, but also treats her like a friend. "He cares for me—I can feel it in the way he talks to me and the way he treats me," she says. "He actually yells at me sometimes, but that shows he cares."

Does considering a patient a friend cloud a doctor's judgment and objectivity? "Absolutely not!" explains Remzi. "I'm her physician and surgeon first, but is it too much for me to care for her as a person?" Remzi explains how this brings more to the table: "If caregivers feel personally engaged, they will be sharper and more in the moment." As a physician, he knows the boundaries. "I'll never compromise what's right for her care, but I'll always see myself as her partner and advocate in helping her to conquer this terrible disease. We are friends in the foxhole together. I have her back, and she helps me be a better doctor—she keeps me sharp."[3]

Remzi provides Dana with medical advice and treatment, but he also helps guide her and her family through the right decisions. Dana's mother describes Remzi as one of the most compassionate and caring people she has ever met, saying, "His empathy is real!" The family's trust and confidence in Remzi's medical ability is bolstered by his concern for Dana as a person, not just as a patient.

Is it truly possible to expect both high professional competency and compassionate care with a human connection? I had the honor of being a guest speaker at an advanced executive leadership course at Harvard Business School when we discussed this very question as part of a Cleveland Clinic case study. We were considering the patient experience, how it factored into the treatment of patients and whether there could be a financial return on investment to help drive these concepts across an organization. I posed a dilemma to the students: You're a patient needing heart surgery and have the choice of two surgeons. One is absolutely the best in the world by every measurable objective outcome, but she is mean and doesn't communicate well with patients or their families. She's a true technocrat who has no empathy or humanism. Your other choice is a surgeon renowned for compassion and empathy, but his outcomes, while within the standard of care, by reputation are not quite as good as the other surgeon's. Whom would you want to do your surgery?

Interestingly, the students were about equally divided in their choice. Some said they didn't care whether the surgeon ever talked to them, as long as the operation was a success with a great outcome. Others took what I call the more "humanistic" perspective: they wanted someone to care for them as a person as well as perform a competent operation, arguing that if the compassionate surgeon's outcomes were within the standard of care, that was good enough.

As a surgeon who has seen excellent, marginal, and poor surgeons up close, I used to believe that technical proficiency was the most important element of surgical care and that if I ever needed an operation, I would surely choose technical prowess over everything else, including whether the doctor talked to me. I have seen very nice and empathetic but technically challenged surgeons navigate terrible complications and avert liability by building strong connections with patients and families. This illustrates a fact that's often revealed in malpractice litigation: Doctors don't get sued because they are incompetent. They get sued because they don't communicate or build relationships with patients and families.

I wonder how the Harvard students would have responded if my colleague Shannon Philips, Cleveland Clinic's quality and safety officer, had first educated them about the culture of safety. Technically proficient but disruptive physicians actually create an environment that is unsafe and stifle other caregivers from stepping forward to protect patients. These physicians can actually have worse outcomes because they foster a culture of fear. I suspect the students who favored the technocrat might have reconsidered.

Being on the other side of healthcare, both as a patient and as a family member of a patient, changed my beliefs about what I want from a physician. Patients deserve—and should demand—a physician who is medically competent as well as empathetic and compassionate. I also believe that as healthcare leaders responsible for safeguarding quality medical delivery, we should work hard to ensure that we provide both.

Brian Bolwell, chair of Cleveland Clinic Taussig Cancer Institute, is, like Remzi, among the smartest physicians I know, and also a caring and compassionate human being. I was in his office one day, and he seemed subdued. I asked what was wrong, and he said, "A young woman I took care of for a long time just died. It's impossible not to be sad." She was not merely a patient to him; he knew about her life, shared a journey with her, and cared about her. If I am ever diagnosed with a terrible disease, I want physicians like Remzi and Bolwell to care for me. I want to have a connection with the persons treating me. I want to know that they care about me personally, that they are as invested in my recovery as I am. Yes, I demand that they be competent and objective, but I want to know that they will be there with me and for me. I don't want some brilliant technocrat to just perform a procedure and walk away without an afterthought as to how I will get back to my life. I want my doctors to know something about me as a person, listen to what I think, and understand that outside the hospital I have a life, a family, and friends. Why is this important? I want my doctors and other caregivers invested personally in my outcome.

Empathetic care that transcends the human condition is what I aim to provide to my patients and is the standard we should all expect for ourselves as patients. A personal investment in empathy and compassion by all caregivers is the foundation of the future for healthcare. We must align our organizations and people around patients and how we deliver care to them.

A focus on the patient experience has become a differentiator for Cleveland Clinic. Dana travels 2,000 miles for high-quality care and high-quality caring at our institution. Our alignment around the patient impacts everything we do, not only improving patient satisfaction, but ultimately enhancing our delivery of safe, high-quality care and high value. Any healthcare system in the world can and should adopt putting patients first as its primary purpose.

When we began our patient experience journey, there was no textbook or playbook telling us how to start. The healthcare scholarship doesn't often consider the competency of how to deliver care. Trial and error became our modus operandi. We created our own strategies and tactics, adopted some from others, and applied lessons from businesses outside healthcare. Our approach has been based on living the challenges at the front lines of a diversified and heterogeneous healthcare system with incredible patient needs and demands. Our physician champions, including me, still see patients. Our nurse champions are at the patients' bedside. This frontline involvement and commitment is one of the reasons we've been successful. You cannot fix the patient experience from a 50,000-foot strategic perspective; most of the work must be operationalized at the patient touch points and carried out by frontline caregivers.

From a practical standpoint, improvement required us to frame a strategy concisely and then focus on key elements that allowed us to implement it. Everything patients—and their families—see, do, and touch is considered by us as the patient experience.

This book focuses on how to think about the patient experience, how to define it, and the factors we feel are critical to enhance it. Improving patient-centeredness also impacts how we deliver safety and quality. These are important not just for patients, but for caregivers as well.

In the subsequent chapters, I describe how Cleveland Clinic's leadership determined to make the patient experience a priority, defined it, and set a strategy for improving it. I discuss the foundational elements of culture, physician involvement, and understanding patients. I share our execution successes and failures, including how we organize, recruit, train, and measure for service excellence; how Cleveland Clinic has evolved its culture and aligned its workforce around Patients First; and how we improved the critical element of physician communication. I convey my beliefs and experiences regarding cutting-edge issues such as making patients our partners in ensuring a quality experience and sharing approaches with caregivers worldwide so that patients everywhere can hope to receive better care.

I have written about Cleveland Clinic's journey because we have made a difference and our approach is working. It is just one of many possible approaches, and you may find that it can help your organization. And just as we have learned from a variety of different businesses outside of healthcare, I believe that our strategy and many tactics hold lessons for other businesses as well. Aligning a workforce around the customer is applicable to any business that has customers, which is every business.

No doubt some reading this book will look at parts of our organization and say that our approach is not functioning as well as we think. Improving the patient experience is hard work, and we still have a lot to do. But just as Cleveland Clinic historically has had relentless focus on medical excellence, there's no question that we now pair that with a relentless focus on improving the patient experience. We have gone from being among the lowest-rated hospitals in the country for patient experience metrics to among the highest.

This book is not meant to be a comprehensive resource for every patient experience tool available or a technical manual of all that we do. I discuss our strategy and many of our tactics, and I describe some of the roadblocks we encountered. If you peer under the hood of our organization, we look like most other healthcare systems—perhaps even like yours. We have the same needs and challenges, and we all face an uncertain future.

There are some elements unique to our journey that have granted us unusual success. Cleveland Clinic's appetite for innovation allowed this program to gain hold and flourish, giving us a head start. But at the time we began, external pressures were not as intense. Today, the forces pushing hospitals to get better are much stronger, so this should help others gain the foothold they need to climb the path of improvement.

It's my hope that you will find something in this book that can help your organization. Perhaps the book will reinforce that you are on the right path and provide you with a reassuring pat on the back. My goal is simple. If you deliver healthcare, you must think about how to align your organization around the patient. In such an environment, Remzi, Bolwell, and millions of other caregivers throughout the world can deliver high professional competency and compassionate care with a human connection. It is what patients like Dana Bernstein want. It is the right thing to do, and it should be the focus of healthcare. It is what you would want for yourself and your family.

Acknowledgments

would not be the person I am today without what my patients have given me since I started this journey called medicine. From the very first patient I saw as a medical student to the ones I treat today, they teach me, inspire me, and challenge me to think differently and to care more. They have taught me the gift of empathy, and it is an honor to have been a part of their lives in such a personal way. The same is true for the incredible people, my caregiver colleagues across healthcare, who share the profound responsibility of delivering care for people.

I would not be successful personally or professionally without the support and encouragement of my wife and best friend, Amy. She was at my side when this patient-centered epiphany occurred, and has supported me during my journey at Cleveland Clinic. Writing a book like this requires the sacrifice of nights and weekends; they were her sacrifices as well.

My father's name was Carmen, and I owe who I am to my family: my mother, Shirley, and my siblings, Sue and Tom.

Toby Cosgrove, CEO and president, and Joe Hahn, chief of staff of Cleveland Clinic, have given me this awesome opportunity to help shape an organization and start a movement. Toby's vision to drive the patient experience was a disruptive innovation in healthcare at a time when no one else was talking about it. Together, Toby and Joe have taken the Clinic to heights many thought not possible. They have never wavered in their support, and there is nothing I will ever be able to do to thank them.

Kelly Hancock, our executive chief nursing officer, has been my friend, confidant, and an early and critical ally in all our efforts to improve the patient experience at Cleveland Clinic. Our success belongs as much to her as it does to me. We would not have achieved what we have without her passion, support, determination, and keen instincts. She is an incredibly gifted leader highly respected not only in our organization, but in healthcare across the United States.

Feza Remzi is my clinical mentor, my friend, and the department chair of colorectal surgery. My first rotation during my fellowship was with him. He taught me the value of a personal connection with patients and is a role model for compassion and humanism. He got me back on track after my father died, and he was the first to enchant me with what Cleveland Clinic is about. I am at Cleveland Clinic because of him, and I will be forever in his debt.

Brian Bolwell, chair of Cleveland Clinic Taussig Cancer Institute, is likely more responsible than anyone else for my holding the position of chief experience officer, encouraging me to persevere during the search process. He is a remarkable leader from whom I learned never to fear speaking up for what's right, especially when it concerns the patient.

Ananth Raman has been my mentor, friend, and, more important, patient experience soul mate from the beginning. He has tutored me in the nuances of execution and continually challenges me to think differently regarding opportunities we face so we may find success in what we do. He has been a constant and consistent navigational beacon in this journey.

David Longworth began his career at Cleveland Clinic and, after 10 years at the Clinic, joined a Boston health system. He returned to Cleveland Clinic 10 years later as chair of medicine. He is my barometer of the "before and after" comparison, constantly reassuring me that where we stand today is better than where we stood yesterday. David has a great mind and has been my muse for many ideas about the patient experience.

Adrienne Boissy has been by my side on this journey from day one. She is passionate, committed, and driven to provide what is needed and right for patients. Her incredible work has enhanced our physician culture and likely will effect meaningful change in the practice of medicine worldwide.

Cindy Hundorfean, our chief administrative officer, is responsible for leading the clinical enterprise. This is the engine of Cleveland Clinic, and there are few people whom I have ever met who can boil down such an enormous operation into something manageable. Cindy has been an important mentor from the beginning. If I owe Brian Bolwell the credit for keeping me in the race for the job, I owe Cindy credit for keeping me in the job. She has been an important source of encouragement, guidance, and support throughout this journey.

Linda McHugh, executive administrator to the CEO and Board of Governors, has been at Cleveland Clinic her entire career, most of it at Toby Cosgrove's side. She knows the organization's history well and has lived through and assisted in leading our tremendous growth and success, including helping to propel the heart institute to the number one position in the world. Through my years as chief experience officer, she has been a guide, mentor, and friend. I am indebted to her for reading the entire manuscript and providing her historical, candid, and objective advice.

Beth Mooney, chairman and CEO of KeyCorp, is a member of Cleveland Clinic's Board of Directors and chairman of its Safety, Quality, and Patient Experience Committee. She is an incredible leader who rose to the top in part by differentiating on the customer experience. She taught me how to think and act like a professional and, from the very beginning, guided me in framing our capability, enhancing it for short-term success, and innovating to drive long-term differentiation. I am indebted to her for her critical review of the manuscript and for writing the wonderful Foreword to this book.

We developed our international patient experience footprint with Bill Peacock, Jim Benedict, Rob Stall, and the late Bill Ruschhaupt, MD, from operations. They taught me volumes about international healthcare and challenged us to think out of the box to meet the needs of other cultures.

Marc Harrison and I both started in the Clinic's C-suite at about the same time; he with much more healthcare leadership experience than I. He is a smart and gifted leader who personally knows the other side of healthcare better than most. He was a beacon in the early fog and has taught me the importance of skepticism, healthy debate, accountability, and integrity.

Tom Graham serves as our chair of innovations. He has a brilliant mind that brings unmatched business acumen to the world of medicine, and he and his team have taught us how to take our success and push it into the market.

I find it a little amusing to tell people "I have an editor." Casey Ebro from McGraw-Hill has shepherded this work from the beginning. Her incredible mind and engaging and inquiring personality match no one I have met. She has made me smarter and this book better.

Writing was never my strength in school, and there was always something attractive to me about the unintelligibility of a doctor's handwriting. Beth Brumbaugh shaped my words and made this book readable. I am indebted to her for taking this work and making it concise for all to understand. She is extremely talented, and from her, I have become better as well.

A colleague of mine often remarks that leaders are not successful without a great team of people to support them, and my work in the patient experience is no exception. I have been successful because the people around me are gifted and exponentially smarter than I: Jennifer Fragapane, Carmen Kestranek, Stacie Pallotta, Mary Linda Rivera, Tom Vernon, and Donna Zabell.

We become better leaders through a variety of methods, but the best way is to acquire the skills and attributes of those around us whom we respect and admire. I am honored and fortunate to work with some of the brightest and most talented leaders in healthcare, including my colleagues on the Clinic's executive team, our medical and nursing leadership, and our administrative leaders across the organization. From you, I have learned much, and together we have created success.

There are many people who have worked very hard to transform this organization around the patient and create a world-class patient experience; I cannot possibly list and thank everyone individually. But this book is about you, and the tremendous achievement we have accomplished is your achievement—thank you!

Finally, Toby often talks about the incredible platform that is Cleveland Clinic—meaning that bright, innovative people working in this incredible organization create synergies that allow success beyond what any one person can bring on his or her own. Toby is right! Anyone who believes that what happens here is the result of one person is mistaken. The Clinic provides a unique, innovative platform to drive collective success; it is an intangible that is hard to describe, but one that produces results that are real!

Chapter 1

Transformed by the Patient Experience

n 2004, I was a colorectal fellow at Cleveland Clinic, in my final year of medical training. The institution had one of the preeminent colorectal programs in the world—and still does. It had among the highest case volumes in the world, as well as several leading colorectal surgeons, including department chairman Victor W. Fazio, a world-renowned, pioneering colorectal surgeon considered by many to be one of the grand masters in the field. Training under Fazio would not only mold me into a great surgeon; it would virtually guarantee an exceptional career. The day I was accepted into the fellowship program, I was ecstatic, knowing that I was joining one of the best programs in the world, if not *the* best. All of my hard work and sacrifice from years of training had paid off.

Six months into my fellowship, my 77-year-old father noticed blood in his urine. He was quite healthy, save for minor high blood pressure. He had an office cystoscopy, which confirmed multiple lesions in his bladder. At first, Dad did not want to come to Cleveland Clinic, preferring to be treated at a community hospital closer to home. I was insistent that he be treated at Cleveland Clinic, for several reasons. We had a world reputation as a top hospital and had the number two–ranked U.S. urology program. More important, consistent with Cleveland Clinic's reputation for clinical innovation, we were providing minimally invasive urological surgery, clearly preferable for a 77-year-old.

Dad was admitted to the hospital on December 15 for a biopsy, to be discharged later the same day. His biopsy evolved into the removal of the lesions, as they were thought to be superficial—good news, because this would prevent a more invasive bladder resection. The procedure generally went as planned; however, Dad's abdomen was distended afterward, necessitating a small incision in it to ensure that his bladder had not been perforated. This complication required him to stay in the hospital for observation. I went to the postanesthesia care unit shortly after his surgery. He was still not quite recovered, but he opened his eyes when I touched him. He was having some difficulty breathing and still had an oxygen mask on his face. He pulled the mask down, and I reassured him that everything was OK. He looked at me and asked, "Am I going to die?"

My father's stay in the hospital was rocky. He was admitted to one of the surgery floors and suffered continuous respiratory problems, requiring supplemental oxygen and respiratory treatments. He developed an ileus, where his bowels were not functioning, and required a nasogastric tube, which is placed through the nose into the stomach to decompress air and remove fluid. I walked into my father's room as one of the staff colorectal surgeons was placing the nasogastric tube. I had performed this procedure hundreds of times on patients, but I had never seen it done from the perspective of a family member. It was difficult. Dad was clearly distressed, and I could see desperation on his face. He looked over at me, and I had to leave the room, unable to bear seeing him in pain. I was traumatized. My father, whom I viewed as a man of strength and determination, had been reduced to his most vulnerable state, and I had no idea how to help him. I wanted to cry.

What was supposed to be an ambulatory procedure evolved into a several-day stay that ended the night of December 22 with him arresting in his hospital room and dying. The complications that caused him to be admitted or that took his life were no one's fault in particular. While an autopsy was not performed, Dad likely succumbed to either a heart attack or a pulmonary embolism. His last days in the hospital, however, were wrenching, both for him and for our family. I am certain Dad died believing that Cleveland Clinic was the worst healthcare institution in the world. I know my family would not disagree.

His experience during those seven days was a test case for how *not* to manage a patient's experience. It's ironic now, because we didn't use the words *patient experience* back in 2004, but when you dissect his hospital stay, you can absolutely overlay a template of the factors that today we consider important to patients. Dad complained about pushing the call button and the nurses responding slowly or not at all. When he was finally able to eat, he ordered menu items that did not appear on his food tray. He wanted to go for walks, but there was no one to help him. Physical therapists were supposed to see him every day but did not. Probably most difficult for me, the physician covering his stay did not round on him every day. His care was managed primarily by the urology house staff.

I vividly remember the night Dad died, a memory indelibly seared into my mind. It was three days before Christmas, and I had come home late after shopping and gone to bed. I heard the phone ringing but tried to ignore it because I was exhausted and thought it probably wasn't important. I finally answered the call. A urologist colleague and friend of mine who had helped take care of Dad was calling from Florida. Away for the holidays, he had been alerted to the situation by the house staff. Because of our friendship, he wanted to be the one to break the news: "Jim, I'm really sorry, but they lost him." He told me that Dad had arrested and they were unable to bring him back. My friend didn't know what had happened. If you've never experienced such a call, there is nothing I can say that will describe it.

My brother picked me up, and along with my mother and sister, we drove to the hospital around midnight in one of the worst snowstorms in years. Dad was the closest family member I've ever lost, and the drive was surreal. What actually happened had not sunk in. I think we believed that we would get to the hospital and learn this was a terrible misunderstanding. But it wasn't.

When we arrived at the hospital, we were taken to his room. His body lay on the bed. Everything else had been removed, and the nurses had covered him up. They spoke with us briefly. A resident from the primary service, who looked very tired, was on call and answered questions as best he could. We believed we were a pretty strong family that could cope with anything, not realizing how much of a fallacy that was at a time like that. The nurses tried their best, but they just could not supply the medical information we sought: Why? What went wrong? Wasn't he getting better?

Someone from mortuary services was available and delivered a very mechanical recitation of our next steps, including inquiring whether we wanted an autopsy and who should be contacted about the final arrangements. It seemed highly impersonal that we were being asked who would take care of the arrangements just after we'd been informed, in the middle of the night, that Dad had unexpectedly died. Arrangements? Seriously?

Finding There Was an Other Side to Healthcare

This experience with my father was the first time someone very close to me became ill with a serious disease. Even though I was a physician and a current trainee of the organization, I found myself grappling with emotions and beliefs that I had not previously felt because never before had I sat on the "other side" of healthcare. Of course, I had seen my share of serious illness and witnessed many people die. I'd had *that* conversation with a lot of family members, but I'd never taken much time to consider what it was like to be on the receiving end of such heartbreaking news. This painful personal experience made me realize that patients and families deserve much more compassion and humanism than the healthcare workforce appeared to be capable of delivering at such a difficult time. And if Cleveland Clinic wasn't able to adequately and consistently "check the box" on delivery of compassion and empathy when someone died, when *were* we doing it?

As a member of that healthcare workforce—a doctor—my entire education on how to treat patients thus far had been based on observation. It was essentially on-the-job skills training, observing the caregivers who taught me. That must be the way patients should be treated. After all, I was taught by some of the best in the world! Many cautioned about getting too close to patients, advising me, "Don't get emotionally attached, as it will cloud your objectivity." I was taught to be a consummate professional: objective, detached, thoughtful. In medical school, we were told that touching the patient was an important sign that you cared. But some physicians cringed when patients or their families reached out to hug them. A faculty member said that if a family member touched *your* arm, "Stare at her and stop talking until she removes her hand."

Physicians like Fazio and Remzi (introduced in the Preface) touched and hugged patients all the time—it was part of their magnetism. I suspect that many trainees mimic the behaviors of the people with whom they most closely identify.

Healthcare is not always humanistic; caregivers are not always compassionate; we don't always display empathy. Just as patients should expect to have consistent and standard-of-care reproducible medical care, they deserve and should demand a consistent approach, but medical training is often contradictory.

A diligent trainee, I had planned to model the behaviors of my teachers. But after my father's experience, I knew that the way we had been taught was wrong. There was something missing. I decided I would be different—I had to be. While I had not yet started to practice medicine independently and could probably not articulate how I should practice, I knew that this experience would forever steer me going forward. I would take much more time to focus on the humanity of the patient and the environment in which I practiced.

Dad's death was a wake-up call, reminding me why I had gone into medicine in the first place. Medicine is not about treating patients. It's about taking care of *people*—people who have lives and loved ones, with unique identities, hobbies, passions, successes, and failures—with a history. Patients are *not* objects, numbers, or diseases. Patients are people we encounter in what is frequently the most challenging and difficult time in their lives. And everyone employed in healthcare delivery should not have to go through an experience like mine to understand why patient-centeredness is important.

Determining to Leave Cleveland Clinic

The month before my dad died, I was offered a coveted staff position in Cleveland Clinic's colorectal surgery department. This was an exceptional opportunity. Fazio informed me that in his 35-year tenure as department head, he had offered staff positions to only two fellows right out of training, and I was one. Having set my heart on staying in Cleveland, I was fortunate to have also been offered positions at two competing local healthcare organizations. When the official offer from Cleveland Clinic arrived on my desk, there was little question where I would practice. I could barely contain my excitement. But after my experience on the other side of patient care, I was thinking very differently about my decision and career plans. I wanted to practice with a strong focus on establishing relationships with patients and their families. My father's experience greatly changed my perception of Cleveland Clinic and whether I could achieve such a practice in this environment.

The first months after his death were very hard for me for a couple of reasons. First, I felt like I had failed my father in some way, that if I had paid closer attention to his care, perhaps I could have altered the outcome somehow. My guilt was overwhelming. I was the physician son who should have done more. Second, I started 2005 on a new service within our department, paired with a physician who had a notorious reputation for bullying house staff. I thought that my strong work ethic, aptitude for building relationships, and ability to get along with people would carry me through the two months on his service. I was wrong. The inappropriate treatment, which consisted of very personal bullying and insults about my professional competence, began on day one.

Driving to work every day, I was sick with fear that I'd be fired for being incompetent and that my career would be over. Intellectually, I knew this was not true and that I was experiencing some departmental rite of passage. But emotionally, I was eviscerated by the constant, capricious bullying. What made it worse was that everyone knew it was going on, that it had happened to many others before me, and no one did anything to stop it. A culture of fear permeated the department around this individual, and the commonly held belief was that you just had to grin and bear it. While I had witnessed bullying behavior in my residency, this was the first time it had been directed at me. It was very personal. The experience was degrading and emotionally draining. I transitioned off the service with my confidence as a surgeon shattered.

The fellow who followed me experienced the same oppression to the point that she broke down in the operating room, scrubbed out of the surgery, and went to the chairman's office to tender her resignation. She was a top surgeon who had come from Great Britain to do a yearlong training at one of the best programs in the world, but flabbergasted by the treatment she received, she threatened to quit and return home. She was removed from the surgeon's service, but there was no formal action against the surgeon.

My bullying experience was the second strike against Cleveland Clinic. My father's death had reawakened the empathy in me, and I was shocked by his poor experience in the organization. Now I had been terribly bullied as a member of the house staff. There was no way I would practice medicine like this. There must be a better way to treat patients and each other. I informed Fazio that I would not be accepting his offer and would join MetroHealth Medical Center instead. I believed that Cleveland Clinic was an evil place that treated patients poorly and fostered an environment in which people did not work together or support one another. I could not wait to walk out the door on June 30, 2005. When my fellowship concluded, I left Cleveland Clinic what I thought was for good.

You Stop Seeing Patients as People in Medical School

I was no stranger to choosing the unexpected path. I did not follow the traditional track of high school, college, and medical school. I was what's known as a "bent arrow" going into medical school, not taking the straight route. While I had always wanted to be a doctor, my original undergraduate degree was in business administration. From my high school days, I had worked in public service and had been involved with political campaigns, which influenced my initial educational choice.

Enthralled by government service and administrative management, I found public advocacy and political campaigns intoxicating. But there was a downside to politics. I never quite felt that I was doing anything to benefit people or that I was making a meaningful contribution to humanity. After five years, I reevaluated my career trajectory and ultimately decided to pursue my dream of being a physician.

I had to go back to school to take science prerequisites before applying to medical school. I was accepted into Case Western Reserve University (CWRU) School of Medicine. It was my first choice, because I wanted to stay in my hometown of Cleveland, but also because the school had a unique curriculum. CWRU pioneered early patient exposure: new first-year students were required to follow a pregnant or geriatric patient. This was believed to make medical education more patient-centered.

I remember my nervousness and apprehension the first day I met my patient: young, single, and pregnant. I followed her through prenatal care and was with her the night she delivered. At the hospital, she was not progressing and the fetus began to exhibit signs of distress. She was rushed for an emergency C-section. Fortunately, both the baby and mother did fine. When I visited them the next day, she thanked me for being there for her. I was the only person she knew during her delivery, and I had seen her through the entire event. She admitted that she had been terrified and that it meant a lot to her that I was present. It was a moment that confirmed my calling for me: I was here to help people.

During my first two years of medical school, most students spent just a few days learning how to interview patients, chiefly how to take comprehensive medical histories. I was fortunate to be one of six students selected for a special program sponsored by Drs. Susan and James Carter. Susan was an oncologist, and James was an internist and former chairman of medicine at MetroHealth Medical Center. They felt that in-depth exposure to patients early in training would strengthen students' compassion and empathy. Once a week for two years, we trucked over to Metro and spent time with the Carters, discussing physical diagnosis skills, practicing taking histories, and examining actual patients.

During the final two years of medical school, the clinical years, there was little time to cover compassionate care delivery, empathy, or much of the human side of medicine. The work and pace ramped up, and like all medical students, we were thrown into the rat race of hospital floors. We were eager to see patients and act like real doctors. Subjects such as empathy and humanism were the furthest things from our minds, displaced by checking labs, running around for reports, and getting "scut," or daily tasks, done for the house staff.

I ultimately chose general surgery for my residency. I was captivated by the ability to "fix" problems for people. Surgeons can make a patient better. They do not manage chronic disease, from which patients are never quite cured. This aspect was very appealing.

I trained in surgical residency when there were few of the regulations that are in effect today. There were no work hour restrictions, and residents would spend up to 20 hours a day in the hospital, often on call multiple days in a row. We became experts at getting things done. We came in early in the morning, rounded on 20 patients as fast and efficiently as we could, checked labs, put in orders, and reported to the OR by 7:15 a.m. We operated all day and rounded on the same 20 patients, plus a few more, before we went home. We would eat, sleep, wake up the next morning, and do it all over again. We were lucky if we were off one Sunday a month. We were there to take care of patients, assist with surgery, and try to learn as much as possible. It was exhausting, often dehumanizing work.

While the program I trained in was benign relative to other surgical training programs, there still were some attending surgeons who were oppressive and just outright mean and nasty to virtually everybody, especially the house staff. This behavior surprised and shocked me. Coming from the world of public and business administration, I had never before witnessed such childish and narcissistic behavior. These doctors who were supposedly focused on care were driven by ego. What kind of world had I entered? I thought we were supposed to take care of people.

After years of training under these conditions, we stopped seeing patients as people. The patient-centered experience I had during my first two years of medical school was gone. Patients were not people; they were diseases that needed to be treated. They became "the small bowel obstruction in the emergency department," or the "SWM with the gunshot wound." Patients and family members who asked too many questions were annoying, and anyone who challenged us was met with aggression. We didn't see our colleagues as people, either. Instead of wanting to work as a team or help each other improve, we mocked what we thought was others' incompetence. On pediatric surgery during the fourth month of my internship, my chief resident informed me, "If you don't make a pediatrician cry during this rotation, you won't pass." I was told by attending physicians that if I could not get a patient's diagnosis in three questions or less, I was stupid.

Did my medical training change me? It certainly did! In my drive to become an exceptional surgeon, I had partially forgotten the reason I went into medicine in the first place, which was to care for and help people. My fellowship year at Cleveland Clinic was a searing reminder and rousing wake-up call that I needed to change course.

A Pioneer in the Patient Experience

At the conclusion of my fellowship, determined to follow a more patient-centered approach, I began my practice at MetroHealth Medical

Center, the public hospital for Cuyahoga County in northeastern Ohio. I made sure I got to know all of my patients personally. I made it a practice in follow-up conversations to ask for an update about something I remembered about my patients as individuals. I routinely rounded on them twice a day and called when I was unable to do so. I called family members when we missed seeing one another at the hospital. Half of my patients were on Medicaid or uninsured, but everyone got my cell phone number. These were practices that many of the doctors at Metro followed.

I was the only colorectal-trained surgeon in my group. When you're responsible for finding your own patients, you learn very quickly the power of relationships and the fact that they are often driven by the experience you provide to referring physicians and patients. High-quality care isn't much of a competitive differentiator when you're in the backyard of an organization perceived as among the premier institutions in the world. But being superior at providing the care around the care—improving the patient experience—was a critical differentiator for me in competing against the giant Cleveland Clinic.

I also leveraged the "other" customer in the market, physicians. Federal law prohibits financially incentivizing referrals, but I "incentivized" them by providing better service. There's an old adage in private practice that physicians get more patients by being affable, available, and accessible, and I strove to be all three. I visited providers in the community to ensure they knew who I was and the type of care I would give their patients, and I communicated comprehensively with them about their patients. My volume of new colorectal surgery patients tripled, as word of mouth drove more referrals—referrals that likely would have gone to Cleveland Clinic. The county hospital was successfully differentiating experience against one of the top colorectal programs in the world.

Cleveland Clinic Gets a New Leader

For the next several years, I stayed in close touch with my fellowship clinical mentor, Feza Remzi. He kept me regularly informed about changes at Cleveland Clinic, and he often remarked how the organization was transforming itself for the better under the leadership of Delos M. "Toby" Cosgrove, who assumed the position of president and CEO midway through my 2004 fellowship year. Cosgrove had identified patient-centeredness as one of his strategic priorities and launched an effort to march Cleveland Clinic in that direction. I remember his initial efforts during my fellowship: He had the organization adopt a "Patients First" motto. He later established an Office of Patient Experience and hired a C-level executive, the chief experience officer (CXO), to lead it. Fledgling patient-centered programs were begun.

Cleveland Clinic Gets a Second Chance

In 2008, when I had been at Metro for almost three years, Remzi called to say he was going to apply for the chairmanship of colorectal surgery, recently vacated by Fazio, who had been named chairman of the Digestive Disease Institute. Remzi asked me to help him prepare for the search committee presentation, saying that if he were successful, he would hope to recruit me back to Cleveland Clinic.

Remzi was aware of what I had been doing at Metro to build my practice by focusing on relationships. He had a similar vision: to differentiate Cleveland Clinic's colorectal surgery department with service to patients and their physician partners in the community. Historically, the department had been successful because referring physicians simply sent over patients. Remzi wanted to build and improve relationships with physician practices all over the state and country to differentiate on service. He was my mentor and friend, so of course I agreed to help him prepare to secure the chairmanship. But I said I would never come back to Cleveland Clinic.

The chairmanship search took eight months, and Remzi and I talked nearly every week. He reiterated his recruitment pitch to me multiple times, and I always declined. But I was becoming intrigued. Remzi is a passionate and compassionate doctor and human being. I could not completely dismiss and ignore the perspectives he was sharing about the changes at Cleveland Clinic because I knew we had similar beliefs regarding a patient-centered medical practice. And Remzi was truly energized about what was growing possible under Cosgrove's leadership.

When Remzi called to tell me that he had been selected as chairman, he offered me one more chance to come back. He pledged a culture of service and respect and unwavering support of the patient-centered initiatives that I believed important. With that promise in hand, I said yes.

I rejoined Cleveland Clinic as a colorectal surgeon in 2009 with trep-idation, but hope. In honor of my father and our family's experience, I'd give it another try. I came back with the aspiration to evangelize other doctors in our department with what I'd learned in my patient-centered private practice. I came back the son who could not make a difference in the care of his father, but who would try his utmost to make a difference for future Cleveland Clinic patients and their families. Little did I know where that decision would lead.

I busied myself with patient care while launching some patient expe-rience–related programs within the department and then across our Digestive Disease Institute. In 2010, seven months after I returned, I was recommended as a possible candidate for the position of CXO. I had had no idea that the position had become vacant, and I was initially not inter-ested. When I was contacted for an interview, I assumed that the organi-zation had already picked a successor and that it was just going through the motions.

During my interview with Cosgrove, he asked why I thought the patient experience was important. I told him the story of my father and said that I did not think anyone else should die in our hospital believing it is the worst place in the world for patients. He was stunned—but it was the truth. He asked me how we should improve, and I said I wasn't quite sure. I asked him the same question, and he had a similar answer. We agreed to figure it out together.

Patients First as True North

magine the practice of medicine a hundred years ago: a time before antibiotics, complicated imaging, and the advent of miracle drugs that cure disease or at least significantly alter its course. There's a picture I use in presentations of a solo practitioner walking through a farmyard carrying the iconic black medical bag. Most of the medical miracles of a hundred years ago were contained in that black bag, but most of the healing that doctors did rested in the hands that carried the bag and the relationships and interactions that the physician had with patients and families.

As the leading early-twentieth-century physician, researcher, teacher, and humanitarian Francis Weld Peabody observed to a group of Harvard University medical students in 1927, "The good physician knows his patients through and through, and his knowledge is bought dearly. Time, sympathy, and understanding must be lavishly dispensed, but the reward is to be found in that personal bond."[1] Physicians and nurses of that day would deliver whatever medicine they had and dispense whatever care they could, but for the most part, they were providing comfort and compassion. They talked with patients and families, and they touched people, giving them reassurance and hope when there may have been little.

When I consider how we deliver medicine today, I think of my operating room or an intensive care unit. Both are filled with teams of highly trained professionals working with the best medical technology on the planet: the practice of medicine has evolved from an individual pursuit to a team sport. When I was an intern, patients who had an inguinal hernia repair often stayed overnight in the hospital. Today they spend a few hours in the postanesthesia care unit. Inpatients today are older and sicker and have multiple medical problems. We often note that large tertiary-care hospitals around the country are becoming gargantuan intensive care units.

Patients First as Founding Principle

Cleveland Clinic was founded close to a hundred years ago, when four solo practitioners with their black bags determined to form a unit to care for patients. Beginning with its unique group practice model in 1921, the organization differentiated itself on innovation, one of the key drivers of Cleveland Clinic's success today. Coronary angiography was invented here in 1958, and it revolutionized the treatment of heart disease. This was soon followed by the first cardiac bypass surgery in 1967. These and other innovations helped Cleveland Clinic grow in size and renown, bringing patients from all over the world and driving a high volume of procedures that further enhanced its reputation as a clinical and academic powerhouse. Today, 14 medical and surgical specialties rank in the top 1, and the hospital overall is ranked number four in the country according to *U.S. News & World Report*. The organization's focus on clinical excellence and its unique model of medicine have brought it to the ranks of greatness.

But over the years, Cleveland Clinic's singular concentration on clinical outcomes caused it to lose its way from the tenets of its founders, who believed that the *patient* was the most important part of the organization. While very good at medical care, the organization had lost some of its caring. Missing in the orchestration of complexity and high-pitched care was often the human touch. Cleveland Clinic was recognized for clinical excellence, but it was not known as a place to be cared for as a human being. Nor was it known for being a collegial unit as the founders had envisioned. My own experience was testament to that. Something needed to change.

Patients First as New CEO Motto

That change process began when Cosgrove became CEO in 2004. One of his first efforts was to immerse himself in what he describes as "CEO school."[2] He consulted and spent time with business experts such as Jack Welch, past chairman and CEO of General Electric; Michael E. Porter, the Bishop William Lawrence University Professor at the Institute for Strategy and Competitiveness at Harvard Business School; and others. Among the compelling issues that Cosgrove identified through this schooling was the need for healthcare to return the customer—the patient—to chief focus.

Shortly thereafter, Cosgrove introduced the "Patients First" motto. His visionary goal was simple: for everyone in the organization to have a clear understanding why they come to work every day and why Cleveland Clinic exists. The single most successful move in transforming the patient experience at Cleveland Clinic was to align the organization around Patients First.

Like any other business, healthcare institutions exist for their customers. As one of Cleveland Clinic's founders, William E. Lower, said, "A patient is the most important person in the organization."[3] Without patients, there would be no hospitals, no healthcare jobs, and nothing for us to do.

We in healthcare might not like to refer to our patients as customers, but patients are indeed customers before they become patients. And patients don't just need our services. They come to us at their most vulnerable and often at the most frightening time in their lives, and they put those lives in our hands. Patients expect us to provide comfort and healing in a compassionate environment, to be concerned for their emotional and spiritual needs as well as their medical care.

Is there any more intensely focused service industry than healthcare? Every decision in the organization must first consider what is best for patients. This is the idea behind the Patients First motto and the reason Cosgrove chose it. Introducing a motto as a first step may appear to be superficial. However, it was neither simple nor insignificant. By introducing the Patients First motto, Cosgrove created an important early talking point and simple strategic statement of why the organization exists.

Patients First would provide the rallying point to align the organization's culture, to set the organization's purpose, to serve as a burning platform for change, and to be a strategic imperative. Patients First would become our "true north," our reason for existing as an organization, our navigational reckoning.

I remember when the new motto was introduced. Cosgrove had been CEO for just a couple of months, and an internal campaign was launched around the concept of Patients First. Everyone in the organization was issued Patients First lapel pins, which we all wore as dutiful employees. Patients First was widely communicated across the organization, and it became part of our branding. We still wear the lapel pins.

At first, a lot of people were skeptical. I recall walking with a colleague down one of the skyways that connect our buildings, joking that the new motto was superfluous. "We are doctors. When do we not put the interests of our patients first?" In our sleep-deprived and overworked state, we ridiculed the motto. And we were not the only ones poking fun; many frontline employees mocked the new motto as well. Every time something didn't work or a patient ran afoul of a hospital process, people would blurt out "Patients First." I'm not sure anyone truly believed this was an important effort that would revolutionize Cleveland Clinic.

Many staff members and physicians even poked fun at what they perceived as Cosgrove's hypocrisy. People would make comments such as, "Have you ever met the guy? He's far from Patients First." They talked about Cosgrove's own behavior as a physician and how he often would not see patients after surgery, relying on his team members, who would make excuses for why he was not in the postoperative environment. One of his patients, a physician from another hospital system, remarked to me several years later that he actually got to meet Cosgrove after his operation. He relayed this excitedly, having heard that Cosgrove never rounded on patients after surgery.

Although Cosgrove didn't routinely appear to be patient-centered does not mean that he didn't care about patients. Quality technical care was his patient focus. He recalled, "During my training, 10 percent of patients were dying during heart surgery. I focused on fine-tuning what I was doing in order to bring down the mortality rate. I didn't spend much time talking to patients or thinking about their feelings. I didn't think about society, the whole patient, or how an organization works. All I did was heart surgery—all day, every day. I spent my life in pursuit of technical excellence."

He shared a story with me about when he was in training as a resident. "Our goal was to keep people alive. Patients were happy if they even survived heart surgery, let alone thinking about how they were treated as human beings. . . . Imagine our perspective—we were around death every day. During my time at Boston Children's, five children died in one day! . . . Do you think we didn't develop a coping mechanism that shut off our emotional side of care delivery?"[4]

Patients accepted his remoteness as a trade-off for his expert surgical skills and anticipated high-quality outcomes. These are facts that Cosgrove freely admits today—and adamantly states are not the right way to practice medicine. Introducing the Patients First motto launched an incredible transformation, not just for Cleveland Clinic, but for the new CEO as well.

Patients First as Organizational Alignment

It might seem intuitive that service-oriented businesses, especially in healthcare, would understand the need to put customers at the center of everything they do and even message it with a motto, but this is not the case. We've all experienced service failures, when it felt like we were the least important part of the equation. Think about the service businesses in your daily interactions. How many demonstrate the importance of customers?

An ongoing study by Watermark Consulting illustrates the point.[5] Each year, the firm analyzes total returns for two model stock portfolios composed of the best and worst publicly traded companies in Forrester Research's annual Customer Experience Index.[6] Watermark calls the top 10 companies customer experience leaders and the bottom 10 customer experience laggards. Similar to Cleveland Clinic's Patients First philosophy, everything that the leaders do is aligned around the customer. Customer experience laggards are the opposite. Since 2007, Watermark has analyzed the stock performance of the leaders and laggards against the S&P 500 Index. On average, the leaders generated a total return three times higher. They also performed more than five times better than the laggards. The conclusion is simple: companies with alignment around customers create greater shareholder value.

It would seem logical that all hospitals share a common patient focus, but most do not. Alignment around patients is discussed or even bragged about, but often there is no accountability or management, and if you evaluate these hospitals' operations, there is no evidence of alignment around the patient.

The purpose of Cleveland Clinic's motto and focus is not about care delivery, nor is it about making patients happy. It's about alignment: getting everyone to put patients at the center of everything we do, always thinking about what is right for the patients—and their families.

Initially, many Cleveland Clinic employees viewed the Patients First initiative as a superficial marketing ploy. But our rejection and mocking of the concept illustrated Cleveland Clinic's failures as an organization and reinforced the need for transformation. If we could not understand or take seriously the importance of a patient-centered focus, regardless of whether or not we felt the CEO believed it, what was the point of being in the business of taking care of people? In healthcare, adopting a Patients First alignment should be a mandatory part of your brand. It is not a gimmick or a marketing ploy; it is a cultural underpinning.

Recently, someone asked me to defend my position on "customer first" versus "employee first," arguing that we should put employees—instead of customers—at the center of what we do because they are the ones who deliver on customer centricity. I disagree. Alignment around the customer is an organizational strategy that articulates why the company exists and gives everyone working for the organization a common purpose—the reason for coming to work every day—which is to serve the customer. Are employees important? Absolutely! An organization must take care of its people. But the primary purpose of any service business, especially in healthcare, is to keep the customer (the patient) at the center of the organizational strategy. Organizations don't exist for their employees. They exist for their customers.

It was not until I left Cleveland Clinic after my fellowship and started treating patients on my own that I recognized the true meaning of employees aligning around patients. I quickly learned that there are numerous factors that affect a patient's perception of care.

At MetroHealth, I had a patient who vomited in his bed, soiling his sheets. He asked the nurse on multiple occasions if he could get his bed changed, and no one helped him. Finally, a cleaning person came into the patient's room, and he asked for help changing the sheets. The cleaning person came back with a fresh set of sheets, but instead of changing the patient's sheets, the individual merely placed the folded sheets on the edge of the bed and walked out. Apparently in this person's mind, he or she had helped the patient, but now it was up to the patient to change the sheets. Frustrated, the patient went ahead and changed his own sheets. He did not want to complain. As he explained to me, "I see these people every day. I don't want to make them mad." Fortunately, he was a nice guy with a great sense of humor, and he did not want to make a big deal about it. But after he was discharged, he told everyone he knew the "sheets story."

Patients First as Purpose: Why We Exist

While healthcare organizations often fail to grasp the importance of customer centricity, other industries provide exemplar models. Contrast the "sheets story" with the employee alignment around the customer I observed when visiting Walt Disney World Resort in Orlando, Florida. Early in my career as CXO, I was interested in understanding how Disney delivers great customer service. I received an overview from one of its executives regarding how the Walt Disney Company frames its organizational culture, spending enormous amounts of time and resources teaching employees, known as cast members, about the organization's mission and how members are to portray it. Each cast member is expected to live the six cultural values of innovation, quality, community, storytelling, optimism, and decency.[7]

I was given a behind-the-scenes tour of parts of the resort. I certainly knew Disney's reputation for great service, but I was a little skeptical and a bit cynical that an organization with nearly 70,000 employees in Orlando alone could get everyone to recite the organization's values upon demand. To poke fun at my host, I performed a little test. As he was giving me the tour, I asked every cast member whom we encountered to recite for me the six Disney values. Initially, it was a little embarrassing to my host because none of the people we met could recite the full list, even with coaching. But it was amazing that each cast member could articulate that he or she felt part of something big and important, something truly magical with a higher purpose, much more than just a job. They all believed their mission was to "deliver happiness" to people. It was an eye-opening experience for me, and I was captivated by these interactions. Delivering happiness is Disney's Patients First motto, their organizational purpose, and everyone we encountered seemed to live it. My colleague from Disney was grinning (mouse) ear-to-ear. The idea of organizational purpose is not new. Patients First is not just a motto; it is a *purpose*.

Alan Siegel, the CEO of Siegelvision, a premier international branding firm whose mantra is Clarity Above All, says that organizations must use the concept of simplicity in defining their purpose.[8] Siegel was the genius behind the design of the IRS 1040EZ one-page tax form. He successfully took a very complicated process (filing taxes) and simplified it to a single page. Siegel believes that our goal as leaders is to devise a simple message or a single purpose that frames what our organizations are about. It should not be something people need to think about; it should be something people understand intuitively. Siegel argues that this is the best way to effectively and powerfully communicate a common reason for existing. For organizations involved in healthcare, what simple phrase communicates purpose better than Patients First?

I observed another great nonhealthcare manifestation of a customers-first purpose when I stayed at the Trump International Hotel & Tower while attending a conference in Chicago. The constant proselytizing "The Donald" makes about quality was evident from the moment I arrived. One would expect a customer-centric and quality focus from an organization in the hospitality business, but I have stayed at many top hotels throughout the world and never quite experienced what I encountered at Trump's hotel. From the attendant opening the door when I arrived, to the time I departed when the valet put my bags in the taxi, everyone and everything I encountered in between was a seamless representation of high quality. Everyone embodied the organization's purpose perfectly. While there were numerous contributors to this exceptional experience, a few details really stood out, making it personal and special.

When I entered my guest room, on the bed was a personalized letter signed by Donald Trump. It acknowledged me as a customer and thanked me for coming, set my expectations by highlighting why my stay would be an exceptional experience, and let me know that the staff, *his* people, were there for me. Communications kept coming. When I returned from my meeting, there was a card from whoever had turned down my bed: "We wish you a pleasant stay and hope you have a wonderful evening. Please let me know if you need anything." I had a drink at the bar that night, and the server was present but never intrusive. He seemed to anticipate my every need.

As a service-industry leader responsible for customer centricity, I know some of the activities and devices that set appropriate expectations and drive a positive experience. But what impressed me most about this property was that, at every step, my experience was exceptional. The hotel had very successfully discerned the touch points critical to customers. The things I cared about were all covered, with additional enhancements.

Hospitality industry companies, especially the top brands, are well known for delivering a great experience. But there is a great experience, and there is making someone feel special. My experience at the Trump property impressed me, and I walked away feeling special. Making the customer feel special was clearly the organizational purpose. I still have that letter.

No one really believed that one simple motto, Patients First, would transform Cleveland Clinic. But that motto did something I'm not sure anyone recognized at the time: it started a cultural alignment of the workforce around the patient and began to define the organization's purpose.

I think most people in the organization today understand the importance of this simple purpose. Several years into Cleveland Clinic's Patients First transformation, and after I had become CXO, I received very powerful patient proof. I was sitting by the pool after attending a meeting in Florida when I learned that an out-of-state patient was trying to reach me. At the time, Felix Rappaport was president and COO of the Mirage Hotel and Casino in Las Vegas, part of MGM Resorts International. I had no idea who he was or why he wanted to talk. Rappaport and I connected, and he told me what a wonderful patient experience he had at Cleveland Clinic. While his organization was dedicated to achieving great customer service, he thought we—a hospital—did a better job.

I asked Rappaport to tell me what in particular about the experience was special. He observed that all the people he encountered, from the attendant who parked his car to the employee transporting him around the hospital, seemed as though they were all there for him and no one else. Everyone worked together, as if the entire organization was focused on making his experience exceptional. Over and over, Rappaport described feeling he was the focal point of everyone in the hospital. He described what I believe is one of the greatest achievements we have made as an organization.

At Rappaport's invitation, I visited the Mirage. It is an amazing property, and I was intrigued to test his observation that Cleveland Clinic delivers better service. Similar to my visit to Walt Disney World, from the moment I was picked up at the airport to the time I was driven back, I asked every Mirage employee, "Do you like working at the Mirage, and why are you here?" Incredibly, all the employees I encountered loved working there. They all had a story to tell about their jobs: The limousine driver had a sick child and remarked how the leadership went the extra mile to take care of him and his family. The desk clerk appreciated the environment and flexible hours so she could finish school. The person who managed the hotel's iconic volcano attraction thought he had the "coolest job in the world" and was proud to tell his friends and family what he did. The energy and job satisfaction from the employees I encountered was admirable.

The next day, I spoke to the Mirage's senior leadership, explaining Cleveland Clinic's Patients First philosophy and how I thought the concept might apply to their organization. I was pretty certain they understood the concept's relationship to healthcare, but I wasn't convinced they believed customer centricity affected all businesses. After conveying accolades about the employees I had encountered, I hit my audience with a bombshell. While observing that employees were happy and satisfied in their jobs—making a personal connection to the organization is an essential tactic for employee engagement—I did not perceive a high level of engagement around the customer: me. For example, when I came off the escalator at the airport, instead of seeing the limousine driver waiting with a sign with my name on it, I had to search for him. I described how there were several burned-out lightbulbs and a nonfunctioning television remote control in my guest room.

I asked my audience to imagine everyone in the organization completely focused on the customer. There would be a synergy of productivity: the organization would have satisfied employees performing their jobs well, and employees would always look out for the customer. The limousine driver would know to meet me at the bottom of the escalator closest to my gate. The housekeeper, whose job it is to clean the room, would check light switches to make sure all the lamps were working. All employees would go out of their way to think one step beyond what they do to what is important to the customer. This is the difference between job satisfaction and job engagement.

You can do a great job taking care of your employees and keeping them satisfied, and they can perform well in their jobs, but the idea of alignment around the customer is something that elevates service to the next level. I'm sure some of the Mirage managers viewed my anecdotes just as process breakdown. But with engaged employees aligned around a common purpose, the culture could compensate for process failures.

That night Rappaport invited me to dinner with another MGM senior executive, Renee West, president and COO of the Excalibur Hotel & Casino and Luxor Las Vegas properties. My companions wanted to try a new restaurant at Caesars Palace Las Vegas, a competing resort. We met at the restaurant, and I chatted with West about my talk, the importance of cultural alignment, and our Patients First philosophy. I was excited to continue my test of employee responses to the question, "Why are you here?" so when our server returned to the table, I asked her, "Why do you work at Caesars?" Immediately, she said, "I am here for you. You are the most important person in our business, and we want you to come back." It was like putting a quarter in a slot machine and hitting the jackpot. In one line, this waitress, who had no idea she was serving leaders of three of the strip's most prominent properties, immediately articulated the concept of cultural alignment with the customer at the center of her responsibilities. It was a true "customers-first moment," and I could see in West's expression how struck she was by the response. We offered the waitress no more explanation or discussion, and we went on with the dinner. Her service was excellent.

The need for customer centricity extends beyond consumer-services companies to include business-to-business enterprises as well. Cisco Systems, Inc., is a world-renowned technology innovator. Its longstanding chairman and CEO, John T. Chambers, met with our executive team and shared personal leadership insights when he appeared in our *Ideas for Tomorrow* lecture series in 2012.[9] Part of Cisco's success comes from its merger and acquisition activities. We asked Chambers what key attributes he seeks when considering an acquisition. He responded that a critical component is an absolute focus on the customer.

Customer focus is an essential ingredient for success in any industry. It doesn't matter whether you serve consumers or businesses. Ensuring that your organization is focused on the customer is an essential ingredient to successfully move your product or service against competitors. Organizations must place their customers at the center and ensure alignment around them. Employees, managers, and leaders must clearly understand that the customer is the organization's purpose. As Forrester Research's Harley Manning, vice president and research director serving customer experience professionals, put it, "Customers don't need you. You need them," and "Everybody wants your customers."[10]

Patients First as Both "Burning Platform" and Strategic Priority

In addition to Cleveland Clinic's alignment and purpose, Patients First has also become our "burning platform" for change. The metaphor of the burning platform is about a sense of urgency in motivating change: if you find yourself on a burning oil-drilling platform, you must jump off or die.[11] In his highly regarded article "The 8-Step Process for Leading Change," Harvard Business School professor John P. Kotter, PhD, cites creating a sense of urgency as the first step.[12]

When I started as CXO, our patient experience scores, as measured by the Centers for Medicare and Medicaid Hospital Consumer Assessment of Healthcare Providers and Systems (HCAHPS) survey, were terrible. Our institution scored near the bottom of all hospitals reporting in 2008. How could a hospital ranked as one of America's best by *U.S. News & World Report* be among the lowest performers with regard to the patient experience? It was inconsistent with our reputation and brand. Here was quantitative evidence that we were not putting patients first, and we used it to light the platform on fire.

Burning platforms can also be used to take an organization beyond just average, as Radboud University Medical Center, a 1,000-bed hospital located about 75 miles southeast of Amsterdam in the Netherlands, learned. In 2005, the government closed Radboud's heart program because of poor quality metrics. I had the opportunity to sit with Radboud's chairman of the executive board, Melvin Samsom, and Lucien Engelen, director of its REshape & Innovation Center.[13] According to Samsom, who was appointed as the chief medical officer after the crisis and later became the CEO, it "was a huge shock on the system." If the heart program was so bad that the government had to shut it down to protect patients, where else was the hospital deficient? This crisis became Radboud's burning platform. "We were determined to not just fix the program, but to become the best," Samsom said. "Quality is measured on a bell-shaped curve. We were at the bottom or far left of the curve. Most organizations sit in the middle. We wanted to use this crisis as our burning platform to propel us to the top or far right of the curve." They have been successful, and today Radboud's heart program, as well as many of its other clinical programs, is rated among the best in the Netherlands. Samsom persists in using the shutdown of its heart program to beat the drum for staying focused on quality.

The mandated closing of an important service line such as cardiac care at Radboud University Medical Center certainly grabs attention. But identifying a burning platform and creating a new motto are not enough to drive an important effort to improve service. Simply creating a new motto and talking about patient complaints puts the effort at risk of becoming just another "flavor of the month." New initiatives like this can easily be swept under the rug as insignificant and ineffectual. When Patients First was introduced, I imagine some employees were anticipating that the new initiative would go away, speculating that it would eventually lose steam and Cosgrove would forget about it. But Cosgrove did not forget about it, and his early steps were critical to ensuring its success.

We had no playbook for organizational transformation; we had no next steps or pages of well-described tactics ready for deployment. However, one of Cosgrove's early actions was to set improving the patient experience as a top strategic priority for the organization. He recognized that mottoes and anecdotes don't change organizations. If Patients First was going to work, it would need to be a topic that stayed on every leader's and manager's agenda. Patients First and the patient experience improvements were here to stay. Setting Patients First as a strategic priority meant there would be an organizational goal to improve patients' experiences, metrics would be identified and made available, and leaders and managers would be held accountable.

One of my primary responsibilities as CXO is ensuring there is plenty of gasoline around to fuel the fire, continually stoking the importance of staying focused on the patient as our alignment, purpose, and strategy. My associates may tire of hearing it, but Patients First is our reason for existence, and I'm determined to keep that fire alive. Adopting a Patients First or customers-first platform is also a no-lose proposition. In healthcare, it's impossible to argue against something successfully framed as right for patients.

Cleveland Clinic Became an Early Pioneer in Patient Experience

Cosgrove introduced Patients First and set a strategic goal of improving the patient experience for Cleveland Clinic before the topic came in vogue for most hospitals or was elevated in importance through the Medicare Hospital Value-Based Purchasing Program. With passage of the 2010 Patient Protection and Affordable Care Act, hospitals and physicians are required to pay attention to improving the patient experience or risk both financial penalties linked to reimbursement and damaged reputations. But should we need "sticks" to drive hospitals to a more patient-centered focus? Cleveland Clinic started this because it was the right thing to do, but quite frankly, we needed to do this because we had a reputation risk that patients would see a connection between how they felt treated as individuals and how they perceived their quality of care.

One might believe hospitals make it a priority to put patients at the center, but they don't typically frame their strategies this way. Hospitals are in the business of taking care of patients. It's the most important thing they do. Customers in healthcare enter the system not as consumers in the traditional definition of the word, but as patients. A patient is a sick individual who needs medical attention. Patients are anxious, confused, and fearful and have a significant information disadvantage about their condition and what to expect during care. Whatever brings them to the hospital is enough to worry about. Patients don't want to be in the hospital, and we have an obligation to treat them in the very best possible way we can.

Framing it from a purely business perspective, we also need patients to be successful. Patients have a choice, and we should be thankful they chose us. We have an obligation to ensure that our organizations are aligned around them so that every employee or caregiver has the patient in mind and ensures that all services and deliverables are wrapped around the patient.

When I became CXO, I said the goal of Cleveland Clinic was to become the world leader in the patient experience. I specifically used the word *become* because I knew it was not a destination, but a journey we would always be on. In 2013, I employed tactics that I had used while observing Disney and the Mirage in our main campus hospital in Cleveland. I randomly asked 10 employees, "Why are you here?" Eight of them gave an answer related to our Patients First philosophy. This is a "B" grade, demonstrating we are just above average and still have a lot of work to do.

Cleveland Clinic has directed significant resources toward understanding how to deliver to patients the ultimate healthcare experience. This is not our imperative solely because it's the right thing to do; it also defines our brand and industry. Ranking as a provider of top-rated specialty care, including being the world's number one heart center, carries with it a responsibility to deliver an exceptional patient experience.

One of our most important accomplishments has been successfully introducing Patients First and aligning our people around it. Healthcare organizations—or those in any other industry, for that matter—that want to start a transformation program that is centered on the customer should begin with these steps:

1. Set your customer as the true north of the organization. Help your people understand that they exist to serve the customer and that the organizational strategy and operational processes must support that.

2. Define your purpose, and message it simply to everyone as the reason you exist. Having a mission statement is important, but employees often do not remember it or know what it truly

means. Having a succinct purpose will allow you to more clearly articulate what it is that your organization does. Your employees will also remember it.

3. Set the platform on fire and fuel it with gasoline. Healthcare organizations do not typically provide an excellent experience. Use your organization's data and tell patient stories to get people to pay attention to this issue. Constantly reminding employees why they come to work and what it is that the organization does will help keep the focus on the customer.

4. Make improving the customer experience a top strategic priority. Simply introducing a purpose will not improve the organization; it must be top-of-mind for all leaders and managers. Ensure that it drives the strategy of the organization.

Leading for Change

C leveland Clinic has made significant improvements in the patient experience, not because there is a CXO or an Office of Patient Experience, but because our president and CEO owns the patient experience as a strategic initiative. Our success in transformation occurred because the top person in the organization led the way.

When I confer with senior hospital leaders having responsibility for managing the patient experience, I often find their CEOs have little hand in leading or messaging it. Others tell me the CEO occasionally says it's important, but holds no one accountable for improvement. This is confirmed in a HealthLeaders Media survey finding that 48 percent of hospital leaders think the patient experience is a top strategic priority,[1] but only 15 percent identify the CEO as owner of the initiative.[2] Patient experience improvement is often seen as "just another thing we have to do," with responsibility relegated to nursing, quality, or hospital operations.

Disparity between what top leaders say about the patient experience and where it resides organizationally is a key reason why there isn't sufficient traction to drive meaningful change. Improving the patient experience is all-encompassing; it requires every person and every process to be aligned around the patient. No one in the organization can singly achieve that alignment unless the top person is leading the charge. Because everything the patient experience encompasses is inherently comprehensive, only the top leader can effectively impact such a broad scope. In organizations where the CEO owns the patient experience, including Cleveland Clinic, Children's National Medical Center, Houston Methodist, and UCLA Health System, among others, you quickly recognize the impact of senior leadership.

At the beginning of Cleveland Clinic's efforts to improve the patient experience, Cosgrove set the strategy, as well as managed the change. Within a couple of years of becoming CEO, he launched a variety of major initiatives to help improve patient-centered care.

For example, Cleveland Clinic became the first U.S. healthcare system to change the way medicine was organized. Traditional academic medicine is structured around major departments, such as the Department of Surgery or the Department of Medicine. All subspecialties related to surgery or medicine were within these departments.

While surgeons and medical specialists in many of the major service lines, such as cardiac and digestive diseases, were already very good at working closely together, Cleveland Clinic was founded on the model of physicians working together as a unit. Cosgrove felt very strongly that formalizing this model and integrating it across the organization for all specialties would greatly enhance patient care. So our radical institute model was born. The entire enterprise was reorganized around new institutes, a significant restructuring of how care is delivered and how patients interact with the system.

There are no longer departments of medicine or surgery; there are institutes organized around disease and organ systems. The Sydell and Arnold Miller Family Heart & Vascular Institute includes all the medicine and surgical specialties necessary to treat any heart or vascular condition. Physicians and services are colocated so patients do not have to travel to multiple locations. And there is a common leadership team for each institute consisting of a clinical physician chairperson, a nursing leader, and an administrative operations expert. The idea was to reorient care delivery around the patient.

Cosgrove introduced other important but less dramatic ideas as well. In 2005, he established a comprehensive wellness initiative for employees and hired Dr. Michael Roizen, the first chief wellness officer. Cosgrove was always bothered by how hospital gowns undermined patient dignity and determined to change this. He engaged Diane von Furstenberg, designer of the legendary wrap dress, to create a new patient gown, which debuted in 2010 after years of research and development and has become famous. Convinced that art could be therapeutic for patients and families, in 2004, he created the Arts and Medicine Institute and hired a physician, Iva Fattorini, to chair it.

While Cosgrove was doing a lot to improve the patient experience, it was unclear whether his efforts were having any impact. Relatively flat patient experience scores persisted, and he continued to receive negative patient experience anecdotes.

One of the most important catalysts that reinforced Cosgrove's convictions and motivated him to redouble his efforts came in 2006, when he was invited to speak to Harvard Business School MBA students, who were analyzing a case about Cleveland Clinic's model of care. At the conclusion of Cosgrove's remarks, student Kara Medoff Barnett raised her hand. "Dr. Cosgrove, my father needed mitral valve surgery. We knew about Cleveland Clinic and the excellent results you have. But we decided not to go there because we heard that you had no empathy. We went to another hospital instead, even though it wasn't as highly ranked as yours. Dr. Cosgrove, do you teach empathy at Cleveland Clinic?"[3]

Taken aback, Cosgrove had no choice but to admit the truth, that Cleveland Clinic did not teach empathy to its physicians. In one anecdote, Medoff Barnett had very successfully framed financial ROI for the patient experience. For an organization whose brand was incredibly important in attracting patients, she demonstrated the significance of differentiating on the patient experience.

Nearly half of Cleveland Clinic's heart business comes from outside our primary service area. When the demographics of those patients are analyzed, it's clear they had a choice; they could go wherever they wanted for care. The student's father, also a physician, recognized that from a quality standpoint, he would probably be fine at any of the top U.S. medical centers.[4] But he and his family were more concerned about how they would be treated as people, not just as patients. The family differentiated on the experience the patient would have, not the reputation for quality. And because of that, Cleveland Clinic lost his business.

Another galvanizing incident occurred 10 days later, when Cosgrove attended the dedication of King Saud Medical City in Riyadh, Saudi Arabia. The hospital president was addressing what the new medical center would bring to the kingdom and the importance of attending to patients' and families' emotional and spiritual, as well as medical, needs. The speaker continued that providing medical care was scarcely enough; there must be a focus on the human condition. Cosgrove noticed that the king and other members of the audience were weeping. Cosgrove was moved by the impact of these words and began to realize he was missing something. He needed to do more and invest more.

A C-Suite Executive Leads and Manages Day to Day

Cosgrove recognized that while it was critical for him as CEO to maintain engagement and to message the importance of the patient experience, an organization as large as Cleveland Clinic needed management of day-to-day patient experience operations. This would ensure that the patient experience received appropriate focus and attention from all key stakeholders, including physicians, nurses, and employees in all operations. The person responsible would report to Cosgrove and, he reasoned, would also need to be a physician.

This was an important inflection point in Cleveland Clinic's efforts to improve the patient experience. While the CEO led the initiative, appointing a separate senior executive responsible for the patient experience became important to ensure successful, consistent execution.

Many service organizations have one person, such as a chief customer officer, responsible for managing the customer experience, and while the position is not new to industry, it is new to healthcare. Forrester Research published a report evaluating the role of senior executives who lead customer service.[5] In a review of 155 positions across several industries, Forrester found that these leaders typically sit on the company's executive team and more than half report directly to the CEO. Many may have a small staff and limited budget, but because of strategic scope and reporting relationships, these executives have influence over the entire organization and huge resources. Some serve in a strictly advisory position with no operational areas, while others have large operations with thousands reporting to them.

Hospitals often have numerous people managing pieces of the patient experience process. Their proximity to senior leadership is frequently unclear, making progress difficult. *HealthLeaders* magazine[6] published an interview of four individuals leading and managing the patient experience. The article sought insights regarding why healthcare is unable to move this important initiative as quickly and as successfully as the leaders think necessary. The interviews included four different roles: a director of inpatient services, a chief nursing officer, a director of quality and risk management, and a director of operations. The diversity of these roles and their reporting relationships, in some cases multiple steps away from the CEO or senior leadership, helps illustrate the challenges of a cohesive approach to managing patient experience strategy. Each person was knowledgeable and passionately committed, and each presented a slightly different perspective of challenges in improving the patient experience.

Cosgrove decided to create a new C-suite position, that of chief experience officer (CXO). He read the article "The New CEO—Chief Experience Officer,"[7] which discussed how this role could impact healthcare organizations. The new CXO would report to him and would be responsible for managing day-to-day execution of the strategy.

Bridget Duffy became Cleveland Clinic's first CXO, the first such position at a major U.S. healthcare organization. Duffy fit the profile perfectly. She was a physician who had been serving in a similar role for Medtronic, Inc. An early leader in this new field, Duffy was passionate about the patient experience and possessed the insight to strengthen Cleveland Clinic's strategy.

The role of CXO began as a consultative function, and Duffy became an important change agent. She further developed the infrastructure necessary to drive organizational change. She initiated better messaging about the patient experience and helped people across the organization understand what the patient experience was about and why it was important. She formed the Office of Patient Experience and with Cosgrove's support assembled what they felt were appropriate resources to make it successful. She also helped to elevate Cleveland Clinic's brand in this space, as news of Cosgrove's seriousness at driving improvement became more well known nationally.

I first met Duffy shortly after moving my practice to Cleveland Clinic in 2009. I was struck by her passion and clarity of thought on the importance of the patient experience. I shared with her the story of my father, and she immediately empathized and articulated the challenges the organization needed to overcome to move toward greater patient-centered-ness. I remember walking out of her office knowing that I had made the right decision to come back to Cleveland Clinic.

Duffy served as CXO for two years before deciding to move back to California, just a few months after I returned. While she was success-ful in introducing the concept of the patient experience, raising its level of importance, and expanding the infrastructure, she was burdened in executing on the strategy, partly because she was inhibited by Cleveland Clinic's culture. While she was a physician, she was viewed as an outsider by the medical staff because she did not practice in Cleveland Clinic's environment. She had difficulty changing an entrenched culture. Duffy continues to be a highly regarded and respected thought leader in the patient experience space.

After Duffy left, Cosgrove decided to seek internal candidates to fill the CXO role. He wanted to find a practicing physician who "came from the culture" to lead it. Knowing that physicians would be the toughest stakeholder group to change, he wanted an established clini-cian to lead it.

Shortly after taking the CXO role, I quickly realized the reality on the ground. The cultural tides of the organization were strong and not aligned. I recognized there would be no honeymoon. Duffy had mes-saged the change, but now we needed to figure out how to execute. I met with a respected elder surgical statesman who told me that many peo-ple believed the patient experience was just lip service and no one really felt that Cosgrove was serious or committed to changing the culture four years after the program had begun. I was also cautioned that the patient experience would not just improve on its own. "Just because Cosgrove talks about it and there is a CXO does not mean anyone is going to pay attention to it," the elder statesman said. His point was that it would take real engagement of the frontline nursing staff and physicians to truly make a difference.

This was a sentiment echoed by many physicians. Practically all of the administrative leaders I met with were 100 percent behind the strat-egy, and nearly every physician I spoke with questioned what it meant and how it would be successful. This is not to suggest the physicians were against it; it demonstrates that physicians were giving us a more honest answer. I recognized that the patient experience would improve only when our leaders recognized its importance and led the change, not because I had an impressive title and Cosgrove and I told them the patient experience was important. I decided that the patient experience implementation needed to go underground. The change would have to come from the bottom up, not the top down.

Shortly after I got the job, Cosgrove said, "So you're going to be in charge of the patient experience." I laughed and replied, "If you want me to be in charge of it, then you have the wrong person, because the reality is that we're all in charge of it." While key strategic priorities of any organization must be set by its top leaders for operationalization by others, effective change management requires that everyone—leaders, managers, and employees across the organization—buy into the initiative. If all leaders in the organization did not "get" that the patient experience was important and that they needed to be part of fixing it, there was no way we were going to be successful.

I had this conversation with Marc Boom, MD, president and CEO of Houston Methodist, when I interviewed him about leadership in the patient experience for an article for the Association of Patient Experience.[8] He believes that the top person needs to drive it, because otherwise organizations won't be successful, but acknowledges that it's everyone's responsibility to ensure that it becomes a reality.

One of Cosgrove's leadership attributes that really helped kick-start our success in the patient experience is his ability to think at a very strategic level but get tactical when necessary. Leaders certainly must be the visionaries who drive innovation. Equally important, however, is the ability to get into the weeds. Transformational change happens because leaders can get into the detail when needed and start fires to ignite processes to support change. This helps to ground and activate change initiatives at the front line.

Some early tactics that we deployed were Cosgrove's ideas. As leader of the heart center, he was tasked with consolidating a collection of heart practices throughout northeastern Ohio. One of his first moves was to distribute unblinded program and physician-specific performance data. He correctly believed that communicating this data to all physicians would help drive improvement, as no one wanted to be at the bottom of the list. So another of the early patient experience improvement projects initiated by Cosgrove was to rank and distribute physician scores.

He reasoned that physicians needed to know how they were judged and what patients were saying about them.

Cosgrove also routinely made decisions that were important for patients but not very popular internally. Marketing and complaint data revealed that patients often viewed Cleveland Clinic as difficult to access. One patient commented, "The Clinic takes only rich people or rulers from Arab countries," for example. Cosgrove felt this misperception had to be attacked head-on, and in 2010, Cleveland Clinic mandated the offering of same-day appointments. Any patient calling Cleveland Clinic is offered to be seen that day—by a generalist or a specialist. We embarked upon a major marketing campaign, "The Power of Today," running television, radio, and print advertising that states, "Call today for an appointment today."

It was an unpopular decision, not universally supported by the medical staff; many physicians were unhappy and voiced concerns. Offering same-day appointments created some schedule bottlenecks and quickly revealed a few areas where capacity was lacking, such as dermatology. Imagine the number of parents calling for appointments in pediatric dermatology in June right after school lets out and public pools open: offering a same-day appointment to every parent calling became a challenge and did not quite achieve the success we desired. However, for every patient that we could not accommodate for a rash, there were incredible success stories, such as a young woman with rectal bleeding who needed to be seen by a doctor. She called for a same-day appointment and, within 24 hours, had a colonoscopy that diagnosed colon cancer. She was seen by a colorectal surgeon, and a plan of care was developed that same day to treat her cancer.

Same-day access was groundbreaking in healthcare. As far as we could tell, there was no other U.S. tertiary-care hospital so bold as to implement a similar program. New-patient encounters jumped 20 percent the first year, and now Cleveland Clinic records approximately one million same-day appointments annually. We meet 96 percent of same-day requests.

Some criticize CEOs like Cosgrove for being too much in the weeds. We occasionally tease him about asking during an executive committee meeting how much sidewalk salt we use in winter. But we really mean it as a compliment, not a criticism. Many of our early successes came because of his direct involvement. His deep understanding of hospital operations, coupled with his vision for healthcare, helps to make our change efforts both practical and successful.

David T. Feinberg, MD, the CEO of UCLA Hospital System, is not unlike Cosgrove in this regard. To help combat the problem with pressure ulcers, Feinberg demands that their incidence be reported to him personally any time of the day or night. He says, "I want to know when patients are harmed—it is unacceptable."[9] Contrast this with other organizations in which the CEO is not engaged or where top leaders don't walk the patient experience talk.

Cosgrove's decisions and his unwavering support of our implementation helped thoroughly ground the Patients First philosophy in Cleveland Clinic's culture. His leadership demonstrated that we were not just talking about improving the patient experience; we were serious and willing to make difficult decisions to dramatically change our practice of medicine. Seeing Cosgrove in the weeds proved his commitment and got the organization thinking about change.

It is incumbent upon leaders not just to be visionary but to have the capability to execute, the ability to go from a 50,000-foot strategic perspective to a 5-foot tactical one instantly. That talent is not micromanagement; it's called knowing your organization.

Cosgrove also recognizes when collaboration is warranted versus a "command and control" approach. Moving from the old academic department model to the new institutes structure was disruptive innovation in healthcare, and he knew it would require collaboration with physician leadership for acceptance. However, with same-day appointments, he decided it was important for patients, so he leveraged his CEO prerogative and mandated it.

Owning Change at All Levels

Our most successful move was to align the organization around Patients First. Our second most successful move was getting people to own leading this change. Just as Cosgrove has done it for Cleveland Clinic overall, the physician staff has done it for our more than two dozen institutes. Institute chairs are leaders in their fields and understand what they do better than most in the world. Incorporating the patient experience as a competency is making the same impact on their areas that Cosgrove made on the enterprise as a whole.

I once was told that successful leaders develop strategy and ways to implement it and then motivate people to adopt it as their own and carry it out. We ignited a "burning platform" to focus people on improving the patient experience, and I am most proud of our success in inspiring others to own and drive the improvement. Cosgrove's responsibility is to keep the patient experience top of mind. My responsibility is to ensure there is plenty of gasoline to throw on the burning platform. But it's everyone's responsibility to own and drive the change. Leaders in our organization who were initially reticent now drive it with incredible passion and believe that it is absolutely the right thing to do.

I first met Joseph Iannotti, chair of the Orthopaedic and Rheumatologic Institute, shortly after I became CXO. Iannotti is a world-renowned surgeon and researcher and a hard-core, outcomes-based thinker who probably didn't give much consideration to the patient experience during his training and early career. He was of the mindset that "It's about the quality of what we do and nothing else." When I went to his office as part of my early institute-chair "meet and greets," I observed that his office furnishings were colorful and stood out from the typical Cleveland Clinic doctor's office. I'm sure I offered some sarcastic comment about his decor, and he remarked, "This is about the physician experience."

Iannotti was courteous and complimentary when discussing the patient experience. Of course, no one criticized it, knowing it was Cosgrove's baby. But I quickly sensed he was not convinced of the importance, and questioned whether he would spend any time focusing on it. I clearly remember walking away from that meeting thinking this was going to be very hard. If we could not convince the top leaders beyond the C-suite, especially clinical leadership, this endeavor would never be successful.

Iannotti came to understand that the patient experience has national urgency and is a differentiator in healthcare. He embraced the patient experience as a priority for his institute and leads it at his level. Today, his institute has among the highest patient experience scores in the organization. Each physician and staff member knows the patient experience priority, and while some may still not believe it to be important, they drive it because they know they will be held accountable for it.

Four years after that meet and greet, Iannotti remarked, "You have really fixed the patient experience here." I laughed and said that it wasn't me, it was people like him. His institute does well because he owns the issue.

I recently received a call from the chairman of orthopedics at a major academic center, one of the country's largest orthopedic programs. Referred by Iannotti, he opened the conversation saying, "Our patient experience is really bad, and Joe says you can help me fix it." We discussed a variety of tactics, but eventually I pointed him right back to Iannotti. The patient experience is tops in our orthopedic department because of its chairperson's leadership. To be similarly successful, my caller needed to start there too.

Leadership Can Change a Hospital

Lutheran Hospital is a small, 125-bed hospital located in Cleveland's historic Ohio City neighborhood. A stalwart example of a local community hospital, Lutheran was an important anchor to neighborhood economic viability. This institution was acquired by Cleveland Clinic in 1997. For years, its overall HCAHPS scores were low, with very little change. In January 2012, a new leader, Brian Donley, was appointed president of the hospital. Donley was vice chairperson of the orthopedics department and headed Cleveland Clinic's foot and ankle center. It was his first time in a major leadership role, but he quickly set key organizational priorities. While the patient experience was already a strategic initiative for the enterprise, Donley immediately renewed its emphasis as a top priority for Lutheran.

Donley increased his visibility by rounding on patients and talking to caregivers throughout the hospital. He made physician engagement a top priority and started hosting small dinner meetings with physicians. Early on, he was challenged by a senior staff member who declared that a lot of patient experience programs had been trialed at Lutheran and hadn't worked. Donley pushed back and said the hospital would continue to pursue improvement in the patient experience. The new president also needed new resources to assist him in the transformation. I hired a patient experience director for the hospital, and K. Kelly Hancock, executive chief nursing officer of the Clinic System, hired a new chief nursing officer for the hospital.

In the early quarters under Lutheran's new leadership team, the hospital achieved some of the highest single improvements in patient satisfaction across the entire enterprise. After one year, every HCAHPS domain jumped nearly 40 percentile points. If you asked Donley how he made such incredible improvements so rapidly, he would attribute it to the great people working at the hospital—leaders, managers, and every caregiver. The metrics improved because of his leadership and his team driving the improvement. He recognized the importance of the patient experience as a hospital priority, and as president, he owned it, messaged it, and sent a clear signal to everyone that improvement was essential.

It's not just the clinical leadership that has to drive patient experience improvement. Steven C. Glass is our CFO, and if there's a nonclinical executive who really gets the clinical side of what we do, he's the one. Well before we started enterprise leadership rounding, Glass rounded on hospital patient floors. He visited patients, talked to staff, and sought to truly understand our frontline work. Rounding in clinical units is a leadership competency he has cascaded to his entire team.

I am often invited to speak to our various finance departments about the patient experience. Many finance executives spend time rounding with me and our clinical leaders. Once, I drove back to Cleveland Clinic with Glass after we visited another health system. He shared with me his thoughts on leadership as a CFO. "Jim, I am not just someone who manages the finances. I see myself as an executive with a role in the organization's strategy. I don't set strategy, but if I am not participating, what good am I to our mission of serving patients? Everything I do from a finance perspective directly impacts our ability to deliver care to patients."[10]

Finance in general and Glass in particular have received a lot of undeserved criticism in our organization because many feel that finance "runs the ship." Nothing could be further from the truth. Glass and his team do what no one else likes to think or talk about: they manage the budget. Glass has worked exhaustively to help senior and frontline leaders understand hospital finances. He has involved physicians in his department, created a standing budget committee that includes doctors, and integrated other clinical leaders into nearly every level of the finance function.

This type of leadership perspective is important. Many are capable of managing healthcare organization finance, but we should not see that as solely adequate. We should look for people who "get it," who understand that it's not just about leading one silo; it's about understanding how that silo supports the mission of patient care.

The Impact of Leadership Rounds

Senior leadership visibility is critical to improving the patient experience. Leadership rounding is one of the tactics Glass and many other leaders regularly employ to better understand what is going on at the front lines. This important tactic gives leaders visibility to both caregivers and patients, and those interactions help them to better understand how their decision making affects the organization.

In 2011, I visited David Feinberg at UCLA Health System. He told me that he occasionally will hold meetings with people while rounding in the hospital. "Time is short. I can accomplish two things at once: conduct a meeting and see our patients and employees," he said. Rounding has a reciprocal effect, demonstrating to frontline caregivers that senior leaders are engaged about what the staff does every day.

My visit to UCLA coincided with a day when Feinberg's hospital was doing what it calls executive rounding, and he invited me to attend. We started in an auditorium, with about 60 senior leaders. The meeting opened with stories about the great work two employees had done for patients. Smaller groups of three or four were then deployed to various areas of the hospital. For about an hour, each group talked to patients and caregivers and evaluated the environment. The group reassembled in the auditorium to discuss patient stories and organizational opportunities. I immediately was impressed and told Feinberg that leadership rounding was something we were going to implement at Cleveland Clinic. I remember asking whether I could "steal" his idea. He laughed and said of course, but for full transparency, that he got the idea from another hospital.

Today we conduct leadership rounds once a month. We follow the same format as UCLA, with a few enhancements. We use three checklists: one for patients, one for caregivers, and one for the environment. We collate the information and distribute it to every manager and leader. As a result, we have made very significant process improvements, including completely changing the way we deliver and maintain supplies in the nursing units and developing a new process to inventory and deliver patient IV pumps. Both problems were tremendous nursing dissatisfiers.

We also have started group recognition at our leadership rounds. In addition to calling out two outstanding caregivers, we recognize an entire group of caregivers who are critical to the mission but frequently have little exposure to our leadership. We have recognized the police force, environmental-service workers, pharmacists, and case managers. In medicine, doctors and nurses are commonly identified as heroes, but we send a message that there are heroes in different roles across the organization and that everyone is important.

Leadership rounding has been a great tool for finding areas of opportunity, but using it for leadership visibility has been the most important benefit. Leadership rounding is also easy to do and can be started right away. If you are a president and CEO of a hospital, or any company for that matter, how often do you get to the front lines and talk to employees and customers? How often does your senior team do it? Start today!

Rounding across the organization keeps our leaders grounded in the reality of what the organization does every day for patients. Cosgrove was rounding with our executive chief nursing officer, K. Kelly Hancock, and they walked into a room where the patient was obviously delirious and trying to get out of bed. They immediately attended to the patient, and a third person, Eileen Sheil, executive director, corporate communications, who was also rounding with them, went for help. It was right after morning shift change. The first nurse Sheil encountered said that it was not her patient and she could not help. The second nurse encountered said she had just signed out and was going home. Sheil went back into the patient's room and told Hancock what had happened, and she immediately got someone to help. The point is that while we work very hard to manage an effective, efficient organization, there are little things that happen every day—whether process or people related—that lead to significant difficulty in achieving our goals. Having top leaders at the front lines exposes them to the real world of what we do, but also sends the message that we are visible and engaged with what is happening.

To be successful in improving the patient experience, we must get people to help us lead the change. We cannot be successful trying to do it ourselves. At Cleveland Clinic, we've created a broad coalition of leaders who understand that the patient experience is important and take responsibility for driving its improvement. Having the patient experience as a top strategic priority allowed us to discover people who recognized the significance of the initiative. We started with these early adopters, people who understood immediately why the patient experience was important, and slowly worked to convince others.

For example, J. Michael Henderson, MD, our chief quality officer, recalls locking a lab door to prevent physicians from using substandard equipment. They were analyzing patient urine samples there and not sending them to the lab for evaluation. This practice had been in place for decades, but it no longer met national quality standards. Henderson tried to change their behavior, and when the physicians would not comply, he removed the equipment and locked the door.[11]

Because we have been successful in cascading the patient experience message, everyone owns responsibility for driving it. All leaders, whether managing huge operational divisions with a thousand people or supervising just a couple of employees, must lead it in their areas. For customer-centric organizations to be highly successful, every leader in the organization must own and lead the customer focus.

One of healthcare's challenges is that patient-centeredness can appear to be the responsibility of only the people who deal directly with patients. Nothing can be further from the truth. For hospitals to be successful, all clinical and nonclinical leaders must align around the patient. Failure will cause the patient experience messaging cascade to stop.

The patient experience, like any other major organizational initiative, requires visionary leaders who own the strategy, talk about it, and have the ability to occasionally take charge and execute a tactic. Persistence is required to prevent the patient experience from becoming a "flavor of the month." Every leader and manager must be made to understand why it is important and how he or she is critical to its success. Accountability must be present for those who don't believe it and don't want to adopt it as an organizational priority. Leaders also must be willing to try new things and challenge others around organizational dogma.

In summary:

1. The top person at the organization must own improving the patient experience as his or her priority. If the leader is not

talking about it, people will not pay attention and it will not get the consideration it deserves. Likewise, since the patient experience is inherently comprehensive, the only leader with the authority to impact such a broad scope is the CEO.

2. While the top person owns the issue and messaging, a C-suite executive who reports directly to the CEO is necessary to execute for meaningful operational effectiveness. Improving the patient experience will require resources, management of data, and specific tactics. There must be a person who is responsible for day-to-day operational improvement.

3. Just telling people in the organization that the patient experience is a priority will not fix it. Every leader and manager in the organization must understand the burning platform, know that it is a priority from leadership, and take responsibility for implementing it. This includes nonclinical leaders as well as clinical leaders.

4. Leadership rounding is an easy tactic that can be implemented immediately in any healthcare environment. It's a way to drive executive-level visibility to caregivers and patients and identify important issues that can impact operations.

Describing the Elephant: Defining the Patient Experience and Strategy

A solid definition of the patient experience is elusive. But before we can improve it, we need to have a working definition of how to think about it. There are two reasons why a concise definition is critical. First, we must define the patient experience *for* patients regarding what is important; otherwise patients will define it for us. Generally, patients are unsophisticated healthcare consumers. A particular experience equates to quality in a patient's mind. Patients often use proxies to judge our effectiveness. These proxies are things they do understand and can easily relate to their personal experience. We need to make sure that they pick the right proxies or at least understand their environment as it relates to their proxies.

Second, before you can improve an organization's patient experience, it must be clearly defined so that everyone in that organization—every caregiver—knows how it relates to his or her job and what must be done to improve it. If you cannot clearly communicate to caregivers the patient experience definition and expectations, it will be impossible for them to understand how to frame improvement tactics. Caregivers will not be sure what they are improving. Successful change management requires

that all personnel in an organization, at every level—from the reception-
ist scheduling the appointment to the director of supply chain—understand exactly what the initiative means to them and what it is that you
want them to do. Not having a unifying definition creates confusion for
leaders and managers trying to affect it, as well as for frontline caregivers
who are trying to deliver on it.

The definition also must account for the clinical realities of hospital
operations and everyday patient care. People must understand how the
definition fits into the overall scheme of what they do every day. Nurses,
doctors, and other caregivers must go about the business of delivering
care to patients. These professionals are very busy, and they don't have
time to study and understand a definition. There can be no room for
interpretation. Getting people to understand the definition quickly will
make it practical and drive rapid adoption. Adoption will also improve if
the framework naturally fits with what people do every day.

A concise definition of the patient experience must factor into other
hospital programs that are well established and critical to the functioning of a healthcare system, namely safety and quality. Patient experience
cannot be viewed as a stand-alone hospital initiative. Patient experience,
safety, and quality are inextricably linked, and tactics that improve the
patient experience, such as cultural development, certainly impact safety
and quality as well. An effective definition must align these links. If we
define the patient experience too narrowly, such as related to patient
perceptions or satisfaction, then we run the risk of marginalizing more
important issues, such as patient safety.

Shortly after I became CXO, the chief nursing officer and I convened
an enterprise retreat on the patient experience. We wanted to involve as
many key stakeholder leaders from across the organization as possible
early in our change process. We invited a variety of C-suite members,
physician leaders, nurse leaders, and operations leaders from all across
the enterprise, including our main campus, community hospitals, and
ambulatory centers. At the opening of the retreat, we asked the 60 attendees to break up into small groups and discuss a vision for the future state
of the patient experience at Cleveland Clinic. In essence, we asked them
to define the perfect patient experience. Results ran the gamut from free
parking, happy caregivers, more smiles, quality medical care, and new
and clean facilities to improved communication with patients.

I liken the patient experience "definition challenge" to the parable of the blind men and the elephant.[1] In this tale, six blind men touching different parts of an elephant are asked to describe the animal. The man who touches the leg observes that the elephant is like a pillar, while the man touching the tail describes the elephant as a rope. The fellow who touches the ear says the beast is like a large hand fan. Each man recounts something different because none of the men can see the elephant as a whole. They could not agree on what the elephant was like, despite all of them correctly describing a feature of the animal.

Our early enterprise retreat validated that the parable was an apt analogy. Everyone knew that the patient experience was important, everyone knew that it needed to be improved, and everyone wanted to help. But everyone had a different idea of what the patient experience meant and how to fix it.

A survey conducted by HealthLeaders Media[2] found that U.S. hospital leaders believe the patient experience to be the number one strategic priority for their organizations. Yet I find that few C-suite hospital leaders agree on the definition of patient experience. Nor do they concur on how to organize and lead patient experience improvement efforts. When I speak with leaders at all levels, I find that patient experience improvement efforts are disorganized and inconsistent across U.S. hospitals.

Part of the challenge is that the patient experience as a focus area is relatively new. Traditionally, it has been defined as patient satisfaction, and responsibility for measurement and management of improvement efforts was relegated to the marketing department. The Affordable Care Act and Medicare have now linked inpatient reimbursement to hospitals' performance on HCAHPS scores. Medicare is also working to expand patient experience measurement tools in the ambulatory, pediatric, and emergency department environments. Other payers have followed Medicare's lead, with many private health plans now negotiating with hospitals to link a portion of payments to patient experience performance metrics.

Data transparency and its link to reimbursement are also driving increased consumerism. Patients have a choice, and they are using publicly reported data to exercise their options regarding where to go for care. These external pressures are forcing hospital leaders to pay attention and determine what the patient experience means to their organizations and how to improve it.

Why Definition Is Difficult

If you ask any healthcare worker if the patient experience is important, most everyone will say, "Yes, absolutely!" It's hard to disagree with the need to provide a great experience for patients. Our enterprise patient experience retreat discussions certainly validated that. While everyone agreed on the importance of outstanding patient experience, few could actually define what it means or how to achieve it. We also faced definitional challenges because we all believed we knew what was important.

What fascinated me most from our retreat was not only the group's passion about why the patient experience was important, but our collective belief that we were better able to define it because we have the benefit of experience both as caregivers and as patients ourselves.

Part of the problem of gaining universal adoption of the patient experience as a top priority is directly related to difficulty in defining precisely what the patient experience means and how it fits into everything else of concern to healthcare organizations. As a 2010 *Gallup Business Journal* states in an article on the patient experience, "After all, if you can't define it, you can't provide it."[3]

To achieve organizational adoption of a new concept like the patient experience, you must define the what, the why, and the how.

When I first started talking about the patient experience, people would often ask me, "But what does it mean?" and "How do you define it?" and "Why is it important?" I remember the feeling of helplessness as I tried to message what it was, what we were doing, and why. Giving presentations to our individual medical departments, I saw blank stares from the audience members. No one grasped what I was trying to say, and as I rambled off lists of different things that I thought were important to patients, I was unsure myself.

After my appointment as CXO, one of the people I met during initial meet and greets with senior leaders across our organization was the president of our regional hospitals. At the time, these hospitals had terrible patient experience scores. He was very supportive of the importance of the patient experience, and we discussed the overall strategy and what might make a difference. Our conversation then veered off into specific tactics we might implement. In retrospect, I recognize that we were jumbling emotional conviction regarding the importance of improving the patient experience with ideas for strategy and tactics. He pledged his support and committed to do whatever was necessary to fix it. We were both on the emotional "can't disagree with the importance of the patient experience" bandwagon without really knowing the scope or definition of what we were talking about.

The early days of my career as CXO were peppered with conversations like that, repeated across the enterprise. Everyone agreed that it was important and pledged to help—but no one knew exactly what it meant or how to fix it. Everyone was committed to it, everyone wanted to share his or her ideas and thoughts on tactics, and some were running out in front trying to implement things they were convinced would make a difference.

After fumbling through what I thought the patient experience meant, most conversations got worse, with the inevitable follow-up question, "OK, great, so how do we fix it?" Shortly after my meeting with the president of our regional hospitals, he gave all of his COOs a mandate: "Fix the patient experience." One of them called to tell me about it, and then asked, "Jim, tell me how to define the patient experience. What is the scope?" At that moment, I finally realized it was imperative to nail down a definition that people could grasp. Here was an operational leader ready to execute, but we hadn't identified what he should be executing.

Nationally among hospital leaders and healthcare providers, the words *patient experience* carry an unfavorable association. The definition has been hijacked, and the patient experience is frequently considered synonymous with making patients "happy." A 2014 article in *Forbes* reported that an emergency medical department with poor patient satisfaction rankings began offering "Vicodin goody bags to discharged patients in order to improve their ratings."[4] The article went on to suggest that if patients don't get what they want, they will not be happy and, therefore, will rate their providers poorly. That "more of what they want" includes expensive diagnostic tests that may not be beneficial. Similarly, when patients seek antibiotics for themselves or their children, if the physician believes the drugs are not warranted and does not comply with the request, poor ratings may follow. These suggestions are preposterous and dangerous.

Patient Perceptions of the Experience

Patients' definition of their own experience is quite divergent as well. We ask patients for feedback, and the results are fascinating. We've found that patients often use the word *experience* in their comments: "I can't believe how the experience in this hospital was." "This place is amazing—everyone is so friendly and caring." A patient remarked to our CEO on one of his leadership rounds, "Where do you find all of these angels to take care of patients?" Occasionally, patient comments are less complimentary: "My experience was terrible!" Patients tend to define their experience based on an "in-the-moment" encounter or a specific significant occurrence. Regardless of the quality of the entire journey, it will be the one or two great—or bad—events that will define a particular patient's experience.

Patients' perceptions, and, therefore, their patient experience definitions, are also influenced by the people around them. Once, when he was chairman of the Department of Thoracic and Cardiovascular Surgery before becoming CEO, Cosgrove was summoned urgently to a patient's room after surgery. The operation had gone well, and he believed the patient to be recovering without incident. Concerned, he ran to the room, finding the patient visiting with family and doing fine. A family member implored Cosgrove to look under the bed, where she pointed out dust bunnies. She asked the world-renowned surgeon, "How can this hospital provide top care if you can't even clean the floors?" Cosgrove was stunned. Why were the family members evaluating the organization's quality on dust bunnies when their loved one had a successful outcome from a difficult operation? He was getting firsthand insight into how patients judge our overall effectiveness based upon seemingly minor things that they readily understand.

I once rounded on one of my patients, and in the room were several family members. They knew of my role in patient experience and immediately wanted to relay a terrible experience they had had in our hospital cafeteria. They went on to describe, "We waited at the counter and the employees just ignored us. People down there were not helping us. The cashier person was rude. She was too busy talking to her partner." The patient, who had not even been in the cafeteria with his family members, piled on, "Yeah, that is no way for a hospital cafeteria to function."

I thought this patient's experience so far had been very positive. He had a good medical outcome, the nurses and I were attentive, and he was happy with our interactions. Does the bad experience of a family member in the cafeteria impact the patient's perception of his experience while in the hospital? I am not sure anyone knows the answer for certain. However, to ignore the possibility would be to diminish the impact of family dynamics on perceptions and opinions. We must assume that occasionally the patient's personal and family experience in the hospital environment outside of the patient's room will impact survey results.

There may also be a disconnect between patients' perceptions and how care was delivered. One patient wrote to our organization, "Your hospital is really bad. They hurt me." Those are tough words for a healthcare professional to hear. Yet often, when we review a dissatisfied patient's medical record and discuss the experience with the team that took care of him or her, we discover that, in fact, the outcome was very good, it met our standards of medical care, and all the members of the team thought that they were going above and beyond what was required to ensure that the patient and family experience was exceptional. When I asked this particular patient what he meant by "hurt," he expressed disappointment at having to undergo treatment in the first place. We were not being judged on the care or the caring; we were being evaluated on the patient having the disease—a battle we could never win, but a very important illustration of how some patients think. Often patients' definition of "quality" is not our definition of quality. Patients relate to things they understand, and that drives their perceptions.

Patients frequently use their experience with service quality to define their perception of the healthcare they received. If you ask patients to tell you "What is it about your stay that made the experience great," they often zero in on a specific item such as "The doctors explained things well and were very nice," "The nurses were very attentive," or "The building is new and clean."

This global grab bag of comments demonstrates the challenge: if the patient experience can mean anything, then how do you define it as an organization and, more important, how do you fix it? Patients have widely varying perspectives, and it is unreasonable to hold patients to a single definition of how they think about the patient experience. The patient experience can mean anything, can differ from patient to patient, and is highly perspective- and experience-based. A patient will define the experience from his or her unique vantage point, which is often determined by a single good or bad event. This is what patients remember.

Professional Definitions of the Patient Experience

Harley Manning of Forrester Research, who focuses on understanding and enhancing customer experience in a variety of industries across the world, including healthcare, defines customer experience simply as "How customers perceive their interactions with your company."[5] Patients are our customers, and they can define their experience any way they want. An astute observer once remarked to me that the patient experience is what patients say it is to their family and friends when they are out of your healthcare environment.

Merriam-Webster's Collegiate Dictionary has several definitions of the word *experience*, but the one that fits most appropriately in this context is, "the act or process of directly perceiving events or reality." An additional definition is, "something personally encountered, undergone, or lived through."[6]

There are consultant reviews and reports that try to explain it, but consultants may have a bias and the tendency to wrap their definition around their services. In a 2009 white paper published by Deloitte Consulting LLP, the authors state, "The patient experience refers to the quality and value of all of the interactions—direct and indirect, clinical and nonclinical—spanning the entire duration of the patient/provider relationship."[7]

Gallup's definition centers on engagement and the need to fulfill psychological elements of confidence, integrity, pride, and passion, combined with providing top-of-line medical care.[8] This definition's central component, engagement, certainly is an element of delivering a great patient experience. Patient engagement is a major focus of Gallup's healthcare consulting business.

Further, there are definitions built around consensus statements and surveys from healthcare leaders. The Beryl Institute, an industry-sponsored organization that works to synthesize thought leadership in the field of patient experience, composed a work group of health professionals to tease out a consensus statement that defined the patient experience as "The sum of all interactions, shaped by an organization's culture, that influence patient perceptions across the continuum of care."[9] I believe consensus statements are compromises, as they amalgamate a variety of ideas. There is the risk that something truly important is missing. Our own retreat demonstrated this observation.

Healthcare's inability to articulate a concise definition of the patient experience, in conjunction with our individual beliefs regarding what we think it means and how to fix it, makes fixing it very difficult. I realized early on that if Cleveland Clinic was going to improve the patient experience, we first needed to define it. Ultimate success in our efforts to improve would mean controlling the perspective on the "elephant."

Additionally, fixing the patient experience has an impact on hospital operations, an element that cannot be managed by consensus. The problem with definition lies not only with frontline people but with the very people who are trying to drive and manage change. We all want to do the right thing for the organization. But without clear leadership and direction, there develops a *meandering definition* of the patient experience: each person has an idea of what the patient experience means, and everyone has individualized thoughts regarding how to improve it, which leads to decision-making paralysis and ineffective change.

Early in my role as CXO, I believed that the patient experience was all about patient perception and that there was little we could do to affect it. Many still have this belief, and while perception may drive how patients view their experiences, providers and systems have tremendous power to set and manage those perceptions.

An interesting study examined whether patients' recollections of past events could affect their perceptions of an experience.[10] Two groups of patients underwent colonoscopy. In one group, patients had procedures done according to normal practices. In the other group, the scope was kept in the patients longer before it was completely removed. The researchers theorized that the longer procedure would be viewed as more favorable. This hypothesis seems counterintuitive, as one would believe the shorter procedure would be perceived as better. Patients tended to zero in on the part of the procedure where they had the least amount of discomfort—which was at the end, where the scope was in longer, but not really doing anything clinically significant. That last part of the procedure defined the patients' perception of the experience.

This study suggests that there are critical events in a procedure that define the patient's perception of how that procedure was performed. The study also suggests that the entire experience can be influenced by the provider. There are critical touch points that define the patient experience, and we have the ability to influence those touch points. Imagine if we knew where the critical points were for every patient's journey—the interactions that were really meaningful. Our efforts and resources could be targeted to ensure that those were exceptional points of contact. Having seamless processes and aligning our efforts around those touch points is achievable. This not only will have impact on patients' perceptions of their experience, but will improve the way we deliver care.

Cleveland Clinic's Definition of the Patient Experience

I have devoted considerable thought to what the patient experience actually means and how it can be improved. It is pretty clear that everything has impact upon patient perceptions; therefore everything *is* the patient experience. It is everything patients see, touch, feel, hear, and think about their interactions with the organization. When asked how I think about the patient experience, I always start out by showing a slide displaying a box labeled "The Episode," as shown in Figure 4.1. Arrows around the box indicate a direction of movement. The arrows represent the patient's journey through and around the medical care. The patient experience encompasses everything before the patient becomes

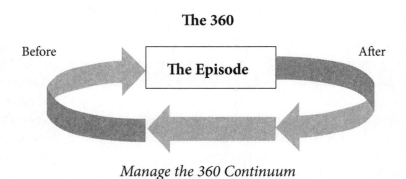

The 360

Before   After

The Episode

Manage the 360 Continuum

Figure 4.1   The patient experience 360.

a patient, such as perceptions of the organization and the ease of access. The patient experience includes what happens while patients are receiving inpatient or outpatient care. The patient experience also includes getting patients back to the starting point, encompassing discharge, follow-up, and so on. I call this the patient experience "360." Managing this 360 is our challenge.

How the definition is used and messaged differs depending upon whether you assume the provider or the patient perspective. The definition is critical to both the inward-facing (provider) and outward-facing (patient) perspectives.

For an inward-facing definition to help drive organizational improvement by focusing strategies and tactics, it must be easy to understand and applicable to the ways hospitals think about and lead their operations. The definition must account for a variety of different priorities in healthcare and help employees understand how to think about the patient experience.

Because for patients the experience can be anything they perceive it to be, the actual outward-facing definition is less relevant and can be less precise. Patients' experience is driven by perception, and their tendency is to define it based upon an in-the-moment experience. They will use this lens to filter everything they see and experience. We need a consistent definition that helps patients understand how to think about their experience. We define the patient experience for them to assist them in focusing that lens on what is important.

If the patient experience is everything, let's contemplate what we want the patient to see and experience. To understand how this concept works and consider how to make improvements, we place ourselves in the role of the patient and ask, "What would we want to experience?" Think about how patients transition through a healthcare encounter and include in that flow their feelings and needs. We did this in several of our areas using patient focus groups and voice of the patient advisory councils. For an effective patient experience, the flow must be seamless and must generally meet the expectations of the patient.

In the 360 concept, patient movement is generally longitudinal. Patients enter on one side, interface with a variety of touch points, whether administrative or medical, and exit on the other side. This basic flow is similar whether describing an ambulatory or inpatient encounter.

The ideal experience for the patient is for each touch point to be effective and each transition seamless.

To illustrate, consider something that happens every night on the Las Vegas strip. As I mentioned previously, in front of the Mirage Hotel and Casino is a volcano attraction. For 15 minutes every night at 5 p.m. and every hour on the hour until 11 p.m., lights, music, drama, and fire coalesce and build to a crescendo of anticipation and excitement that ends in a fiery explosion. The visitor sees magic, unaware of the hundreds of processes and multitude of people working behind the scenes. The day after I first watched this unique entertainment, I was given a behind-the-scenes, under-the-volcano tour of the operation. Management pulled back the Wizard of Oz's curtain to reveal multiple hidden processes that when combined deliver a consistent, reproducible experience for viewers. The Mirage volcano is a model of seamless execution designed to deliver a friendly and fascinating user experience.

Taking care of patients is much more complicated than making that volcano erupt; nevertheless, the point is the same. We should ensure that patients never see or experience the complex support that drives the flow—whether processes, information technology, or human beings. Too much behind-the-scenes exposure can erode patient confidence in our system, as it may appear disjointed and uncoordinated. Creating the ideal patient experience requires a multitude of caregivers from a variety of disciplines employing complex processes that work together to deliver what meets the patient perception of the ultimate. For the patient, the process should be akin to hearing a well-conducted orchestra performing together to create a harmony of experience and ensure consistency, superior execution, and seamless transition. The combination of consistency and accuracy in what we do not only secures the optimal patient experience but also upholds safety and quality.

To understand how we would like our employees to think about the patient experience, let's look at aviation. I have had opportunities to fly on private jets and sit up front with flight crews and better understand how they perform their tasks. On one such flight, just after completing the preflight checklist and right before we took off, one of the pilots informed me that there were times I could not talk to them, specifically during takeoff and landing and during selected events in the air. Once we were airborne, I asked why these sterile cockpit rules existed. The pilot told me that takeoff and landing are the most dangerous times for pilots, and they have to be completely focused and cannot be distracted. Furthermore, when the plane encounters certain types of events in the air, such as heavy turbulence, the same is true. Pilots focus on flying the plane rather than conversing with passengers. I often get nervous during periods of heavy turbulence and wonder why pilots don't immediately announce that everything is OK. It is because my satisfaction is not their priority; it's ensuring that the plane is safe.

Airlines have hundreds of thousands of employees around the world, and their leaders must balance the same elements: seamless execution from the customer experience standpoint, safety, and high quality. Airlines have achieved remarkable safety records partly because of the way they prioritize how they want their people to think about what they do every day. Airlines prioritize safety above everything else, and then comes quality, followed by the customer experience. In the airline industry, safe travel is when landings equal takeoffs. High-quality airline travel is landing and taking off on time. You can personally define the airline customer experience.

Now let's think about how to discuss the patient experience definition with the people who drive the experience, our caregivers. If we accept that everything that touches the patient constitutes the patient experience, then how do we help our people think about it? How do we further define it so that we can begin to understand ways to make it better and also make certain that it fits with everything else we do to ensure great care for patients? At Cleveland Clinic, the patient experience does not equate to patient satisfaction. Rather, we define the patient experience, or our Patients First culture, as, first, providing safe care; second, delivering high-quality care; third, in an environment of exceptional patient satisfaction; and, finally, in a value-conscious environment, or as I like to say, "everything else we do" (see Figure 4.2).

Think about why this definition is important. Healthcare is the ultimate service-delivery business. There's nothing more high touch and personal than how we deliver care to our patients. However, a major problem is that we are in the ultimate service-delivery business in which our customer is not always right. When I operate on a patient and go to her room the next morning, I inform her that she will be getting out of bed and walking. The day after major abdominal surgery, patients are

Patients First

- Safe Care
- High-Quality Care
- Patient Satisfaction
- High-Value Care

Figure 4.2   The Patients First culture.

exhausted, have pain, and generally do not want to move. Often they will say that they cannot do it. This is simply not an option. I don't say "OK, I'll come back tomorrow, and then we'll see how you feel." I tell her that she will be getting out of bed and that the nurses will help her.

This is when patients generally get annoyed with me. And if I don't explain why walking is important, they will then define their experience and perception of me based upon the belief that I was mean and made them get out of bed when they were in pain. But when I inform patients that it is critical to ambulate to avoid complications and that it is a safety and quality issue, they are more willing to comply. I have set an expectation and guided them regarding how to define my care and their experience. I don't let them define me based upon their being upset. I help them understand—and define their experience—based on my looking out for their safety.

While patient advocates may bristle at my suggestion that we help patients understand how to define their experience, I see this as an opportunity to increase the level of patients' engagement in their healthcare. Everything we do for patients is important, but I want them to be able to prioritize the most important elements of their experience. Safety trumps satisfaction every time, and when we ask patients to do things that they may not like or that make them unhappy, it's important that they understand why.

Having a definition that prioritizes how we think about satisfaction relative to safety and quality is also important for our caregivers. I often talk to physicians who are reluctant to get on board, suspicious of our efforts to improve the patient experience. I regularly hear sarcastic remarks from colleagues who accuse me of caring more about "smiling" and "making patients happy" than quality. I refer these individuals to Cleveland Clinic's definition of what is important in a Patients First culture and note that our first priority is not quality. It's actually providing safe care, followed by quality, then ensuring patient satisfaction. Those are the elements of high-value care.

If a world-class surgeon forgets to administer a drug to prevent blood clots after surgery, and the patient subsequently develops a fatal pulmonary embolism, the world-class operation that the world-class surgeon just performed is irrelevant.

The way we've taught our caregivers to define and think about the patient experience is similar to how Medicare wants the public to think about it. When you examine the HCAHPS, you realize very quickly that the complexity and granularity of the questions relate to issues much more important than just whether patients were happy. There are nine questions regarding patient communication, including how nurses communicate, how physicians communicate, and how we communicate about medications. Certainly, if measuring the patient experience were just about whether patients were happy, we would not need nine questions about communication. That's because the patient experience is more about how we actually deliver care.

It's been demonstrated that when nurses communicate better at the bedside, medication errors, pressure ulcers, and falls decrease.[11] So improving nurse communication at the bedside directly impacts how well we ensure patient safety. When physicians communicate more effectively with patients and families, treatment compliance increases, and when physicians communicate and coordinate better with nurses, there is an overall improvement in the quality of care. There's no question that when all caregivers communicate better with patients, they are more satisfied, and this obviously has direct impact upon the patient experience. And when we affect safety, quality, and satisfaction, we also impact the value of healthcare. That's the point: improving the experience of care—the way we deliver care to patients—not only impacts safety, quality, and patient satisfaction; it drives higher effectiveness, efficiency, and, ultimately, value in healthcare.

As Leah Binder, the CEO of The Leapfrog Group, pointed out in a blog post, "Many providers still do not grasp that improving the patient experience requires something more than studying the issue and implementing a few new policies. It requires a paradigm shift in the way they think about their role in the patient's life and the fundamentals of their practice."[12] Her statement grasps the complexity of and difficulty in developing a unifying definition. Her comments further reinforce that this is about not just satisfying patients or affecting patient's perceptions, but also how we actually transform the interaction, which is about care delivery.

Physicians, nurses, and other healthcare professionals spend many hours every year improving their knowledge of disease and how to treat illness. Yet how much time do we spend thinking about better ways to deliver that knowledge to patients? The fact is we spend little time. Physicians in training are instructed to deliver care by modeling their teachers and mentors. They learn their communication styles, interaction styles, and overall approach to patients by mimicking the people that are teaching them. While we are beginning to spend more time with medical students and house staff teaching basic things like communication skills, we spend very little time teaching them how to interact with patients. Furthermore, we spend very little or no time, nor is there significant coursework offered, in teaching physicians better ways to interact with patients. Providing a clear, concise definition of how to think about the patient experience allows every caregiver in the organization to clearly understand our expectations of them.

Putting It All Together

Once you have defined the patient experience, the next important element is to operationalize the improvement. My Harvard colleagues invited me to present with them at the 2012 Production and Operations Management Society annual conference in Chicago. I was asked to describe how we execute on improving the patient experience. I talked about setting the patient as true north, the importance of making the patient experience a strategic priority, how we define the patient experience for caregivers, and the consequences of effective and accountable leadership.

I then discussed how we frame execution. If we accept that managing the experience requires us to think about the "360," then we can unwind that 360 into a linear journey, with an arrow representing direction to consider how everything we deliver to patients is connected

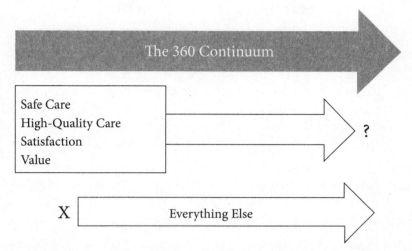

Figure 4.3 Cleveland Clinic's definition of the patient experience in the 360 continuum.

along that flow (see Figure 4.3). Our challenge is to manage everything we do across that continuum in a consistent, reproducible manner, whether related to safety, quality, or the patient experience. Every patient touch point must be consistent and the continuum seamless. Indeed, for any organization as complex as ours, everything we do for customers must be done consistently across the continuum. This is the foundation of systems thinking. When we solve problems with a systems mindset, we are always thinking about how changes or improvements will impact other processes downstream.

To successfully manage seamless continuum flow requires bucketing execution into three critical elements: process, people, and patients, which I call managing the 3Ps (see Figure 4.4). Process is the first P. Hospitals are replete with processes, and the first priority must be to ensure that basic hospital processes function efficiently and effectively. Then you can consider what additional processes or tactics will directly improve what you're already doing. People, the caregivers who are foundational to the organization, are the second P. This represents everything done to manage, invest in, and develop caregivers in a service-oriented culture aligned around and focused on the patient. The final P is for patients. There is likely no business that requires development of more and stronger customer partnerships than healthcare. We are in the busi-

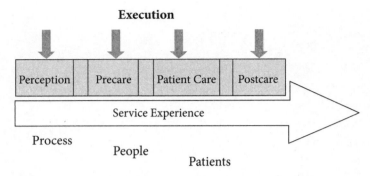

Figure 4.4   The 3Ps framework for executing a great patient experience.

ness of helping people, but we also need those people to help *us*. We cannot do it alone, and how we educate, engage, and activate patients and their families, as well as manage their expectations, is critical to achieving the collective goal of a great patient experience. As you contemplate improvement strategies and tactics and consider how to budget resources, understand how they fit into the 3Ps framework to help structure your thinking and execution.

The patient experience is paramount, but it is more than making patients happy. The definition must provide healthcare leaders and employees with a framework to prioritize their thinking. Just as in the airline industry, we must never compromise what is the most important element, which is delivering a safe product. If we lose sight of what is important, our efforts to improve the experience and patient satisfaction will become irrelevant. Along with providing a clear definition, we must deliver a framework to think about execution. As you continue to read this book, consider how every strategy and tactic discussed helps to drive safety, quality, satisfaction, and all that we do in healthcare.

In summary:

1. The patient experience is about how we deliver care, not whether we can make patients happy. Questions and domains on standardized surveys are designed to evaluate the process of care delivery by nurses, physicians, and others involved in healthcare. If the patient experience were just about satisfaction, we would not need to evaluate as many patient touch points.

2. The patient experience can mean anything to patients. The patient experience includes everything patients see, touch, feel, hear, and think about regarding their interactions with the processes and the people in the organization during their journey through medical care. Our challenge is to get them in, deliver what they need, and return them to where they started, which we affectionately label "managing the 360."

3. Cleveland Clinic defines and manages the patient experience as processes that deliver safe care, high-quality care, and maximum patient satisfaction in an environment of high value. Healthcare delivery is the ultimate service business, but we must ensure that the most important elements of healthcare—safety and quality—are prioritized above service. This is necessary to ensure that all of the elements are linked and the organization can message the priorities to employees and caregivers clearly.

4. Employees need a clear definition of what the patient experience means and what you want patients to do. Patients also need help framing how to think about their experience so that they understand why things are happening. Failure to set and manage appropriate expectations will result in patients evaluating your performance based on their understanding of the environment.

5. Improving the patient experience, or our ability to execute on a strategy, requires a framework to operationalize what we do. Using the 3Ps of process, people, and patients helps managers and leaders understand how different tactics fit into an enterprise strategy. The framework also allows organizations to better understand how their patient experience strategy fits into the overall strategy of the organization.

Culture Is Critical

T he entrance to our old executive offices was across from the elevators to the main hospital. One day I was walking in the lobby about
to get on one of the elevators when I noticed a puddle on the floor.
I immediately went to find something to wipe it up. As I was returning
to the lobby with my paper towels, I stopped and observed all of the people that were either avoiding or stepping over the puddle. People were
taking appropriate evasive action, but no one did anything to take care
of it. Many were our employees—doctors, nurses, other staff—who were
ignoring a problem that could have caused harm to a patient.

I'm often asked what I might have done differently along our patient
experience journey. While quick to admit the trial-and-error process that's collectively led to our success, I unequivocally respond "the
culture"—turning our attention to aligning and developing it earlier.
Culture in healthcare is critical!

Culture impacts safety, quality, and satisfaction, everything in
healthcare—or in any organization, for that matter. Human talent is our
most important asset, responsible for delivering everything we do. But
it would have been difficult, having just taken over the patient experience initiative, for me to raise the specter of culture change. How could
a relative neophyte challenge the culture that has made Cleveland Clinic
highly successful since its foundation in 1921? It wouldn't have been a
credible first step.

Cleveland Clinic was founded by four physicians who were friends and colleagues in Cleveland, Ohio. Three of the four served together on the battlefields of Western Europe in World War I, where teams of physicians worked closely to care for patients. Back home in the United States, the practice of medicine was very competitive and independent, with no incentives for teamwork. Believing there was a better way, these men founded Cleveland Clinic "to act as a unit" in the group practice of medicine.

Over the years, while it was generally true that our physicians collaborated closely on patient care, many felt the founders' ideal had faded as the organization grew. We started as a small, single-location, tertiary-care specialty referral center. Today we are big and growing: an enormous organization with some 43,000 people throughout the globe. We have more than 3,000 physicians and scientists. Those still here after more than a quarter century talk about how different it was when there were only 150 physicians on the medical staff. While our culture supported physician teamwork, the concept of team has been eroded by our size, and there certainly wasn't a workforce uniformly focused on patients.

The organization also didn't have a reputation for being particularly nice to employees or patients, confirmed by engagement and satisfaction studies at the time I assumed the role of CXO. At a recent executive leadership retreat, I asked my colleagues to select adjectives to describe Cleveland Clinic before Cosgrove became CEO. A longtime physician didn't hesitate to say "mean" and "vindictive," not a very conducive culture for patient-centered teamwork! We provided excellent medical care, but we were *not* excellent at caring or treating patients with empathy. Nor were we consistent in treating our own people with respect, something I experienced firsthand during my fellowship.

Cosgrove often joked in speeches that patients came to us for clinical excellence but did not like us very much. One of my patients, also a Cleveland Clinic financial supporter, ribbed me about our culture every time I saw him. He'd had heart, prostate, and back surgeries with us. He said he came to Cleveland Clinic for surgery because of our master technicians but went to his primary-care physician, employed by our chief regional competitor, when he wanted to be cared for as a person.

There were two strong elements of our culture: one, the physicians, employed in a large group practice, and two, everyone else. You would often hear nonphysicians joke that Cleveland Clinic was all about the doctors—a hospital founded by doctors, for doctors, and because of doctors. Within the "everyone else" group, there were large, defining stakeholder subcultures, such as nursing, which made up about a third of it. But in general, doctors were perceived as the proverbial king of the hill. One early patient experience initiative was to reserve for patients all parking spaces close to our buildings, forcing doctors to park farther away. One angry physician cried, "What does Patients First really mean? Doctors last?" Cosgrove's comeback was "Yes!"

We had drifted away from what our founders believed necessary for delivery of great care, namely, high-performing teams. I'm sure they didn't use the words "high-performing teams" back in 1921. But a review of our history and founders' statements leaves little doubt what they hoped to create.[1] They espoused the importance of teamwork: your role didn't matter, but your contribution to the overall goal did. Cosgrove often emphasizes that one of his most important priorities is to protect this ideal.

In addition to our "us-them" challenge, the other main obstacle to alignment around our founders' vision was that we were no longer just one hospital. We were a heterogeneous healthcare system functioning as a holding company. We had nine community hospitals across northeastern Ohio; each had been a stand-alone hospital or system with its own culture. We had hospital operations in Florida and Canada, and we managed hospitals in the United Arab Emirates. We had lost the small-town feel as we grew into a vast healthcare system. One of Cosgrove's top priorities when he became CEO was to transform our holding company into a healthcare operating company, integrating services and operations across all sites—truly creating one Cleveland Clinic. And part of this integration task was cultural alignment.

Culture Is Hard to Define

There are two critical elements that compose culture: first, the people who make up the organization and, second, how intensely those people are committed to what they do. Do they come to work to perform a task and collect a paycheck? Or do they believe they are part of something special, working for an organization with a compelling vision and mission and giving everything they have to make that organization great? Some would call this engagement; others would call it creating a culture of ownership.

Many employees go to work, perform their job, go home, and start the cycle all over again the next morning. They know what is defined in their job description, and they do it, and do it well. But in healthcare, that is not enough. A. Marc Harrison, MD, chief executive officer of Cleveland Clinic Abu Dhabi, points out, "I want people to come to their job every day like they are owners of the company, personally invested in our success."[2]

Owners live their mission, vision, and values. They care and are passionate about what they do, but they go the extra mile to understand everything around their environment. They hold themselves accountable to a higher standard. It's a culture that chief quality officer J. Michael Henderson, MD, says is necessary to achieve high levels of safety and quality, as well as patient experience. A successful culture of ownership would have everyone stopping to take care of that spill by the elevator. Developing that culture of ownership is a challenge all healthcare organizations face.

I don't claim to be an organizational culture expert, whether at defining, measuring, or changing it. I even challenge the notion of experts in this field. When you review the "culture" scholarship, the "experts" don't even agree about the definition of culture or how to measure it. There are also different types of "experts," including those who study culture and those in leadership positions who write about how they've developed their organizations' cultures. One finding I believe is certain; the top person must protect and define the culture. Joseph M. Scaminace, chairman and CEO of OM Group, Inc., and vice chairman of Cleveland Clinic's board of trustees, once told me that when he became CEO, his first act was to get rid of the external organizational development consultants. "I know how to lead, and our team will define the culture we need to be successful."[3]

Large nonhospital corporations tend to be driven strictly in a top-down fashion; the CEO is responsible for minding the mission and managing the culture. In academia, there are unique and powerful stakeholder groups to be considered. A university faculty tends to function independently, cannot be underestimated, and must be consulted about culture change.

Hospitals do not fit the corporate authoritarian leadership model and are more analogous to academia, owing to large, influential physician and nursing stakeholder groups. Community-hospital structures are classically defined by a triangle, with each tip representing a key stakeholder group, including administration, trustees, and medical staff. With the evolving importance of nursing, some might suggest that the classic triangle has become a square.

So what cultural framework should Cleveland Clinic have? There are unique cultural attributes from the original group practice model and hospital, now joined by community hospitals and other units with their own historical identities and cultures. We have large physician and nursing stakeholder groups and competing identities, such as clinical excellence, education, and research. How exactly would we frame a culture-change program, and what would we want that culture to be?

I don't like the expression "change the culture." The messaging of everything we're doing in the patient experience is very important, but no one wants or likes to be changed. Cleveland Clinic was immensely successful at the time we started thinking about culture *vis-à-vis* the patient experience. We needed to celebrate who we were and what got us there. There would be people, especially longtime physicians who had joined the organization when there were only 150 doctors, telling us that the culture was just fine and we didn't need to change anything.

Coming out aggressively that we were going to "change the culture" had the potential to send shivers down our collective spine and likely result in no support for the initiative. There's a terrific *Harvard Business Review* piece about "organizational immunology" that compares an organization attacking change to the immune system attacking disease.[4] Recalling the cliché "culture eats strategy for breakfast," I was concerned that our strategy to change the culture would be eaten by the culture that existed at Cleveland Clinic.

Culture in its present, prechange state is what I call the organization's bedrock. I could never define the totality of Cleveland Clinic's culture. However, I could cite several specific elements, such as innovation and high quality. Our culture is the amalgamation of nearly a century of layered success and failure that led to the rise of a highly successful organization. We would take that foundation and layer on what we needed to enhance it, rather than change it.

A practical and much more understandable alternative to *changing* culture is to seek what elements to add to it. Or what elements to modify because we don't like them. Or how to collectively develop culture to where we want it to be. I recognize this is wordplay in a sense, that *modify* and *develop* also mean *change*. But this represents a much more subtle tactic than *change the culture*. Our organization's culture is foundationally solid. We don't want to change what we are but to determine what we want to be and develop to that level. This is the approach we have taken. I've joked with Melvin Samsom of Radboud University Medical Center about the nuances of cultural change and the importance of respecting the past while building the future state. He agreed about overtly avoiding the word *change* and has coined the phrase "culture change in stealth mode,"[5] which is exactly what we were considering at Cleveland Clinic.

The problem with developing the culture is very similar to that of improving the patient experience: few can actually define or impact it. There are multiple definitions of culture. One of our leaders used to say that culture is "how we do things around here." This always seemed too simplistic. Is it how we deliver food, wash gowns, or inject medications? Those are the types of things we do in a hospital, and if culture encompasses all that, then where do you start?

There are two definitions of culture I especially like, because they directionally define an organization. The clearest definition of culture for a service organization is from Forrester Research: "A system of shared values and behaviors that focus employee activity on improving the customer experience."[6] Substitute "patient" for "customer," and you have a definition of culture for any healthcare organization that not only states why it exists but also states who exists at the center and is most important. My other preferred definition is from Edgar Schein, professor emeritus at the Sloan School of Management at the Massachusetts Institute of Technology: "A pattern of shared basic assumptions learned by a group as it solved its problems of external adaptation and internal integration."[7]

These definitions allow practical flexibility in grappling with an intellectually challenging and complicated topic. Our goal as healthcare leaders is to get our people focused on what is right for patients: creating a Patients First culture. Who can argue with defining the culture as the need to keep patients central?

Applying Cleveland Clinic's definition of the patient experience (safe care, high-quality care, maximum patient satisfaction, and high value), we can revise Forrester's definition as follows: *Healthcare culture is a system of shared values and behaviors that focus caregiver activity on improving the patient experience.* Taking a lesson from Schein about adaptation and internal integration, we can move forward to build on our foundation.

We aligned our culture around the patient. We believed that if people understood that the real reason for coming to work every day was taking care of people, we would improve the patient experience and the culture. We then determined what components were necessary to drive toward this ultimate goal.

Culture Starts with the *Right* People

How well an organization hires and manages its talent will determine its degree of success. Hospitals traditionally have implemented a rather transactional human resources strategy. HR departments advertise job openings, screen applicants, assist with hiring, administer timekeeping and payroll, facilitate performance reviews, and conduct other transactions necessary to manage a workforce. Strategic talent management, popularized by a 1997 McKinsey & Company study,[8] is something very different from transactional HR management. Talent management transforms HR from a strictly transactional function to a strategic function that impacts how organizations "source, attract, select, train, develop, retain, promote, and move employees through the organization."[9] Talent management links strategy with the HR process so that an organization acquires people predisposed to alignment with organizational goals and objectives. It wraps the HR function around the mission, vision, values, and goals of the organization. This is very different from ensuring people get paid.

Great companies spend a lot of time making sure they have the right people in their culture. Zappos, for instance, offers every new employee a $4,000 quitting bonus. Its leaders' belief is that if new employees take the money, then they are not committed to what the company is about and they are not wanted. Jenn Lim, who cofounded a company called Delivering Happiness with Zappos founder Tony Hsieh, describes their philosophy about "hiring slow and firing fast"[10] to ensure that the culture the company is trying to create is protected.

Most people choose a healthcare career from a genuine desire to help care for their fellow humans. While the following has no statistical backing, I estimate that roughly 85 percent of our employees come every day completely dedicated to what they do. Ten percent may not be quite so motivated but probably are aligned with our mission and what's important. Five percent likely don't care whether they work for a hospital or a fast-food chain. The 10-percent group needs to be motivated or probably shouldn't work in healthcare, and the 5-percent group needs to go. This 15-percent club has missed the reason for working in healthcare; the people in this group consider it just a job, don't like or aren't committed to taking care of patients, and probably don't belong. As leaders and managers, our job is to try and elevate the 10 percent and outplace the 5 percent. The scholarship on employee engagement by and large suggests that one important point: one badly disengaged, nonproductive, or disruptive employee can contaminate a big chunk of the workforce.

Cleveland Clinic's HR strategy formerly focused on transactional management of people. When Cosgrove became CEO, he recognized the need to significantly improve our management of human capital. He conducted a national search for a new chief HR officer and found the perfect candidate in Joseph Patrnchak, who had extensive experience in the industry, most recently with Blue Cross Blue Shield of Massachusetts. His primary responsibility was to transform Cleveland Clinic's HR from a very transactionally focused operation to a strategically aligned one.

Patrnchak started by defining key components of our talent management life cycle and realigning the HR organization around our functional areas. He created a talent acquisition department and rebuilt a learning and development organization that had been eliminated. He recruited and hired team members with extensive HR experience.

Cleveland Clinic's hiring strategy had been to find people to fill jobs, a very transactional approach. Patrnchak introduced the practice of "hiring for fit," meaning we assessed candidates for organizational alignment. Similar to The Ritz-Carlton, which "selects only the most passionate and skilled hospitality professionals,"[11] we wanted to make certain we hired only people in the 85-percent category, passionately committed to healthcare and helping people. HR introduced prehiring screening and began to test applicants for predilection for teamwork, service, and other important organizational competencies. This tactic alone eliminated 20 percent of job applicants.

Patrnchak initiated employee engagement measurement and the development of action plans to improve satisfaction and buy-in. He ardently advocated and ultimately achieved wide-scale adoption of a robust rewards and recognition program called Caregiver Celebrations. He convinced leadership that job satisfaction is not dependent on compensation alone, but that a consistent process of recognizing employees with award certificates, trophies, and gift-purchase points is equally important. These tactics and other major HR initiatives were critical to our work on cultural development. We needed to find the right people, orient them to the organization and their roles, and develop them to high performance. Patrnchak was an early supporter of the concept that everyone is a caregiver, not just an employee.

We Are All in This for the Patient

Adopting the caregiver label for everyone in the organization was an important first step to begin alignment of our culture around our Patients First philosophy. When I first became CXO, I asked one of my patients to keep track of all the caregivers she encountered during her hospital stay. At the end of a five-day, uncomplicated stay for abdominal surgery, she had encountered eight physicians, more than 60 nurses, and so many other people (housekeepers, food deliverers, surgical residents in training, surgical fellows in training, phlebotomists, volunteers, medical students, and so on) that when I walked into her room on discharge day, she apologized, "Yesterday I encountered three new people and forgot to ask their names."

The number of people "caring" for my patient was eye-opening. Granted, not all of them were directly involved in her medical care, but every one of those employees had an important role in the overall delivery of care. Each could impact not only how she perceived her experience, but how we delivered quality and provided safety.

My patient's stay was fairly routine. A surgical complication could have extended it, meaning more specialty physician care, more nursing care, more blood draws, perhaps more procedures such as x-rays, more meals, more days the room needed to be cleaned, and, therefore, exposure to yet more people, all playing an important role in care and affecting her stay. My example is limited to the people that the patient encountered. Her family and friends touched places in the hospital that the patient never saw, such as the parking garage, gift shop, hallways, and cafeteria.

How each of those people defines culture is typically overlooked in healthcare. We've all heard similar complaints such as "My hospital stay was great, well, except for the phlebotomist who kept sticking my arm, could not get blood, and never apologized." Or, "That one nursing assistant was really mean to me." Or, "Dr. Merlino was great, but every time his resident came to see me, she flicked on the lights at 6 a.m. and scared me awake." Introducing the concept that everyone is a caregiver was important to begin fostering teamwork and convincing everyone he or she mattered in patient care. Everyone in the organization is important, has a role to play, and must be aligned as a team around patients. This is what Patients First is all about.

The concept of caregiving is not that complicated. If you're raising children, you're a caregiver. If you have elderly parents or an ill spouse, you're a caregiver. Deeming everyone a caregiver is no different from what's done at a lot of other high-performing service organizations, such as Walt Disney Company, which calls its employees *cast members*, or The Ritz-Carlton hotel company, which refers to its employees as *ladies* and *gentlemen*. Caregiving is also not just about service and patient satisfaction. You don't have to be a doctor or nurse to help a patient. If a food-service worker delivering a tray sees a patient having a seizure, he or she can help the patient by summoning aid.

Calling everyone a caregiver is not meant to imply that everyone is the same. But it does imply a common purpose. It also implies that we're in this together, that equality exists, and that everyone should be treated fairly. To foster a highly engaged culture of caregivers, there must be zero tolerance for ill-treatment of patients and each other. Successful implementation also requires that everyone, regardless of role, is held accountable. A healthcare organization must not have two standards, one for doctors and one for everyone else. We could not permit physicians to get away with bad behavior that we would never tolerate in another employee. Leveling the organization by calling everyone a caregiver resets our purpose and, at a very basic level, reminds people why they come to work every day. It's also an important step in having people recognize they are part of a highly functioning patient-care team. If you work for Cleveland Clinic, you're part of the organization's mission, which is providing care to patients. Therefore, you are a caregiver.

The conversation about labeling everyone a caregiver was not a smooth one. We had some physicians who vigorously argued that if you weren't a nurse or doctor, you weren't a caregiver. Likewise, we had many employees who never directly impacted a patient contending they were in no way caregivers. We listened to these views but held firm. As Patrnchak often pointed out, this is not just about a name we call each other, but about changing how we think about our talent. Cleveland Clinic long referred to physicians as the "professional staff," which implied to many that if you weren't a physician or scientist, you weren't valued as a professional. Caregiver sends the subtle but important message that everyone is valued.

Everyone Must Know the Goals

All these points about alignment around caregiving apply equally to organizational alignment around important goals. Early in my tenure as CXO, we held a retreat for one of our community hospitals. Every leader and manager was in attendance, and the purpose was to engage the group in improving the patient experience. The retreat opened with a *Jeopardy*-like icebreaker. The five or six people seated around each table were considered a team and took turns answering questions from the "*Jeopardy* board." One table chose the category "safety," and the card was flipped to reveal the statement "Identify patients correctly." The moderator inquired whether anyone at the table could answer what the statement meant to the hospital. The team passed, so the statement was reread to the entire room. Again, silence! No one knew the meaning or how it related to healthcare. This was remarkable to watch. No single manager from the entire hospital—all senior leadership included—could correctly name one of the Joint Commission's six national hospital patient safety goals for the year.[12]

This incident provoked another striking realization for me. We can train members of the general public to call 911 in an emergency, avoid elevators during a building fire, and put on their own oxygen masks in the event of airplane cabin depressurization before assisting a child. But not a single leader in that large, Joint Commission–certified community hospital could correctly identify a key requirement for hospital safety, which all of them were responsible for managing. Were they incompetent? Unaware? Did they go to their jobs every day ignoring basic safety requirements for which all hospitals are held accountable? Not exactly.

Juxtapose this story with my account regarding the number of people who helped care for my surgical patient. Each person affected not only the patient experience but how we delivered quality and provided safety.

If we agree that the top priority in a hospital is safety and everyone is responsible for it, then we need to ensure that the entire organization is wrapped around it. Every one of those people caring for my patient could have an impact on safety. For me as a surgeon, it's making certain we adhere to specific processes, such as doing a time-out before starting the operation. For nurses, it's double-checking what medications are being administered to a patient. For the food-service worker, it's verifying that the patient receives the correct diet. For the environmental-service worker, it's making sure the room is clean and uncluttered to prevent germs and falls. Everyone has an important individual role, but we also have a collective role to be there for the patient. We have to take ownership of what is at the center of what we do, which is Patients First.

If we see a disoriented hospital patient trying to get out of bed or having a seizure, we don't need a medical degree to know something's wrong and that we must immediately call for help. The same goes for walking into the room and seeing a puddle on the floor. Any one of our multitudes of caregivers should be aware that this poses a danger and do something to correct it—either wipe it up or warn people and call environmental services. We all have a role in safety.

Now apply this concept to the satisfaction side of the patient experience. Every person interacting with the patient and family should demonstrate the same courtesy, empathy, and compassion. We should all be kind, project caring, and try to be helpful. Everyone entering the hospital room should utilize a basic framework for interacting. The point is that everyone needs to align around the patient.

Standardizing Who We Are

In our journey to develop our culture, Cleveland Clinic had adopted the Patients First motto, made the patient experience a strategic priority, and rebranded employees as caregivers. Now it was time to pull together other essential elements, including shared mission, vision, and values.

Some of the hospitals we had acquired had different mission statements and values. Our move toward integration required us to finally think about a unified *One Cleveland Clinic.* Our founders' original mission, "to provide better care of the sick, investigation into their problems, and further education of those who serve," became the unifying mission for the entire Cleveland Clinic health system. This meant that longstanding mission statements of some acquired entities went by the wayside, as Cosgrove felt strongly that our success stemmed from the defining mission of our founders. With input from the entire organization, the executive team created a new vision statement further galvanizing organizational focus on the patient and reinforcing that our quest for excellence would be continual.

Our vision became "Striving to be the world's leader in patient experience, clinical outcomes, research, and education." To our existing four values known as the "four cornerstones"—quality, teamwork, innovation, and service—we added compassion, to speak of the human side of care delivery. Integrity was also added to reinforce what we wanted caregivers to bring to work every day.

At the same time we were committing to a common mission, crafting a new vision, and augmenting our values, the organization was at work on a variety of other major initiatives. For example, there was a significant impetus to improve quality. We were beginning to integrate our health system operations. HR was transforming the workforce with employee wellness programs and engagement planning. In the fall of 2009, as our executive team rehearsed presentations for a year-end organization-wide leadership retreat, it became utterly apparent that we lacked a connection between all of these endeavors. Our presentations were clunky and uncoordinated, and a frustrated CEO left the room.

As we regrouped to tackle the problem of a cohesive focus and message, C. Martin Harris, our chief information officer, who was organizing the planning retreat, started to sift through our accomplishments and undertakings. He pointed to our Patients First orientation and our vision of a great patient experience. Patrnchak remarked about our "most important asset," our people. We all chimed in about important safety, quality, and other initiatives. Harris kept pushing us to think about a unified theme. That's when we had a corporate epiphany. Our efforts to improve safety, quality, and the patient experience would align our caregivers. We had renewed commitment to ensuring those caregivers were satisfied and engaged. The key to achieving our enterprise goals was an engaged workforce. We made the connections, and we finally recognized that we needed to treat our people (our caregivers) like we treated our patients (our customers).

At our strategic planning retreat a few weeks later, I presented a slide articulating that improving safety, quality, and the patient experience would require us to build and sustain a culture of highly engaged, satisfied caregivers, which would allow us to achieve our enterprise goals (Figure 5.1). The unified message resonated with Cosgrove and our leadership. One of the institute chairs e-mailed me after my presentation, saying we had nailed it. The message was simple and the linkages were clear, and it launched our development of Cleveland Clinic's culture.

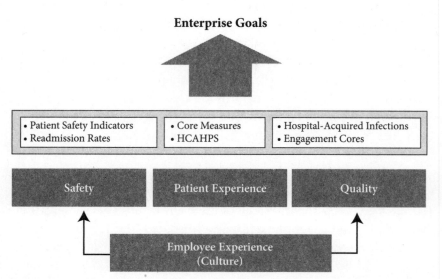

Figure 5.1   A caregiver culture would allow us to achieve our enterprise goals.

Under Cosgrove's leadership, our organization had laid significant groundwork to strengthen our organization's human capital. We modernized our HR infrastructure, focused on development of our people, and started to change how we referred to each other to take us back to our roots. We had reinforced our mission, strengthened our vision, and added critical components to our values. Next would come the daunting task of actually getting people aligned.

Here are critical steps for success in considering culture revitalization:

1. Define or refresh a unifying organizational mission, vision, and values. It is important that the M/V/V fit the organization in its current form. If the enterprise is made up of different business units, the M/V/V should be standardized.

2. Don't try to change your culture. People don't like to be changed, and organizations represent the net value of their successes and failures, good and bad. This is especially true for organizations with a long legacy of success. Ask what you want the organization to become or what it will be in the future, and then shape a strategy to identify what you are in your current form and what you need to do to achieve what you want to be.

3. Leverage your organization's legacy to drive your efforts. Every organization has a story to tell. Organizational history is likely what drove the mission and can be an important starting point for discussions about culture development. Use your organization's history to ignite passion and frame the road map for the future.

4. Recognize that the key to your success is your people. Great organizations invest heavily in their people. Make sure that you treat your employees well. Their engagement will drive the organization's success and enterprise goals.

5. Implement a talent management strategy that includes the following vital elements:

    - Find the right people. Not everyone should work in healthcare. The goal is to ensure that they are the right cultural fit for the organization.

- Onboard employees extensively about their new role, goals, and the organizational expectations, not just for whatever they are being hired to do but for cultural alignment.

- Provide development opportunities so that your employees have a career trajectory.

- Measure engagement to keep a handle on the "pulse" of the organization.

- Recognize and reward people to validate their worth to the organization and call out achievements. Employees want to know that management is paying attention to the good work that they are doing to support the organization.

- Off-board people who don't belong. One disengaged employee who does not support the organization or the mission can have negative consequences for an entire department. The hardworking and engaged employees will resent these people being around.

6. Promote the concept of teamwork: "We are all in this together." For healthcare, "We are all caregivers." It does not matter what an individual's job is in an organization, but each must support the mission. Everyone owns the "customer" experience, and beyond that, everyone needs to own the delivery of whatever it is your company does for customers.

Cultural Alignment: The Cleveland Clinic Experience

Since the introduction of the Patients First motto, there had been discussions about how to instill that purpose more strongly into the culture of the organization. Creating the motto, making patient experience a strategic priority, revamping the mission, vision, and values, and appointing a chief experience officer proved not to be enough. And while we could point to a number of success stories in improving the patient experience in the units and in addressing physician communication, caregivers were not aligned and did not *live* the patient experience. It became increasing clear that we needed to do something so that everyone would comprehend the importance of the patient experience. We needed to shock the system. We needed an all-hands-on-deck training program.

Although we had little granular patient experience research at the time, we all knew anecdotally that patients paid attention to virtually everything. It didn't matter how good the medical care was or whether every safety contingency was covered. If a phlebotomist was rude when awakening the patient, a nurse seemed preoccupied, or a doctor didn't explain things completely, the patient left with a negative perception. We needed to evoke something dramatic to get everyone wrapped around the patient.

The *why* was pretty clear. Despite our early efforts, we still had terrible patient experience scores. Patients were continually complaining, often about simple things like rude behavior, not knowing what was going on with their care, and poor coordination between caregivers. The pressure on the culture was mounting for all of us to change.

We were relatively new at patient-centered thinking, and no one in our organization had experience with culture-change initiatives on the scale of the entire Cleveland Clinic. At our strategy session in late 2009, we had committed to develop a culture of "engaged and satisfied" caregivers for the purpose of achieving enterprise goals. This obviously meant alignment around the patient. Cosgrove had talked about it for years, but we hadn't done anything yet to achieve that change. We were behind, and he was frustrated.

We Learned from Others

To get started on building our cultural alignment training program, several members of the patient experience team and others from HR benchmarked organizations known for great service delivery. We looked at healthcare organizations but also wanted to learn from outside industries. Natural targets were hospitality companies and other service leaders.

The InterContinental Hotels Group manages Cleveland Clinic's hotel properties, and Campbell Black, regional director and general manager, graciously allowed us to spend a day with his senior leadership. They gave us a behind-the-scenes look at how they developed employees and sustained their excellent service culture. Black made several very important points, highlighting the need for ongoing training and constant individual recognition of great work. He also underscored how InterContinental aligns everything around the customer and holds employees accountable to the organization's values.

Another organization we visited was Houston Methodist, which puts considerable effort into constant culture development. A program called the Houston Methodist Experience, an ongoing training and development effort, begins at an employee's onboarding and lasts throughout his or her entire career at the organization. As president Marc Boom describes, "It starts from our board and goes all the way through our organization."[1] The Houston Methodist Experience is centered on a concept called I CARE, which stands for Integrity, Compassion, Accountability, Respect, and Excellence. Each employee is expected to embody the I CARE values in all that he or she does for the organization.[2] The Houston Methodist Experience is meant to instill these concepts in all employees.

From our benchmarking and discussions with service-sector leaders across the country, it became clear that organizational culture is an enterprise asset. And like any other major asset, it must be developed, maintained, and leveraged as a tool to achieve organizational goals. Organizations that did this well created a culture of ownership we desired. We also found that adherence to a set of values was a recurring theme. In addition, we learned that efforts at cultural alignment are not successful unless sustainability is addressed early and becomes part of the developmental effort. All the programs we benchmarked had long-term operational sustainability elements to ensure ongoing success. Tactics included consistent enterprise messaging and regular manager meetings. Other critical sustainability components included engagement measurement and a rewards and recognition program, important HR infrastructure that we were rapidly developing.

The Delivery Tactic Is Key

In designing our program, it was imperative to deliver information so that it would be remembered by employees and change their behavior. Learning research demonstrates that people retain about 10 percent of what they read.[3] Traditional didactic instruction increases retention to 50 percent. But with learner interaction and engagement in small-group activity—displaying material visually, allowing for one-on-one interchange, sharing stories, making it fun and relevant—people can retain up to 95 percent and will adopt the behaviors you're seeking. Our culture-training program needed to be meaningful and interactive, and our goal was not only to learn new concepts but to adopt new ways of doing things.

The team had recommended building our program around a visual delivery tool called a learning map. A learning map is a visual representation of content and has been demonstrated to be a useful tool for stimulating small-group dialogue. The learning map idea was championed by senior HR executive Reggie Stover, who had been recruited from PepsiCo, where he had used similar tactics. He had begun working on the development of the learning map before I became the CXO.

When the learning map concept was first introduced to me, I admit I was skeptical. I knew nothing about culture change tactics, but I recall worrying that if this was the best we had, we were in trouble. After the program was described to me, I didn't completely understand how it would work. I thought there was no way people would agree to do it, let alone believe it could develop our culture. My predecessor had nearly torpedoed the idea by branding it a "board game," and I secretly agreed with her (see Figure 6.1). Advising Cosgrove that we should give 43,000 people a half-day off work to sit around a table and talk about Patients First using something that resembled a board game seemed preposterous!

I started to change my mind about the learning map concept when I met Arden Brion, managing director of Root, Inc., a pioneer in learning map technology, who had used this tactic with great success at other companies, including several of the Fortune 500. Brion explained the concept and galvanized for me the importance of using a visual tool to drive small-group discussion, explaining that the interactivity of learning map exercises is one of the reasons they are successful. He also discussed the importance of having Cleveland Clinic people populate the content on the map so that it becomes theirs. This was my introduction to the concept of "by us, for us." We settled on the learning map tool because it was interactive and would engage caregivers in developing what is important for the organization and discussing tactics that would help achieve our enterprise goals.

To proceed in developing the training program, we formed a team jointly led by my office and HR. Donna J. Zabell, a member of my team who had been the longtime nurse manager of the cardiac operating rooms under Cosgrove, and Thomas Vernon, an HR executive with organizational learning and development experience, would colead the project.

Root's team elicited input from several key executives to decide what strategic themes the map would include and how the information would be "bucketed." Cosgrove immediately zeroed in on making sure everyone understood why we put patients first. We also wanted to include service excellence education and some practical skill training. After we deter-

Figure 6.1 Learning map.

mined the key elements, we assembled focus groups of employees from across the organization. Brion's team from Root facilitated discussions to determine how the content of the "buckets" would best be messaged and represented in the map. Designers from his company drew the map in real time during the focus groups. Participation from the employees was critical. Not only did they frame how the messages should be delivered; they elevated a number of important issues, such as how we would discuss defining and measuring the patient experience, why it's important, and how it relates to the key themes.

The focus-group exercise also taught me an important lesson about executive presence and sponsorship. At first, I was not scheduled to attend meetings; I was still settling into my role and frankly did not think I was needed. Zabell said that if I didn't attend, no one would come. She said, "No one will take it seriously. You have to tell them it's important." We argued about it, because I was still not sure I was taking it seriously. Zabell politely told me that we really had nothing else and needed to try to make it work. So I agreed, and it was an incredible process to watch. There were a variety of people in the room, from high-level executive leaders, hospital presidents, and nurse leaders to frontline caregivers. Many were skeptical at first, but you could see the conversation and input intensify as the map was drawn in real time. People were engaged and energized, and the most common emotion was passion for wanting to get this right for the organization.

Everyone Must Participate, Even the Doctors

We decided early on that to be successful, every employee—including each physician—would be required to participate. Employees would arrive at the event, sign in, and be randomly assigned to a table with 8 to 10 others. Random assignments ensured that everyone encountered fresh faces and different roles. We wanted employees sharing stories and discussing their experiences and reactions with a range of people, not just those they knew or were comfortable with because they worked in similar careers or units. Around a table could be a neurosurgeon, a parking valet, a nurse, and a cleaning person. I often referred to the Cleveland Clinic Experience as the "great leveling exercise." It did not matter what you did for the organization—for half a day, you were just a caregiver who works for Cleveland Clinic and supports our mission.

The team decided to have a facilitator at each table responsible for managing content flow and ensuring that every critical element of the exercise was covered. For three and a half hours, the facilitators would guide discussion around each of the components in Figure 6.1. Facilitators also were responsible for leveling the emotional intelligence disparities among table participants, toning down the overly talkative and drawing in quieter people, critical to achieving effective group participation. Finding a sufficient number of facilitators would be an enormous task. At first, the facilitators included the planning group and others from the Office of Patient Experience and the Office of Learning and Performance Development. We considered hiring contract facilitators but wanted to stay true to the belief this had to be "our people teaching our people." As we gradually rolled out the program, we observed participants to identify additional facilitators. We ultimately trained more than 400 facilitators from a variety of different disciplines and careers. One facilitator was a painter from operations whom we affectionately referred to as "Joe the painter." He became the poster child for the program being designed and implemented by only Cleveland Clinic people.

There had been several discussions about cost, including one rather heated exchange at an executive team meeting. Our nursing leadership was very concerned about lost productivity. In the usual sense of the measure, there would be lost productivity by taking a half-day of each employee's time. The investment of time could impact patient care if nurses were 100 percent productive 100 percent of the time they're on the clock, but they aren't. This reasoning applies to most employees across the organization, including the doctors. Surgeons, for instance, do not operate every day. For employees like cashiers or police officers, whose efficacy is measured by the number of hours they stand at their posts, then yes, their shifts would need to be covered. But taking most people off station for four hours would likely have a minimal effect on operations and productivity. Managing participation in the exercise would require thoughtfulness and collaboration, but we believed it could be done without negatively impacting operations. And in fact, it didn't. The year we ran 43,000 employees through the Cleveland Clinic Experience, we recorded one of our best years in patient volumes and financial performance. Some lingering critics might argue that the year would have been even better had we not done the exercise. I would argue that the year was as good as it was *because* we did the Cleveland Clinic Experience. Who is to judge?

There also was considerable discussion about how to evaluate the program's success. How do you measure culture change (or development, as I say)? Obviously, this would be very tough. With the items we were attempting to impact, patient experience, complaints, and employee engagement, it could take a year or more to see a difference. There are also no direct outcome metrics to tell you that the culture has been modified. So clearly there was a gamble. We were embarking on a very expensive program that did not have a real ROI measure. There was definitely an element of this being a "leap of faith," with our gut telling us it was the right thing to do. We ultimately determined to define success by how participants viewed the program: did employees consider it effective? We would wait for the longer-term impacts on patient experience, complaints, and employee engagement. Anyone embarking on a cultural development program like this will have to contend with finance, which will want to know the ROI. There just isn't one to defend the expenditure in the short term. Our leap of faith was guided in part by the successes that had been achieved in previous years by organizations conducting similar activities.

You Must Convince People It's the Right Thing to Do

Making the argument that doctors should participate was easy; convincing people the argument is right is a whole different story. When the learning map was first proposed, before I became CXO, there was the assumption that doctors would participate in this program. The nondoctors who were advocating, developing, and leading the initiative could not understand why doctors should not be included. There were no doctors involved in the discussions, however, until I came into the picture. As we got closer to implementation, the issue of physician participation moved to the forefront. Some leaders in the office that oversees the group practice were vigorously opposed. They argued that the doctors were different, and it would have a very serious effect on productivity. I took the matter to chief of staff Joseph Hahn, reasoning that, "What would be the purpose of trying to align the culture if we excluded the group considered the most important element?" We agreed to take the issue to the executive team meeting the next day; this would be our go/no-go decision point. About half the team was composed of physicians. If we could convince them, we would likely get the go-ahead.

I left work that night feeling that the success of the entire patient experience initiative was in the balance. The organization had invested heavily in developing the learning map program, and I had staked my reputation on it. We needed to walk out of that meeting with concurrence to proceed. I went home and started on my presentation. I decided to take the story from the beginning, talk about why we were doing it, how we would measure success, and how we would implement. I proposed a pilot with small groups, working up to a single institute to test effectiveness. We would pilot in the Digestive Disease Institute, my home base, where I felt the most comfortable with the subculture and thought we could successfully navigate the politics. I stayed up all night honing the message. I was on the phone with Brion from Root multiple times until very late, absorbing all I could about the learning map tactic, reexamining evidence of its effectiveness, and reviewing testimonials from Fortune 500 leaders who had deployed it. I studied the evidence we had assembled regarding how people learn and what makes culture change initiatives fail. At the heart of the discussion would be the *how* to do this, not the *why*, and whether doctors should be required to participate. Were the learning map and small-group discussions the best way to align our culture?

The next morning arrived, and I made my best pitch. After setting up the why, going over our benchmarks, and explaining the how, I clicked up a summary slide entitled *current state*, saying, "Here are the tactics we currently have in place to develop and maintain our culture." The slide was blank. I moved on to the next topic, adding, "We have nothing!" It was a shocker, and frankly, I was nervous, being in my position and a member of the group for only four months. But the statement was true, and I challenged the room to dispute it. Hahn looked at me and said, "You have a lot of balls to say that!" He was acknowledging my willingness to call it out, not scolding me. No one challenged me on the statement; everyone knew it was true that there was no program in place. I finished the presentation proposing that we conduct a pilot and see what happened. We had come a long way, and it was worth a shot to see whether this could help us.

Then the fun began. All the concerns regarding cost and productivity were raised again, and there was vigorous debate about physician participation—from the physicians. Cosgrove was silent, letting others be heard, and I was having difficulty reading him and the room. Finally, he smacked the table and declared, "Enough. We'll never know the cost, but what will be the cost of not doing this? Five years ago, we wouldn't have been ready, but today we're a different organization, and we have to try it." He felt that if doctors didn't participate, there would be no point in doing it. Cosgrove gave us the green light to pilot the program in the Digestive Disease Institute with about 1,000 people. But he wanted two things before we proceeded with an enterprise rollout. First, he wanted to be certain of physician support and requested that another group of physicians he selected test it to ensure it resonated. Second, Cosgrove was very concerned about whether we could sustain the program and wanted evidence of sustainability.

We assembled a group of 10 physicians to review the map and test the process. Cosgrove recommended some of the most skeptical physicians on staff to ensure honest, tough feedback. Zabell assembled them in a room, and before we revealed the map, I presented what we were seeking to achieve and why. Then we turned the map over, and Zabell, Vernon, and I talked through the program. I didn't know many of these physicians personally and had no idea how it would go. To our surprise, they all were incredibly supportive. They provided excellent suggestions on how to engage the medical staff, including messaging to physicians deeming them opinion leaders whose participation was essential to demonstrate the program's importance. The pilot physicians also made it clear we had to spell out the *why* to the entire organization. One longtime physician said, "The organization really needs to do something like this." The meeting finally convinced me the program would work.

However, no one on the team was convinced we had checked the box on Cosgrove's sustainability requirement. We decided to delay the Digestive Disease Institute pilot and reexamine sustainability. While we championed the fact that we had built the program without consultants, we decided to bring one in for an independent assessment. It was a very expensive two-day engagement, in which we had him watch focus groups of the learning map in progress. At the end of the second day, he still had given us nothing. Seated next to me, he finally turned and exclaimed, "The managers! The managers are the key to sustaining the program, and they will make it successful." There were about 2,200 managers in the organization. Effectively touching each manager would touch every employee. Our team quickly went back to the drawing board and developed two more pieces to the program that would be required for all managers (Figure 6.2). The first, "Leading the Way," would be a half-day managers' retreat laying out exactly what the Cleveland Clinic Experience learning map exercise was meant to accomplish, setting managers' expectations, and seeking their help in transforming the organization. The second session, "Coaching for Outstanding Performance," would be a full-day course given after groups had completed the learning map exercise. The course would reiterate the goals, discuss engagement strategies, and provide ways to sustain change. These manager retreats were a prelude to the important leadership forums we continue to have today.

The physician focus group and the decision to leverage the managers for sustainability also gave the team important insights into how to communicate the program to the organization. We wanted everyone to know what we were seeking to accomplish and why. Messaging would be targeted for three groups: physicians, managers, and all other caregivers. Following the focus-group physicians' advice, we sent letters to every staff member explaining what we were doing and reinforcing that the other caregivers across the organization viewed them as leaders. To managers, we messaged that they were essential to building the organi-

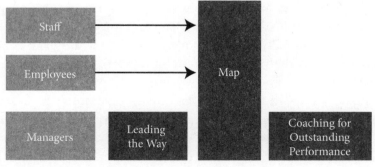

Figure 6.2   Process flow for the Cleveland Clinic Experience.

zation needed for future success. For the entire organization, our marketing team, led by Paul Matsen, chief marketing and communications officer, created a "brand book" that explained the role of the caregiver and how difficult, yet imperative, it is to the organization.

Something to Align the Culture

After extensive piloting, in late 2010, we introduced the Cleveland Clinic Experience program to our organization. The brand book was delivered in advance to all the employees, recognizing the important work they do and ensuring they understood the *why*. Each manager attended a "Leading the Way" session. Finally, each employee attended a four-hour exercise designed specifically to align our entire population to the organizational priority of Patients First. The program explained why Patients First is our guiding principle and described how every person who works for Cleveland Clinic is a caregiver regardless of role. There were exercises introducing expected service behaviors and our service recovery program, Respond with H.E.A.R.T., and there was a discussion of organizational values. Employees were asked to pick one of the values and tell the group why it was important to them in their role at the Clinic. At the end of the exercise, participants graduated and received a special caregiver name-badge backer. Next came the capstone training course, "Coaching for Outstanding Performance," again for all of the managers.

The Cleveland Clinic Experience became the instrument to internalize the concept that we are all caregivers and to begin the sustainability effort. It took a little more than a year to put everyone through the exercise across all of our sites. While the design and execution expense was relatively minimal, the cost in salary and wages alone was an estimated $11 million. This doesn't include the opportunity cost of lost physician productivity, such as forestalling a surgeon from performing operations.

While we agreed in advance that there would not be an immediate impact on outcome measures such as patient experience, complaints, and employee engagement, we did survey caregivers to judge their satisfaction with the program. The surveys were anonymous, and nearly half of attendants completed them, with the following results:

Will assist in my performance	87.7%
Content delivered effectively	92.5%
Satisfied with this course	85.4%
Supports mission of world-class care	93.8%

In addition, we wanted to capture visually what we were hearing anecdotally, so the team designed large posters with columns headed *Skeptical, Neutral,* and *Believer* for the walls where we hosted the Cleveland Clinic Experience. We asked arriving participants to put a blue sticker in the column that most indicated their frame of mind about the experience. At the end, they did the same with a green sticker. Most were skeptical or neutral at the start, but most were believers at the end (Figure 6.3). It was a great visual to demonstrate that people "got it" and were in agreement.

There were thousands of positive anecdotes from our caregivers about how much they liked the program and how supportive they were of Patients First. One of the most common observations was about physician participation: "I can't believe the doctors are doing this, too!" or "I have been here 32 years and have never done anything with one of the doctors." Employees were thrilled to see physicians participating with them to help improve their organization. Nearly all of the physicians participated with gentle appeals and words of encouragement. We had "gotten to" mandatory without "making it" mandatory." I'm a realist and never would have contended that all physicians would like it. Prior to the

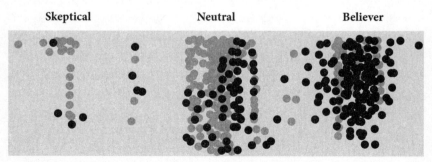

Figure 6.3   Participants' frame of mind before (gray) and after (black) the experience.

sessions, most were skeptical and, in some cases, resistant. But their support afterward was quite surprising.

In October 2010, we received our surprise, but anticipated, visit from the Joint Commission for recertification of our main campus hospital. During the executive debrief at the end of the visit, the lead surveyor said, "You have beautiful buildings, high-tech equipment, and intensely complex patients, but it's your people who are your greatest asset. They are engaged, passionate, and compassionate. Congratulations! You have world-class care here because you have world-class people!"[4] Nearly all of the main campus caregivers had just completed the Cleveland Clinic Experience. It was by far the greatest single validation of what we were doing!

Accomplishing the Impossible

The Cleveland Clinic Experience became our program to modify our culture. We successfully took all of our 43,000 employees, including our physicians, offline for a half-day to align them around Patients First, as well as other critical organizational priorities, such as service excellence. I believe we're the largest company, and certainly the first in healthcare, to take such a bold action to align culture in one fell swoop! People I talk with often express surprise about the project's scale and scope: "You put all employees through it?" Yes, everyone! From healthcare leaders, I'm always asked, "And the doctors did it?" Yes, the doctors did it!

Sustainability has been robust and consistent. Each new employee, including every new physician, goes through the Cleveland Clinic Experience as part of on-boarding. We continually refer to our employees as caregivers in conversation, meetings, and publications. Our service excellence program, Communicate with H.E.A.R.T., was developed to reinforce the expected service behaviors explained in the Cleveland Clinic Experience and is now part of every caregiver's workflow. Patient experience, service excellence, and our values are incorporated into everyone's annual performance review.

To refresh our Patients First theme and reinforce our values, about every four months, all our 2,200 managers attend a leadership forum designed to develop organizational competencies. These are traits we expect everyone in the enterprise to have. Every manager should be familiar with the organizational competencies and cascade them to his or her direct reports. At these forums, we've covered engagement, emotional intelligence, culture of safety, culture of continuous improvement, value-based care, and change management. Each session links to our culture story and thoroughly incorporates the themes introduced through the Cleveland Clinic Experience.

The Cleveland Clinic Experience, along with its associated sustainability tactics, is in my mind the single most important thing we've done to improve our organization. It directly targeted the culture, which is the most important element necessary to achieve patient-centeredness, and it has translated into improved patient satisfaction and enhanced safety and quality as well. The program has been successful because it had absolute organizational leadership and commitment: Cosgrove got behind it and stayed behind it. It also allowed us to reset, not change, our culture by demonstrating to everyone why we're here—for the patient—and aligning us and everything we do around the patient. The great leveling exercise became the springboard for our messaging and development tactics moving forward.

When implementing a cultural exercise, consider the following:

1. What are you trying to achieve, and how does it relate to the enterprise strategy? Our program was designed nearly exclusively for organizational alignment around the customer, with a focus on improving patient satisfaction. At the time, this was the appropriate focus. Our new working definition of the patient experience, which includes safety, quality, and satisfaction, could have been incorporated into the program to directly address those as well as culture and service. Understand what your long-term strategic needs are to adjust your culture first, and then build your program around those needs.

2. Decide if your goal is to inform or to change behavior. If you are going to get people to adopt new behaviors, your tactics need to consist of interactive small-group exercises. People remember what they discuss with other people more than what they learn in a classroom. It is a costly proposition in terms of time and commitment, but one that we believe pays off.

3. Deciding to put your organization through a major exercise will cause people to ask, "How do we know this will work?" The answer is there is no guarantee it will and there is no direct metric to measure that. Our metrics of success lagged behind the effort by a year, if not longer. These programs can be an expensive leap of faith, but if they are carefully constructed, well thought out, and successfully executed, as we and others have demonstrated, then they can be highly successful.

4. The sustainability of the program and the messaging must be determined before you start the program. This is where most efforts fail and are at risk of becoming just the "flavor of the month." If your organization is not going to invest to sustain the change, then don't invest in the program to begin with because it will not work.

5. Big organizations are culture-centric. This means that they tend to reject outsiders and consultants. Our program, the content, and the execution were all developed and accomplished by our own people. We used outsiders to help us think it through and design the learning map, but the program was ours: "designed by us, for us!" This is a powerful statement to the organization that we are leading this for our people.

6. Everyone must participate. There was a lot of pushback from some about requiring doctors to participate. This program would have failed if they had not, and I would not have recommended we proceed. Programs like this cannot exclude important and powerful stakeholder groups. What is the point of an alignment exercise if the group that is viewed to have the most power does not actively engage?

Physician Involvement Is Vital

G rowing up, I always wanted to be a doctor. I had my black doctor's bag, and I played doctor in the neighborhood. My collection of stuffed animals had so many stitched-up surgical scars that the toys could barely contain their stuffing. I saw the family doctor virtually every month, needing shots for bad allergies, and I was in awe of him, his tools, and his book-filled office! I remember marveling that there was no way I would ever be able to read that many books. There were no physicians in my blue-collar family, and we were conditioned to believe that doctors were all-knowing and deserved nearly unequivocal respect.

Doctors have incredible responsibility. They take care of people at the worst times of their lives. Physicians weigh an enormous amount of information and make decisions that impact patients' health and welfare, and patients place immense trust in their doctors to do the right thing. In some cases, doctor-patient interactions involve violating the patient in the most personal way possible. When patients go under general anesthesia, they trust the physicians and entire operative team to bring them back to consciousness. There are few ways to risk more personally violating individuals—or having greater responsibility toward them—than when exercising our sacred duty to ensure patients emerge safely from anesthesia and successfully from their surgeries. This is a profound, frequently challenging, and very stressful responsibility.

Doctors work very hard and train a long time to be able to practice medicine. I was in medical school for four years, residency for seven years—which included two years of research—and one year of fellowship. That was 12 years of training before I was able to see a patient independently. It also requires huge personal sacrifice: surgical residency involves long, grueling hours of work. In addition, there is substantial opportunity cost; I could have been doing something else over the course of those 12 years. Finally, there's the educational debt. I graduated from medical school with more than $200,000 of debt, and my wife and I both still pay student loans. The average physician incurs almost $170,000 in medical education debt, with nearly 20 percent of graduates having more than $250,000.[1]

With these sacrifices, however, come great rewards. By their title alone, physicians are afforded tremendous respect and stature, and very few U.S. physicians are suffering financially. Becoming a doctor essentially guarantees lifetime employment at a reasonable salary—I say reasonable because while some specialties are very highly compensated, others such as primary pediatrics and adult primary care are not. With the United States and the world facing a physician shortage, doctors will likely never be under threat of unemployment.

Patients recognize the sacrifice physicians make and hold them in very high esteem. Physicians remain among the most respected and trusted occupations in the United States.[2] A recent Gallup poll ranked medical doctors the fourth most honest and ethical profession.[3] These findings are anecdotally supported in my conversations with patients, who frequently remark how they respect what I do as a physician. Patients interact with me for a very short period of time without really knowing who I am, but because I'm a physician, I have instant credibility. I'm certain this is the experience of physicians throughout the world.

Doctors Have an Ugly Side

However, there is another side to physicians that the public rarely sees. Prior to applying to medical school, I was appointed to the board of a small community hospital in the city where I grew up. It was the early nineties, and hospitals were very different back then. They were more independent, as this one was, and community hospitals near large urban areas were not part of large systems as they are today.

Most of my colleagues on the board were local businesspeople and community servants, as I was. The board also included a few physician leaders, including the president of the medical staff. All the physicians at the hospital were in private practice. It was a classic community hospital triad model, with three semiautonomous but symbiotic stakeholder groups: the administration operating the hospital, a board providing oversight, and a medical staff delivering care.

Under this model, which is still very much in existence across the United States today, the true hospital customer was the physician, not the patient. A hospital CEO in Arizona once told me that the role of the hospital president was to ensure that physicians were happy, because they were the real customers. Physicians brought patients to the hospital; it was not the hospital that attracted patients for physicians. It was, and in many cases still is, a paradox. Many hospitals depend on private practice physicians to bring in patients, and those patients determine whether the hospital is successful. But hospitals are forbidden by federal law from doing anything to entice physicians to bring patients. So in these situations, physicians very much control the market.

As a board member, I was in awe of the physicians, their knowledge, and the influence they commanded over the organization's governance. It was fascinating to watch my board colleagues defer to physician opinions. When a physician leader spoke, it might as well have been written in stone. While our board included some very successful business leaders, they didn't have the ability to effectively challenge a physician's perspective. The physicians could quickly deflate any issue by questioning how it would impact the patient-provider interaction. You had little credibility to counter if you hadn't been on the front lines of care. Physician omniscience often ruled on critical hospital decisions. For me, it was an early lesson in hospital backroom politics and the power wielded by physicians.

Physician power plays were very much in evidence when our board became concerned with pregnancy-related outcomes. An important quality measure for obstetrical units is the vaginal birth after cesarean section (VBAC) rate, a marker of high-quality care. Pregnant patients who have had a previous cesarean section should be offered a vaginal delivery for their next pregnancy, when appropriate, rather than automatically defaulting to a C-section. Repeat C-sections pose significant risks to mothers and carry the possibility of surgical complications, a longer hospital stay, slower recovery, and ultimately greater expense.

For the obstetrician, C-sections are more convenient (no middle-of-the-night hospital trips to deliver a baby) and lead to higher reimbursement, because doctors are paid more for a C-section than for a normal vaginal delivery. Many of our obstetricians at the time had very high C-section rates and had VBAC rates well below what was normal from a quality standpoint. But some of our competing community hospitals had physicians with rates much worse than ours, and the president at a competitor started to hold obstetricians accountable for poor VBAC performance. This obviously did not go over well with the physicians, leading to an influx of obstetricians applying for privileges at our hospital. During a board credentialing meeting, I asked some of these physicians why they decided to change institutions after so many years of practice at a competitor. One answered that he wanted to expand his practice, while another stated that she wanted to practice in what she considered a better hospital. When challenged about their C-section or VBAC rates, the physicians asserted their need for autonomy to "make the right decisions for my patients." Nonmedical people simply cannot compete in such conversations.

I think most of us on the board knew the real reason these physicians were leaving the other hospital. They had poor VBAC rates and were seeking to escape the increased monitoring at the competitor hospital. These physicians were exercising a very important economic and political trump card, arranging to take their patients to another hospital if held accountable to a higher-quality standard. Proving this is nearly impossible, and denying privileges to a qualified physician is risky business. But more important, we also wanted those physicians to bring us their patients, because it would make our hospital more successful. Remember, in this model, the physicians are the customers, and we wanted them to bring us their customers, the patients. These physicians were leveraging their power against us to get what they wanted, and it was wrong! But all of their requests for privileges were approved.

My experience as a surgical resident and fellow also gave me first-hand exposure to the ugly side of medicine, which showed me just how far administrators and the medical leadership were willing to go to protect disruptive physicians. Most people have heard about the difficulty of internships and residency training—the exhausting hours and hard work of learning and taking care of patients. But much less discussed is the monstrous bullying that many medical trainees face under the tutelage of physicians. Bullying takes on many forms: screaming and yelling, calling people names, telling house staff that they are stupid, making fun of them excessively, and demeaning them in front of other residents and hospital staff such as nurses and, in the worst cases, in front of patients and families. Bullying can evolve to physical violence. Some surgeons throw things in the operating room and occasionally throw things at other caregivers. When I was an intern, a surgeon physically assaulted a chief resident by grabbing his shirt and shoving him against a door. Some of medicine's best-known and well-published physicians are the worst behaved. The doctors in training are not the only recipients of this despicable behavior; unfortunately, it is often directed at nurses and other members of the healthcare team as well.

Fortunately, I was never the recipient of physical violence, but the bullying behavior that my colleagues and I experienced at the hands of various "teachers" was well known, but simply ignored, by our departmental chairs. In my residency, the behavior was always brushed off with the comment, "But he's such a good surgeon." I witnessed nurses in the operating room and on patient floors excusing terrible physician behavior and rudeness toward patients with "But he's such a good doctor." The same was true in my fellowship. Trainee after trainee, nurse after nurse, had been consistently and repeatedly bullied by a member of the medical staff, yet the physician was allowed to continue to practice.

Today I think—I hope—we are better at policing this and holding people accountable for bad behavior. Leaders are better at monitoring and policing these actions, and some hospitals have peer-based professional conduct committees to review incidents when they are reported. We know, however, that not all acts of bullying are reported and many hospitals do not have these types of committees. All of us in physician leadership positions know that bullying absolutely still occurs.

In January 2014, the Associated Press reported that a doctor in Shelby, Montana, had privileges suspended for disruptive behavior after allegedly refusing to delay a surgery, which caused an entire day of cases to be cancelled.[4] He also allegedly threatened to kill an employee if she didn't help him fix a problem with an electronic medical record.

A recent study suggested that a majority of medical students were bullied in some fashion.[5] Interesting, and more disturbing, is that bullying tends not to be overt, but what sociologists call "micro aggressions," which are "subtle interactions that shame employees and undermine their confidence."[6] This is the worst kind of bullying because it's very difficult to catch the perpetrators.

These stories are all too familiar across healthcare. Bullying behavior by physicians toward colleagues and subordinates is well described. There can never be a circumstance where this is right. We should never excuse bad behavior with coworkers or patients in exchange for excellent physician skills. Both appropriate behavior and excellent skills are required to deliver safe, high-quality, and effective care.

Physicians who bully or are abusive put patients at much greater risk than would be created by denying society their "good" physician skills. These behaviors cause unsafe environments for patients. A physician who has a reputation for bullying or angry behavior can undermine a healthcare team's ability to speak up when a patient is at risk. One of my colleagues in training actually had the courage to walk out of an operating room during a surgery because he was being treated so poorly, despite there being no protections in place for him at the time. His willingness to stand up and take action was the right thing to do. In his words, "I was bullied to inaction. I could not function. It was bad for me and dangerous for the patient, and I had to leave." Everyone in the department knew about this act of courage, but there were no consequences for the staff member. While we should all have the courage to stand up to bullying and abuse, all too frequently employees and subordinates fear coming forward, and healthcare leaders are reluctant to take decisive action. My colleague should be a role model for all of us in medicine to call out bad behavior and hold people accountable.

I have met hundreds of physicians over the course of my career that are incredibly talented, dedicated team players focused on doing what's right and caring deeply about their patients and colleagues. But my service on the community hospital board and my experiences in surgical training taught me very important lessons about the physician culture behind closed doors. It can undermine what is right and what most of us represent in healthcare.

Patient Experience Cannot Be Fixed Without Addressing This

"The problem with healthcare is people like me—the doctors," states Thomas H. Lee, chief medical officer for Press Ganey Associates, Inc., and former network president for Partners HealthCare System in Boston. Lee is a world expert in understanding physician engagement. In his 2010 *Harvard Business Review* article "Turning Doctors into Leaders," he describes some of the challenges that physicians face as they adapt to a new world of healthcare where we need their help to drive significant organizational change.[7] He acknowledges that the fundamentals undergirding physicians are solid, but they need to think and act differently to become leaders paving the way for significant progress.

Why are this background and the topic of physician engagement important in patient experience? Because it simply can't be improved without physician leadership and involvement, and if the patient experience is to be fixed, we must recognize and confront this "other side" of physicians.

People make significant sacrifices to become physicians and shoulder incredible responsibility and stress to practice medicine. These circumstances set physicians apart as unique, and they need to be recognized for it. However, we must call out the hypocrisy and mitigate the risks that a few rogues are placing on our efforts to promote the culture required to deliver effective healthcare. Beneath the dedication to care for people, there's an occasional undercurrent of selfishness and greed and dangerous behavior. When combined with the unquestioning respect and admiration that patients have for physicians, these physician attitudes and behaviors can be hazardous to healthcare and are perverse. We also must recognize deficiencies in how physicians are trained and develop methods to enhance their capabilities to lead.

Physicians Must Lead

I'm frequently asked which was the toughest stakeholder group to engage in our effort to transform the patient experience. This is a loaded question with an obvious answer: the physicians. My response is always met with head bobs and comments like, "I thought so." When I speak to hospital leaders, the question is always asked, and the audience response is always the same. Physicians should want to lead patient experience efforts, but the reality is that they're not often involved or engaged.

Physicians are typically revered by their nonphysician colleagues. So they proffer a range of excuses for physician disengagement on important patient experience initiatives: "Physicians are too busy and have more important things to worry about. Their time is valuable, and we shouldn't burden them with this work. They're smart people and know it's important, but we have to lead it for them." Others will admit that while physicians are at the table, they're not really involved in helping to fix anything.

These excuses are unacceptable. We can't improve safety, quality, or the patient experience, or transform and develop the healthcare culture we need, without physicians at the table, engaged and helping to lead. The pressures on hospitals today are such that we simply can't be successful without physician help. Regardless of the difficulty, the challenges to physician engagement must be met head-on. The impact that physicians can have on the patient experience is as powerful today as their influence on individual patients was 100 years ago.

If you acknowledge that the patient experience is everything around the patient, and you accept the Cleveland Clinic definition—that the patient experience includes how we deliver safe, high-quality care, in an environment of satisfaction, to achieve value-driven healthcare—then you also must acknowledge that just as we can't improve the patient experience without steadfast CEO leadership, it can't be improved without physician involvement. Even if you believe that the patient experience is solely about satisfaction and making patients happy, the same holds true.

Taking the position that physicians "have a lot to do" or that "they're smart people who will understand the importance" is inadequate and diminishes the impact physicians can have on patient experience initiatives. Physicians carry tremendous influence on both patients and the organization's other caregivers and are typically viewed as leaders by subordinates. Physicians hold a position of incredible respect, and patients and their families hang on to every word and action; their influence to individually impact the patient experience is unparalleled. They are the most powerful and effective drivers of patient perception and service. I have often argued that physicians are our most important service recovery tool. They can influence patients enormously. Another benefit of physician engagement is that once they're engaged, they become powerful partners in ensuring the success of patient experience efforts.

Getting to Leadership

A critical component of engaging physicians is recognition of their importance to healthcare and their unique role in the patient relationship. I would never argue that what physicians do is more important than the care provided by other critical members of the healthcare team, but physicians deserve recognition that their role is different. Most physicians want to help, but they often are not asked or meaningfully engaged. Cosgrove and Lee argue that physicians need to engage "in a noble shared purpose"; in essence, get them to help "pursue a common organizational goal."[8] In our organization, I've personally asked nearly every key physician leader to help me enhance the experience for our patients, and no one has ever said no. Some would argue that there should be no need to ask for help when it's a requirement of leadership to participate. I disagree, because remember, we're talking about a unique stakeholder group. Physicians are the engines of the clinical organization and deserve some deference regarding their time.

A very good first step is making meaningful presentations to physicians to help them understand what the patient experience is about and how it impacts them. I initially joined small groups of physicians at department meetings to deliver a high-level stump speech explaining why the patient experience was important and ways we could improve it. These early talks, however, were not effective, because in actuality, there was no real meat to my presentation—no strategy and no recommended tactics. In addition, I had no hard data that supported what I was talking about. I just showed our overall hospital HCAHPS scores, and at the time we didn't really understand how they applied to the local environment or how physicians could have impact on the scores.

The physicians' skepticism was palpable, and I could see lack of interest in their facial expressions. Most physicians were clearly just humoring me and paying polite attention. They would ask a few easy questions about the concepts and then inquire what exactly I wanted them to do to help. The doctors weren't rejecting the message; they were simply applying their analytic skills against what I was saying to better understand it. Physicians are trained to interpret and understand important issues. I didn't have any substance yet—the information I presented was just window dressing, and that won't fly with docs. Their reaction taught me that if we were to engage physicians, we had to provide detailed information and convey exactly what we wanted them to do to help—a basic concept of change management.

There was one part of my presentation, however, that clearly got physician attention. Every time I talked about Medicare's Hospital Value-Based Purchasing (HVBP) Program, it was clear that most physicians had no idea what it was. I had a slide that detailed what Medicare at the time was specifically targeting, including safety indicators, quality core measures, and patient experience HCAHPS data. I described the process, formerly referred to as "pay for reporting," in which hospitals had 2 percent of Medicare reimbursement withheld subject to voluntary submission of quality core measures and HCAHPS data. I described how eventually this would transition to a pay-for-performance program where hospitals would receive payments only by meeting specific benchmarks. Physicians were paying very close attention indeed to this part of my presentation. I could tell many had never heard about the HVBP Program.

I understood very clearly that we needed to educate physicians about what was going on in the healthcare environment and why their role in helping to manage it was vital. The HVBP information directly affected physicians. This was not just another hospital initiative; it was personal. At the conclusion of one of my talks, chief of staff Joseph Hahn, who always watches audiences as they listen, concurred that the message was really resonating.

I revised my presentation to show the three specific questions patients were asked regarding how well physicians communicate in the hospital environment. Now this part of my presentation really got their attention. I soon recognized that physicians truly did not know about or understand the government-sponsored survey mechanism by which patients were asked to rate physicians' communication skills. They also didn't appreciate that their individual performance would eventually be reported on the Internet and potentially linked to reimbursement. The epiphany struck them and me. One of the most important ways to engage the docs was simply to educate them about the new landscape and how they were personally going to be judged.

The responses from our employed group practice physicians and our private practice physicians were very similar. Neither group fully understood the implications of the government programs being deployed and how they would eventually affect physicians personally. While Cleveland Clinic's employed physicians were easier to connect with because they had a clear reporting structure in a department or institute, it still required time and commitment to educate and engage them individually. Anyone who believes that employed physicians will just stand up and salute when you ask them to do something really does not understand physician culture. Employed physicians need to be convinced and engaged, just as private practice doctors do.

Engaging private practice physicians was somewhat more difficult. When I first became the CXO, we hosted dinners for our community hospital physicians to discuss the patient experience: what it meant, why it was important, how we were measured, and how we were all held accountable. These presentations were similar to what we gave to our employed doctors. We mostly discussed the HCAHPS data, which is a measure of inpatient experience. While the private practice physicians could certainly impact those scores through their behavior, hospital metrics are not individual physician metrics, so these doctors weren't individually accountable. During one of the dinners, a very successful private practice physician remarked, "I don't care about HCAHPS. That's your problem, not mine." In 2009, what could I say? He was right. HCAHPS was primarily a hospital issue, and there was little we could do to hold private practice physicians accountable. HCAHPS scores included how this particular doctor communicated with his patients, so it was not just about how the hospital functioned. But the hospital was the one penalized for not performing, not the private practice physician.

At a subsequent meeting, we addressed efforts to improve private practice physician communication with patients. We'd developed a physician communication improvement program for our employed staff and wanted to offer it to our private practice physicians to help them improve as well. This same physician said, "When I go over to your competitor, they put their arm around me and ask what they can do for me. When I come to your hospital, you're always beating me up for my quality metrics. Where's the thank you for bringing my patients to you?" It's simply preposterous to suggest that we should be concerned first about making the doctors happy over monitoring quality outcomes for patients! But that exchange pretty much summed up our challenge.

The reality for private practice physicians, however, is changing. Medicare is creating strong levers in the form of quality reporting and transparency that will force hospitals to be more rigorous with regard to physicians' performance. The risk for physicians is not just public reporting of quality and patient experience data and its link to reimbursement. They will be held increasingly accountable in four critical areas: outcomes, complaints, behavior, and the patient experience.

The World Is Changing for Doctors

We are moving from a volume-based world, where physicians are paid for doing more procedures and seeing more patients, to a value-based world in which physicians and hospitals are rewarded for how well they manage patients. Critical to this change is how we monitor outcomes. We presently have very little data on how well specific physicians perform, but progressively more data will be collected, and as a result, physicians will be held accountable for how well they deliver care. Those who perform poorly will lose money, will have their reputations defined by this performance, and could face organizational sanctions as hospitals are increasingly held accountable for safety and quality.

Regulatory agencies are listening to patients and investigating complaints about doctors and hospitals. In my state of Ohio, the department of health aggressively investigates patient complaints. One anonymous patient complaint about a doctor to the Ohio Department of Health or the Centers for Medicare and Medicaid Services can result in a surprise investigation of the hospital. Whether or not the complaint is valid, the investigation may reveal other deficiencies that could jeopardize a hospital's Medicare Conditions of Participation, the minimal standards a hospital must meet to be reimbursed. The actions of one physician could endanger an entire hospital's participation in the Medicare program. From an organizational perspective, this is obviously unacceptable. Hospitals can no longer afford to look the other way, as poor quality or disruptive behavior may place the organization at serious risk.

This new environment links physicians and hospitals much more closely. We're dependent on one another for high performance and must work together to survive. The sooner physicians understand this—and the more we do to bring them into the fold to help us—the more successful we'll be at navigating the difficult waters of healthcare reform.

All my talks with physicians now end with a slide that shows why paying attention to the patient experience is important:

1. It's the right thing to do.

2. It's how you and your family would want to be treated.

3. It's patients' perception of quality.

4. It's the foundation of patient-centered care.

5. The government.

My list always starts with my preferred reason: "It's the right thing to do." Do we really need another reason? For the disbelievers and doubters, I end with "The government." If you don't think improving the patient experience is important for the right reasons, then understand that the government is now telling you it's important and holding you accountable for improving it.

Today, the private practice physician I referenced earlier is one of our strongest supporters and advocates. He did not come along because of some sales pitch regarding why he should but took our efforts at education and came to better understand the importance. This physician is also engaged because we recognized him as pivotal. Identifying powerful peer leaders like him and helping them understand the importance of what's going on creates strong allies in the war to improve.

Currently when I talk to physicians about changes in the healthcare marketplace, I still say, "This is the right thing to do," and "It's how you would want yourself or your family to be treated." For the truly recalcitrant few, I also must occasionally make clear that unless they want to practice outside the American healthcare system on a desert island, they need to pay very close attention. I believe we've successfully taken the significant changes in the environment and leveraged them into a burning platform to get physicians engaged. Helping them to understand how these environmental changes will impact their self-interest is another critical engagement tactic.[9]

Transparency Is a Powerful Tool to Engage Physicians

Transparency is a powerful tool that is changing the face of U.S. healthcare, and it's something that physicians are not quite used to dealing with. Just as individual physician communication metrics are relatively opaque at present, so are individual physician outcomes. But as the government pushes hospitals to collect more and more data on hospital and physician performance, communication and outcome performance will be posted online and available to all. Individual physician metrics that Medicare is developing will engender reputational risk and financial penalties. These environmental changes will create pressure on nearly every U.S. physician, whether group employed or in private practice.

Patients, businesses, and payers will have greater ability to view and analyze physician performance, likely leading to greater consumerism in healthcare. Patients will choose where to seek care based on a physician's performance scores. Public reporting of data and its link to reimbursement will dramatically change physician marketplace behavior and the nature of the doctor-patient relationship. Physicians will be compelled to monitor their performance as it compares to national standards, which will impact reputations.

There have been some pioneering efforts in physician data transparency. Healthgrades was one of the first online companies to provide patients with a one-to-five-star mechanism to rate their experiences with doctors. This is inherently biased, as anyone can rate the physician, even nonpatients who may hold a grudge. Yet the ratings are in the public domain for all to see. Today, Healthgrades not only seeks patient feedback; the company queries public databases to compile information about education, awards, languages spoken, criminal records, board actions, certifications, sanctions, and malpractice. In addition,

Healthgrades provides access information: where patients can be seen and what type of insurance is accepted.

One challenge of publicly reported data is that often the public doesn't know that the data is available. Most healthcare consumers have no idea Medicare publishes hospital data online. The Massachusetts Health Quality Partners coalition found an interesting way to solve this problem by partnering in 2012 with the *Consumer Reports* organization to produce a special report regarding how patients rated Massachusetts physician practices.[10] Some 64,000 adults were surveyed to obtain experience of care data for more than 480 adult and pediatric practices. Consumers rated the practices based upon patient communication, care coordination, familiarity with patient medical records, ease of appointment scheduling, and courtesy of staff. While leaders of the study touted cooperation of the various stakeholders, many physicians were unhappy with the transparency, as not all practices scored highly. Some took issue with using the same visual representation system (Harvey Balls) to rate both medical practices and goods such as washing machines and blenders.

Medicare has a public website called Physician Compare designed to provide individual physician safety, quality, and experience of care data. This will transform public reporting for physicians, because Medicare will establish the standards by which data is collected, including what is reported, how it is reported, and who participates. All physicians who work with Medicare patients will participate—essentially, all physicians. Furthermore, as with other Medicare programs such as readmissions reduction, value-based purchasing, and so on, reporting will be linked to reimbursement, so there will be financial penalties for nonparticipation.

Cleveland Clinic has heavily leveraged data transparency to drive improvement in our organization. For our 3,200 employed medical staff physicians, we are completely transparent with patient feedback. All staff physicians receive specific data regarding how inpatients perceive communication; the number and nature of complaints, including patient verbatims; and selected ambulatory scores. Every three months, all physicians receive unblinded departmental lists. Doctors can see their own data, as well as that of all of their colleagues. This complete transparency is unusual for such a large employed medical group, but it's very important. The data transparency has introduced staff to an important tool for driving personal improvement, as well as helped prepare them for what is clearly coming in the national environment.

Physicians Are Vital, but Others Are Important as Well

When discussing environmental changes, physicians are often quick to point out that they are an essential piece of the healthcare puzzle. As one remarked, "Without doctors, there is no healthcare, so people better pay attention to us." He was certainly correct, but I was quick to observe that without nurses, there is no healthcare either. In fact, there is no healthcare today without a lot of things and different people. Doctors are important, and they are often referred to as the engine of healthcare, but engines cannot fly by themselves without the rest of the plane. Alignment and engagement of physicians requires us to validate their importance. However, we're also required to help physicians face the reality that it's not just about them and that being the "engine" is not a license to do and say whatever they like.

Physician opinions are essential, and their voices must be heard. But physicians also have a responsibility to participate, listen, adjust actions when necessary to support the organization, and be productive participants to help the organization succeed. Physicians also need to keep their emotional intelligence in check. Clinical leaders who are not physicians, as well as nonclinical leaders in healthcare, tend to defer to physicians. I loathe sitting in meetings when a physician colleague confabulates about something he or she knows little or nothing about while the nonclinical leaders stay silent. However, once they are out of the meeting, they will talk about the physician behind his or her back. That is worthless participation! Nonphysician clinical leaders and nonclinical leaders must have the courage to challenge doctors openly.

If we're willing to recognize physicians as unique and deserving of some deference, this requires us to ask something of them as well. Because of their impact and influence on patients and employees, physicians must hold themselves and their colleagues to a higher standard of behavior. Physicians and physician leaders should place greater emphasis on holding their peers accountable for doing the right thing. For example, we should never tolerate bullying. Doctors serve as role models for patients, students, nurses, and others in healthcare. Behavior that breaches that perception undermines the trust we place in physicians to provide care.

Physicians also must understand the subliminal influence they have on other leaders. Holding a medical degree does not impart expertise in managing healthcare organizations. Leadership teams must collectively recognize that everyone brings a unique perspective to the discussion. No one group should be allowed to dominate. I was troubled recently when a colleague and important member of our C-suite team said he did not always feel the doctors respected him because he was not a doctor. This is not the kind of environment we need to be successful.

There also must be a real effort on behalf of hospital leaders to engage physicians. When I spoke to a group of nonclinical hospital leaders from an outside institution about physician involvement in hospital strategy, they expressed significant frustration at the lack of physician buy-in. They complained, "Every time we make a decision that affects something in the operating rooms, it seems as though the physicians are always opposed to it. Nobody supports us!" I asked these leaders how they encouraged surgeon consultation and involved their physician leadership. They responded that key physician leaders were invited to all critical meetings but rarely showed up.

I discovered that their meetings were late in the morning when most surgeons had already started their operating room schedules. Private practice physicians, whose livelihoods depend on doing cases, are not going to reschedule patients or leave blocks of time open to accommodate meetings. The institution also held other meetings where important decisions were operationally vetted, but to which surgeons were not invited. This is where the real decisions were made. The so-called critical meetings were nothing more than presentations of decisions already made.

If we're to be successful at engaging physicians, they have to be present for the real discussions. Inviting physicians to a meeting as window dressing and not involving them in a meaningful way is a superficial attempt at physician engagement that simply won't work. If hospitals want to be successful at any strategic initiative, they have an obligation to get physicians to the table, and this may require a little accommodation and respect for the challenges their practices impose on their schedules.

Another effective tactic Cleveland Clinic has used to engage physicians is to identify early adopters and leverage them into physician-champion positions to drive new initiatives. Early adopters will have an interest in what's going on and understand what you're trying to achieve. They are the first to raise their hands to volunteer, or they may be ones who have a particular interest in a program peripheral to the patient experience. It's also important to seek out the well-respected physician leaders. Not necessarily all who step up to volunteer are people you want driving your initiatives. Identifying a physician leader, even an informal one, who is well respected in the physician culture and who can be developed into a role model and champion, will have significant impact on improving physician buy-in. We tend to select the same people to help with various initiatives. But it's imperative that we seek out a broad selection of physicians to participate. Experience is also critical. It's the wrong choice to select new physicians, who may have more time on their hands, or physicians close to retirement and winding down their clinical practices. We make sure to take a cross section of busy clinical physicians working at the front lines. They command the greatest respect from their peers and have a much more current view of the clinical arena.

We have made an effort to wrap physicians around everything we do in the patient experience. We have physicians involved in our unit teams, consulting with the ombudsman department, and teaching communication skills. As frequently as possible, with anything related to the patient experience, we use physicians to help lead and drive a program and carry the message to others across the organization about why this is important. This is not something that my office developed; it's a best practice that our organization follows for most important initiatives. At Cleveland Clinic, we have integrated physicians into every facet of decision making. The tally of the number of physicians involved in leadership positions totals more than 300, nearly 10 percent of the medical staff. But even involving this many physicians doesn't guarantee there will be universal buy-in of new programs and strategic initiatives. It takes time, transparency of decision making, and authentic leadership. Having physicians at the table is not enough. They must be participating in the debate and integral to key decisions.

As a group, physicians are intelligent, assertive, motivated, driven, data- and goal-oriented, and focused on doing what's right for patients.

Few enter the field of medicine and take the Hippocratic oath without the absolute desire to care for people. Physicians are lifelong learners, with insatiable curiosity.

As I applied to medical school, an experienced physician offered his counsel. He advised me to prepare for a never-ending journey of exploration and discovery—one that would continually fascinate me, make me better at what I did, and have the added benefit of helping others. It sounded like I was about to embark on an epic adventure. The patient experience has been that adventure.

It strikes me that as physicians mature in practice, they continue on their lifelong quest for medical knowledge but often fail to develop their interpersonal relationship and patient-interaction skills. I make this statement based upon several observations. There is a dearth of professional development curriculum offerings compared to the number of offerings on medical science. Also, there is generally no requirement for interpersonal or patient-practice assessment in any regulatory or professional certification, although this situation is evolving. Further, when one looks at national HCAHPS data for the physician communication domain, an 80-percent score on inpatient satisfaction falls in the 50th percentile. This means that half of physicians who are ranked with HCAHPS scores achieve a score of "C" or worse from patients when they're asked whether their physicians always communicated appropriately. Should we accept this? Many believe that doctors just aren't able to improve. Cleveland Clinic's data, and that of other organizations, disproves the point.

Getting physicians and physician leaders to understand the importance of the patient experience takes time, recurrent and consistent education, and consensus building. If you ask any member of our medical staff today, overwhelmingly most will attest to the importance we place on the patient experience. Some may not have bought in 100 percent, but most will agree that it's the right thing to do, and all will know that the patient experience is very important to the organization.

The uncertainty about how the future of healthcare will impact hospitals today is also directly affecting physicians. Robert Coulton, executive director of professional staff affairs at Cleveland Clinic, has been managing the physician group practice for over two decades. He has had a ringside seat to many changes in healthcare and observes, "It is tough for doctors right now. There are a lot of things that are dramatically impacting how they practice." Tremendous disruption is occurring in the physician world, creating anxiety and insecurity. But we cannot drive cultural development in healthcare and lead changes to improve patient-centered care unless our physicians are fully committed colleagues helping to lead through the opportunities. Many observe that there has never been a better time than this difficult era to elevate physicians to help lead.

In summary, for nonphysician leaders:

1. Ask physicians for their help and give them clear suggestions on what they can do to help. Don't just assume that they should be a part of something; often, they may not know how to engage or will not feel valued for their involvement in nonmedical programs. Engage them in the "noble purpose" of helping to improve the way we deliver the patient experience.

2. Create a burning platform by educating physicians about the environment. There are numerous factors that impact doctors today as never before: increasing regulatory burden, transparency, and personal accountability. These are important for improving medicine but challenging for doctors because they do not know how to manage through them and many have no idea how these changes will affect them personally. Educate physicians and help them understand the business side of medicine and how to manage these changes.

3. Leverage your data. Provide doctors with as much information about their safety, quality, and patient satisfaction data as you have. Give physicians every verbatim comment from patients. Doctors should know what patients think and say about them. Leverage the data transparently by making it available to all of the medical staff. This is the future of medicine, and the sooner physicians are exposed to it, the more prepared they will be to accommodate an increasingly transparent healthcare environment.

4. Make physicians your partners: ask them to help set your strategies, goals, and agendas. Merely inviting physicians to

a meeting does not check the box on engagement. Make sure they're involved in decision making and have access to as much of the raw information as you do.

5. Recognize the challenges physicians face in participating in administrative functions and endeavor to accommodate them. Administrators have a great deal of flexibility in their schedules (I can say that because I am one). Physicians need to practice medicine, but we need their meaningful involvement, so accommodate their schedules. Private practice physicians lose money when they don't directly participate in patient care; be willing to buy some of their time. Employed physicians are burdened by productivity standards; give them protected administrative time.

6. Respect the influence that physicians have over patients and recognize physicians as different, but remind them that they are not any more important than other members of the healthcare team. Because of the tremendous influence they have on patients and families, we have an obligation to hold them to a higher standard of behavior and professionalism.

In summary, for physician leaders:

1. It's true. It can't be done without your participation, but that is not license to try to control, obstruct, or change something just because you don't like it. Exercise emotional intelligence, and practice listening more than talking. Develop your team and business skills so you can relate.

2. You are not necessarily the smartest person in the room. Nurse leaders and nonclinical leaders who are professionals in their respective fields are just as smart and important as you are. Respect them for who they are and the years of training and education they have, and recognize that many hold you in esteem because you are a doctor. Do not abuse this perception. Instead, mitigate it. Ensure that your opinions jibe with the system, not just the doctors. And by the way, just because you completed your MBA doesn't make you a business professional.

It took you over a decade of education and training to practice medicine. It took your chief financial officer the same amount of time to attain his or her professional status as well.

3. You're not in Kansas anymore. Real change in healthcare is here, and many of these changes will impact you personally. The only way to thrive is to work closely with your colleagues from nursing and other professions.

4. Help police yourselves. You know where the problems exist. Bullying is unacceptable and must stop. We also know the physicians we would never send our family members to see. Ask yourself why. Should they be seeing members of the public? Ensure that your colleagues are using their influence over patients appropriately.

5. Physicians in administrative positions are not sellouts. The job is difficult. Give them respect.

Want to Know What Patients Think? Ask!

n December 2010, I received a letter from the husband of a deceased patient who said the Clinic had failed his wife. Enclosed was a photograph of the couple at their daughter's wedding. My heart sank. Looking at the beautiful picture, I immediately feared that we had missed something, that there had been a terrible medical error causing a treatment failure that led to her death. His wife had been diagnosed with breast cancer; she was successfully treated and cured. Several years later she had a recurrence, which was treated and controlled. She subsequently developed a final recurrence, and despite aggressive treatment, the disease won the war. She began palliative treatment and was sent home on hospice. She was readmitted to the hospital for dehydration and died after four days.

Her last wish had been to die peacefully at home, with her family at her side. We had failed at helping her realize this last wish. She did not need to be in the hospital the last three days of her life. The patient and her husband told everyone who would listen that they needed to get home. No one could help them. They talked to doctors, nurses, case managers, social workers. No one could make the appropriate arrangements to have her discharged. Furthermore, no one was coordinating her care. She had no hope from further medical treatment; she wanted to be with her family at home. We did not fail in her medical treatment; we failed in her treatment as a person. Our organization was unable to integrate the emotional and spiritual elements of this patient's care with her medical care. We failed her because no one was listening to the patient or the family. Everyone was focused on his or her "job," and collectively they ignored the primary purpose of why we are here, which is to put the patient first.

Today that letter and photograph sit on my desk as a constant reminder that treating patients is about more than just treating disease, and that to be successful, we need an organization where the patient is at the center of everything we do. It is a reminder of why we are here and the purpose of what we do every day for patients.

I have heard it said that up to 90 percent of service businesses say they know exactly what their customers want, but only 10 percent actually take the time and invest the resources to be sure they are right. This is an interesting but shocking statistic. Most people leading service businesses would say they understand their markets and customers. I'm sure many can point to robust market share and sales growth. Imagine how much more successful these companies could be with research to intimately target customer needs.

Healthcare providers—doctors, nurses, and administrators—are guilty of this phenomenon as well. We think we know exactly what's important for patients. We stand at their bedside and tell patients exactly what they need to know and what we think they want to hear. This sounds a little extreme, and I certainly don't mean in a literal sense that we dictate to patients without interaction, but think about it: for the most part, physicians are in tight control of the healthcare environment, and patients are poorly equipped to challenge what we tell them.

Most caregivers perform their functions every day with a marked sense of determination and precision. Nurses flow in and out of patients' rooms constantly, taking vital signs, delivering medications, doing rounds; it's amazing to watch. They are efficient, fast, complete, almost fluid in their delivery.

The way we interact with patients is primarily a function of our training, and the requirement to be efficient and collect a lot of information quickly makes us forget that we are interacting with *people*. We don't listen very well to what patients really want or what they think is important. Patient-centeredness is about encompassing the "quality of compassion, empathy, and responsiveness to the needs, values, and expressed preferences of the individual patient."[1] We frequently fail to remember or even realize that delivery of medical care is not just about medicine; it's also about spiritual and emotional care. It's about addressing the patient's needs holistically.

Imagine you are home on a Sunday afternoon doing whatever it is you like to do—playing with your children, watching a sporting event, preparing dinner—when suddenly you get a headache and start to feel dizzy. The headache momentarily subsides, but as you are walking over to sit down, the dizziness gets worse and you nearly pass out. You feel better the rest of the day, but first thing Monday morning, you call your doctor. She schedules an appointment for the next day, although at this point, you feel fine and consider cancelling. On Tuesday, your doctor examines you and can't find anything wrong. But to be safe, she orders a CT scan of your brain. Wednesday, you get the scan and go back to work. Wednesday afternoon, you get a call from the doctor's office because she would like to see you to discuss the test. In the doctor's office Thursday morning, she reports that the test is abnormal, and there is a mass in your brain. Your life freezes. You experience a sudden visceral reaction; you feel sick; you are confused. "Mass in my brain? What does that mean?" Your doctor says it might mean you have brain cancer.

On Friday, you see a neurosurgeon, who schedules a biopsy for the following Monday. Over the weekend, all you can think about is dying of brain cancer. But you hold out a sliver of hope that it will be one of the more benign diagnoses your doctor talked about. Monday comes, you get the biopsy, and you wake up in recovery. Your spouse is there, looking anguished and scared. You are in pain and confused. A couple of hours later, your surgeon comes in and tells you that the diagnosis is glioblastoma multiforme, the most lethal form of brain cancer. Your life is forever changed. In one week, you went from "normal" to a new "normal" that will redefine everything you do, everything you think about, and everything you experience. You move to a single focus: survival.

This has nothing to do with patient feedback. But it has a lot to do with listening and understanding. In this terrible situation, what would you be thinking about? Sitting at home, in the car, or in the hospital, every day as the world revolves, all you would think about is the cancer.

That is what occurs with patients. It drives their behaviors, reactions, and interactions. Yet we fail to comprehend what's going on in their minds.

Cleveland Clinic collects patient feedback from a variety of comprehensive surveys conducted in six critical environments: inpatient, ambulatory, emergency, psychiatry, pediatrics, and home health. Two of these surveys are standardized instruments developed by the Agency for Healthcare Research and Quality and are part of the HVBP: the HCAHPS and the Home Health Care CAHPS. A third, the Clinician and Group CAHPS survey, is a standard tool used in the ambulatory environment, currently mandated only for physicians participating in accountable care organizations.

Extensive testing went into development of the CAHPS instruments, including validation by Rand Corporation.[2] In 2005, the HCAHPS instrument was endorsed by the National Quality Forum.[3] The Centers for Medicare & Medicaid (CMS) established three broad goals for the HCAHPS tool:

> First, the survey is designed to produce data about patients' perspectives of care that allow objective and meaningful comparisons of hospitals on topics that are important to consumers. Second, public reporting of the survey results creates new incentives for hospitals to improve quality of care. Third, public reporting serves to enhance accountability in healthcare by increasing transparency of the quality of hospital care provided in return for the public investment. With these goals in mind, the CMS and the HCAHPS Project Team have taken substantial steps to assure that the survey is credible, useful, and practical.[4]

The CAHPS instruments are not perfect, and there has been criticism that they prevent hospitals from obtaining the granular data necessary to drive improvement processes. In addition, the surveys measure patient experience perceptions without providing real insight into what's important to patients.

The HCAHPS surveys also lack a robust adjustment process to segment patient medical risk that may bias results. Cleveland Clinic substantiated that when patients are stratified by severity of illness, survey results change significantly. Patients with higher documented severity of illness tend to score the inpatient environment more poorly. Hospitals that have sicker patients may have lower scores and greater difficulty determining what impacts patient perceptions.

Studies have demonstrated that certain groups of patients score hospitals differently; for instance, those admitted for exacerbation of chronic conditions have worse perceptions of inpatient experience than those admitted for elective surgical procedures.[5,6] This is also the reason why the HCAHPS survey methodology adjusts many of the domains down for surveys received from surgical admissions.[7] While the instruments are not perfect, they are evolving; and despite some of these limitations, the instruments and data in fact can be effectively used to drive and monitor performance improvement, as our organization has clearly demonstrated.

Patients have a strong tendency to judge their experience based on their personality, values, and expectations. Healthcare is a very emotional and personal experience, so how can our emotions and personality not impact our perceptions? I was at dinner with a friend who recently went through a healthcare crisis and was extolling her doctor. She emphasized how good this physician was and that she believed he was very talented. I asked how she knew. She described how he was very matter of fact, to the point, efficient, and took time to clearly explain things.

My friend is extremely bright, well-read, and certainly an educated healthcare consumer. I pushed for exactly how she knew the doctor was "good" and "talented." She reiterated her previous comments, and then compared him with her previous physician, whom she did not consider very good, disliking his communication style. She felt he wasted a lot of time discussing trivial things. "I don't want to have a relationship with the guy; I just want him to take care of business," she said.

I observed that such practice characteristics have little to do with whether the physician is "good" or "talented." My friend pushed back at me to define how a consumer determines whether a physician is good. My comment was an affirming "exactly!" When we have few ways to evaluate quality with certainty, we default to attributes we understand. My friend judged her doctor based upon her perceptions and how his practice characteristics aligned with her personal style.

Patients are unsophisticated healthcare consumers, not understanding what we do or the services we deliver. Even the highly educated are not medically sophisticated healthcare professionals. A layperson can spend days studying an illness, but a physician providing treatment can quickly dominate a conversation and delineate what patients don't know.

Patients measure our effectiveness by making comparisons of what we do against things they understand. In other words, they use proxy measures. Proxies are things that patients understand and think are important, and they judge our effectiveness based upon them. My friend judged her physician's quality based upon her interactions, which is what she perceived as important.

Cleveland Clinic has come a long way on its patient experience improvement journey by using standardized survey data. However, we often ask ourselves what we're missing and what more we can do. To better understand the importance of patient proxies, we commissioned two studies in 2012 to gain additional insights.

At our main campus hospital, we randomly survey about half of our inpatient discharges with the HCAHPS survey. For the first study, we randomly sampled 900 patients from the other 50 percent of discharges, those not automatically receiving the survey. We administered the HCAHPS survey exactly how it's done for Medicare, then asked the 900 patients why they answered each question the way they did. We wanted to know how their thinking influenced their responses.

The second study was ethnographic research on one of our inpatient floors, Ethnographic research captures insights by observing processes and subjects in their natural environment. Since we were having difficulties with the inpatient services experience, this type of research would help us better understand what was happening and identify what we might be missing so that necessary improvements could be implemented.

Four researchers were located on one of our floors for about six weeks. They interviewed 124 patients and families, followed them around the hospital, talked to their caregivers, and observed staff interactions with them in providing services. The research team also collected the observations, concerns, and opinions of patients, families, and staff regarding hospital treatment.

These two studies provided quantitative analysis of patient perceptions and ratings of our organization and care, as well as detailed qualitative analysis of the environment that led to those perceptions and ratings. The collective results were illuminating and surprising.

"Patients want more respect" was an early conclusion; when this was revealed, I worried that we had wasted money. Everyone in healthcare knows that. But the inference wasn't so simple. Patients don't merely want more respect from their doctors or nurses; patients want more respect from everyone they encounter in the healthcare environment. And it gets even more granular: It's not just about respect. It's actually about being recognized as an individual, not as a patient.

Hospital patients are bombarded by interactions with people whom they've never met before. Everyone is a stranger. The person most familiar, their "best friend," is their doctor. In many cases, this physician is the only person a patient has met before being admitted. Everyone else a patient encounters—a lot of people—is essentially a stranger.

The number of people increases when patients share a room. Imagine that you're a patient in a semiprivate hospital room. You're not only deluged with a host of caregivers you've never met before; you're also having first- or secondhand interactions with your unfamiliar neighbor in the next bed and his family, friends, and caregivers. From all these people, patients want respect as human beings.

I once heard it said that patients are a lot like prisoners. Fortunately, I've never been a prisoner, but the analogy resonates. Think about the similarities: You are brought to the building; do you really want to be there? No! We take your clothes, give you a gown, and attach a wristband. We put you into a small room with a stranger. There isn't much for you to do. Strangers whom you don't know, and may not like, tell you what to do. We serve you terrible food. There are long, boring periods with nothing to do, and you can't leave. (Well, I suppose you could.) And you are frightened. We need to ensure that everyone in healthcare treats patients and their families with respect as individuals.

Patients use an array of proxy measures to judge us. In addition, a particular proxy judgment can color opinion about all the care patients receive. Physician-nurse communication is one example. When a doctor rounds on a patient at 6 a.m. and talks about the day's plan, the patient expects the nurses on duty that day to know the plan. If the patient asks a nurse about the plan at 8 a.m. and he or she can't answer questions, the patient, appropriately, finds this unacceptable and thinks, "How can they deliver high-quality medicine when the nurse and doctor can't even talk to one another?" The patient uses the communication interaction as a proxy for how well the hospital functions.

Another example of a proxy measure is environmental cleanliness. If a patient's room is cluttered or appears dirty or poorly maintained, patients and families wonder whether the hospital can deliver quality medicine: "They can't even keep the room clean, so how can they perform a good surgery?" What the patient and family see and hear in the healthcare environment is processed against what they believe is important—in some cases, their values—and this directly impacts how they view their care or the organization. A stay-at-home mom who proudly worked hard every day for 30 years to keep her home spotless for her family would naturally be appalled at having to spend time in a dirty hospital room.

Patients also want caregivers to be happy, one of the most baffling findings. Critics of the patient experience movement will view this as validation that they are right: "See, it's about making patients happy. They are focusing on the wrong thing, they don't know how to judge quality, and they're holding us to this ridiculous standard that has no impact on how well we perform our care." The critics are wrong. It's not about caregivers literally being happy; it's about how we conduct ourselves in front of patients and how patients perceive caregivers' actions. If I walk into a patient's room and appear to be bothered by something, look sad, or display negative emotions, patients can have several responses. They may wonder if they did something wrong: "Did I do something to offend Dr. Merlino? Is he mad at me?" Patients are in a very submissive role relative to healthcare providers. Most are afraid to challenge nurses or doctors. They are very afraid of doing or saying something negative, concerned that they'll be treated differently.

While on leadership rounds at one of our facilities, I went into the room of an elderly Hispanic woman. We asked about her hospital stay. Everything seemed OK at first, but the more questions we asked, the more upset she became. Finally she started to cry. Asked what was wrong, she said, "That person, that person." The patient was very afraid of one of her caregivers, who was mean to her, ignored her, and made highly inappropriate comments. Apparently, while the patient, who needed assistance to ambulate, was on the toilet, the caregiver joked that she would just have to sit there all day! The patient didn't want to complain out of fear that the caregiver would retaliate or persuade other caregivers to treat her badly as well. My stomach turned as I listened; joking or not, it was highly inappropriate and, in my mind, was tantamount to neglect. We immediately addressed the situation and filed a patient complaint and grievance. That caregiver will have no other opportunities to treat our patients with such disrespect.

A caregiver's negative expression may also make patients wonder whether there is something of concern with their condition or care: "Is there something Dr. Merlino is not telling me? He looks worried. Should I be worried about something?" Apply this finding to the story I relayed earlier about brain cancer. Patients sit in their hospital beds focusing exclusively on what's happening to them. The more serious the condition, the more intently patients and families search for visual and verbal cues. They seek ways to supplement what we say to better understand their personal situations.

My own experience as a patient illustrates this point—and also strengthened my empathy. My wife, Amy, and I were in an automobile accident in 2010. A young woman, who was texting while driving, failed to yield right-of-way and turned her car into ours, which resulted in a head-on collision. But for the air bags, seat belts, and a well-constructed car, I'm quite certain I'd have been dead. I remember it vividly: as the crash approached, I turned my head to the right and put my arm out across my wife's body. The steering wheel air bag deployed into my left upper chest, neck, and face. Fortunately, we were not seriously injured, and after helping my wife out of the car, I checked on the driver whose vehicle had hit us. I found her clutching her cell phone, a little dazed and crying, but seemingly uninjured. Still at the accident scene, I started to feel pain and swelling in the front left side of my neck. I soon began to have difficulty swallowing. My symptoms progressively worsened. When the paramedics arrived, we refused transport to the hospital—we were physicians; of course we were fine. The accident happened very close to our home, so the kindly police gave us a ride.

I covered trauma call while I was a surgeon at MetroHealth Medical Center, our region's Level I trauma center, so I was familiar with these types of injuries. The differential diagnosis of my symptoms included a handful of possibilities, mostly benign. But one was a serious, life-threatening carotid artery dissection or aneurysm that is a traumatic injury to one of the large vessels of the neck that supplies blood to the brain. An acute dissection can cause critical loss of blood to the brain resulting in a stroke and possibly death. Of course, I immediately thought I might have that, as it is frequently caused by a direct blow to the neck. When we arrived home, I convinced Amy that we should go get checked out. Naturally, I did not reveal my worst fears.

I drove us to the hospital (something I don't recommend). On the way, I called my friend and former colleague, Jeffrey A. Claridge, who is director of MetroHealth's Division of Trauma, Critical Care, and Burns. MetroHealth is northeast Ohio's only Level I trauma center, and part of the Northeast Ohio Trauma System in which the Clinic is a member. It is the appropriate hospital to manage the most severe injuries, such as a traumatic carotid artery dissection, which I feared I might have suffered. As luck would have it, he was in the hospital on call that night. I described my symptoms to him, and he immediately shared my concerns.

It took about 30 minutes to drive to the hospital and another 30 from the time I arrived to the reading of the computed tomography (CT) arteriography of my neck. From the time I first feared a serious diagnosis to the last seconds watching the images unveil on the CT monitor, I had a single focus: Would I need emergency surgery? Would I have a stroke? Would I die?

I remember very little of my time at the hospital before the point I received my diagnosis, which was no diagnosis! I vividly remember Claridge questioning me about my symptoms and examining my neck. I watched and listened intently, waiting for him to say I had nothing to worry about, but it never occurred. I studied his facial expressions, looking for a smirk to suggest I was a typical "doctor hypochondriac," but . . . nothing. My entire life, everything I was, everything I thought about, collapsed around an immediate life-threatening situation.

I remember my relief as I watched the images unfold on the CT scan monitor, revealing there was no injury. In that instant, my life was returned to me and my anxiety and fear disappeared. This is how our patients feel and perceive their environments.

Patients want to know what's going on. I know this sounds simple, and everyone in healthcare understands that patients need to know the plan of care and have appropriate follow-up. But patients' craving for information is much more granular and comprehensive. Remember, all hospital patients have to do is think about what's happening to them. If a physician walks in at 7 a.m. and tells the patient he needs an x-ray of the chest, and the patient goes to radiology at 9 a.m., he wants to know the results. If the physician does not come back until the afternoon with the results, the patient sits around all day brooding, "Did the doctor forget to check the results? Does the test show something bad that the doctor isn't telling me?" Again, patients are stuck with time on their hands to worry about what's going on. If we don't provide information or manage patients' perceptions, they will fill in the blanks themselves.

While patients traverse the healthcare environment, they are concerned and afraid. In some cases, they are terrorized. Triggers for their tremendous anxiety are everywhere and can be very little things. Patients are also confused and have tremendous uncertainty about what's happening to them. We make this worse when we fail to communicate well or coordinate with other caregivers.

A final important point from our studies: patients don't want to be patients. I once proposed a contest to a conference audience, with an expensive prize to the winner. I put up a slide of a private jet, and I told my audience to get ready to quickly raise their hands, because the first hand I saw would be the winner. It was pretty funny to see all their hands at the ready. I told the audience that Cleveland Clinic had the number one heart center in the United States, with outcomes second to none. The first person to raise his or her hand would get a free, all-expenses-paid trip to Cleveland on that private jet to have a heart operation. What a deal! The greatest heart center in the world, with the best outcomes! I implored the members of the audience to raise their hands. No one did, because no one wants to be a patient.

This may be our most obvious study finding, as well as one of the most obvious facts in healthcare. No one wants to be our customer. The studies Cleveland Clinic conducted are a trove of what hospital patients think and experience. If we would query caregivers about the findings, no one would disagree. But we don't think about them. We don't consider them.

Our challenge—our responsibility—is to ensure that everyone in the organization understands what it's like to be on the other side. Think about what I said at the beginning of this chapter. Most organizations don't take the time to really understand their customers. But when we get granular, when we try to put ourselves in their shoes, when we ask how patients think about things, we uncover extremely important information to guide our work.

Equally important to the point that no one wants to be in the hospital or visit a healthcare provider is that no one wants to come back. I see many patients with inflammatory bowel disease, specifically Crohn's disease. It's a chronic disease for which there is no cure, and sufferers can have mild manifestations to terrible, severe, and recurrent manifestations that require multiple hospital admissions. You can feel their anxiety and trepidation when they are told they should be admitted to the hospital. We typically fail to recognize or appreciate patients' post-traumatic stress from previous life- or health-threatening events.

There's no absolute need to hire survey companies like Cleveland Clinic did to help understand patients. Taking time to genuinely listen and understand their comments is what's important, because it provides a wealth of information. Patients tell us things every day, but we frequently fail to listen and reap the knowledge to improve the patient experience. If we take a little time to get to know our patients as people, we not only will establish better relationships; we will be better caregivers.

Healthcare organizations receive a wealth of information in comments expressed through letters, surveys, and personal interactions. We need to study them and absorb what they tell us. I've heard it sneered that the plural of *verbatim* is not data, but *verbatims*. No! Verbatims and anecdotal data are very powerful when evaluated thoughtfully, used in the context of the local environment, and pooled with other data. For example, one of our surgeons received patient comments that he was not seeing them after operations, that he was very short when he did see them, and that he was rude and did not answer questions. Similar comments from eight different patients about one physician over a short time period may not be randomized, validated data. But it provided a pretty accurate representation of what was happening.

This physician was shown the comments and counseled about how to improve his practice, and the negative comments ceased. Verbatim feedback must be used carefully. We cannot condemn a physician as a bad practitioner based on a single patient complaint. Furthermore, there may be local process issues that impact patients' perceptions of what's happening. Suppose patients are cared for by a team of physicians, and one doing a particular procedure does not see patients the next day, but another does. This may indicate not that the practitioner evades patients, but that we've failed to effectively communicate whom patients should expect to see. So just as quantitative data must be used in perspective, single comments can be windows of opportunity when appropriately evaluated.

There are severe limitations to quantitative data as well. For years, we reported a satisfaction measure called "appointment when wanted." We tried new tactics, implemented new policies, and held managers accountable. But despite significant effort to improve access, we never raised the score. While we saw improvement in how patients rated our organization and their providers, we made no difference in how patients perceived access.

This prompted a deep dive into the data and patient comments. What we found is that getting the appointment when wanted was less important than the conduct of the appointment staff and the encounter with the physician. If appointment staff were helpful and courteous, patients rated the overall experience very high. Likewise, if patient-physician interactions were positive, that defined the overall rating of the encounter. "Appointment when wanted" did not accurately capture what was truly important to patients. It wasn't when the appointment occurred, but the positive experience with the appointment staff and physician that were important.

There are ample occurrences along the healthcare continuum that can result in a bad experience or make patients unhappy. But there are many things we *can* do that have great impact on enhancing the patient experience and delivering high-quality care. This was an example. We were measuring something that really did not matter to patients. The root of what was important was the interaction with the staff at all touch points. Using data to better understand such nuances, ascertaining we are employing appropriate metrics, and testing the validity of those metrics are all vital to ensuring that we regard the right information.

The single best way to find out what is important to patients is to just ask them! Don't be afraid of the answers. Each patient suggestion or comment may lead to significant and meaningful improvements in your organization. Cleveland Clinic uses a variety of other tactics to better understand what's important to patients. Several years ago, we established Voice of the Patient Advisory Councils (VPACs). An emerging trend and not unique to us, VPACs allow patients to provide feedback that helps tailor activities. Because of our sizable main campus hospital, we formed VPACs for most large institutes.

Groups like these also help validate our understanding of what's important to patients and amend our views when our thinking is off-track. We've used VPAC input to help redesign the look and feel of selected waiting rooms and to develop a new patient-friendly admission guide. Group members helped confirm why our "hospital quiet at night" scores were so low. We suspected it was less about being interrupted from sleep and more about hallway ruckus and noisy neighbors, and the VPACs confirmed this.

I recall listening to a Digestive Disease Institute VPAC discuss bathrooms, which are very important to such patients. Several floors suffered poor cleanliness scores, and we supposed this was overall room cleanliness. But the actual problem was bathroom appearance. While the bathrooms were not dirty, VPAC members criticized low levels of light and untidy urinal storage, which made the bathrooms appear dirty and cluttered. We changed the lighting and urinal organization, and cleanliness scores improved.

We don't let just anyone sit on a VPAC. Patients are nominated by clinical staff and interviewed, and there are minimal participation requirements. While any ideas and suggestions are welcome, we ensure that participants can work with others and channel their individual perspectives into constructive group feedback. We also have parameters on discussion topics; obviously, we're running a forum for improvement, not airing individual grievances. Additionally, we discourage suggestions unlikely to be implemented. We need to "rebuild the hospital so everyone has a private room" is simply not practical or constructive.

Success of VPACs also requires commitment from the organization and its leadership. John J. Fung, liver transplant surgeon and chair of the Digestive Disease Institute, leads all its VPAC meetings. Such visible commitment demonstrates to patients that leadership cares about their input and that feedback will be considered at the highest levels.

Pragmatism

We're relentless in pursuing patient-centeredness and trying to understand what patients want, but we also must be pragmatic about the challenges we face in healthcare. At our organization and in healthcare in general, the pendulum of patient-centered care had swung too far in the wrong direction. Now that it's swinging back, we must ensure that it doesn't go too far in the other direction. While always keeping the patient as our true north and taking into account our patient experience strategic priority, we must also be mindful of the realities and difficulties of delivering effective care and weigh those against what patients tell us they want.

Excessive surveying doesn't necessary equate to better patient-centered care. We can become distracted by things that are simply unreasonable or lack significant improvement value against the costs of implementation. For instance, is it reasonable to expect that hospitals are quiet at night, an emblematic question from the HCAHPS survey? Hospitals, especially large academic centers, have difficulty achieving top metrics in this area. We simply don't know what patients expect regarding quiet. Does it mean minimal interruptions? Do they expect a good night's sleep? We have to recognize that hospitals are simply not quiet. Hospital patients should not expect to get a good night's sleep.

Similarly, there's a national push to essentially eliminate visiting hours—patients and families want unrestricted access to their loved ones—and few would disagree. However, are unrestricted visiting hours at night reasonable for the privacy and comfort of patients in semiprivate rooms? One of the top patient complaints about noise relates to having a roommate. I have heard estimates that more than 60 percent of U.S. hospital rooms are semiprivate. Certainly, we aren't going to demolish all the hospitals with semiprivate rooms and rebuild them so that patients can have private rooms. We allow unrestricted visiting hours, permitting patients to have family members and friends with them around the clock. Then we ask whether the hospital room was quiet. This reflects a lack of systems thinking. One good idea, unrestricted visiting hours, can lead to noisy hospital rooms at night, and therefore this is probably a bad question to ask patients on a survey.

By posing too many questions, or asking questions that capture the wrong information, we may be driving unintended consequences. In 2013, Cleveland Clinic partnered with the Ohio State Medical Association to survey Ohio physicians regarding their views on pain management. Of the 1,100 physicians surveyed, 98 percent believe they are under increasing pressure from employers to improve patient satisfaction scores for pain treatment. Seventy-four percent agree that, in general, U.S. physicians overprescribe controlled substances to treat pain specifically to increase patient-satisfaction scores. These are troubling findings, and the consequences can be dangerous for patients. There is emerging evidence that heroin abuse is linked to prescription narcotic abuse. Americans constitute 4.6 percent of the world's population and already consume 80 percent of the world's opioid supply. We've set an expectation in this country that pain will always be treated, and it may be wrong to ask patients how their providers performed in treating pain.

Patient satisfaction surveys also measure patient perception. As I've said, patients define their perception of the experience relative to their personal situation. Many of the standardized surveys we are required to use are not well adjusted for important patient factors, such as the severity of a patient's chronic disease or presence of depression; both are important elements that can define patients' perception of their care. One study estimated that up to 30 percent of chronic medical patients who are hospitalized have elements of depression.[8] At Cleveland Clinic, we analyzed our HCAHPS data relative to a patient's severity of illness and self-reported depression. When compared to more healthy patients without chronic disease or depression, patients with chronic disease and/or depression gave significantly lower HCAHPS scores across all domains, an important finding that impacts how we interpret this data and the assumptions we make about our facilities and their ability to deliver patient-centered care.

Tell Patient Stories

Every patient has a story, and we need to take the time to listen. We'll be more insightful as we help patients navigate a very difficult time. Marc Boom of Houston Methodist Hospital opens board meetings by reading a patient letter—a patient's story. "It helps remind us why we're here, and we learn things about our organization," he says. This is why I keep that letter and photo on my desk.

As healthcare professionals, we're very good at persuading ourselves we know exactly what patients want. After all, we are the professionals, and in many cases, we have been patients. Both perspectives tend to convince us we know best. But using feedback and data analytics is vital to true understanding.

Do your people know what customers think? Do you have insights on frontline issues? Do you distribute that information so everyone knows it? Satisfaction surveys provide important data, and organizations should use them to measure specific areas of interest. However, direct visibility and discussions with frontline customers, in our case patients, are crucial to accurately understand what's occurring. Cleveland Clinic has made significant strategy changes and meaningful organizational improvements by paying attention to the data.

Important elements to consider:

1. Get over the bias that because healthcare professionals are both leaders and consumers of healthcare we know what's best for patients. Often we really don't understand what it means to be on the other side, and the only way to be sure that we get it right is to ask our patients and understand what is important to them.

2. There is more to what patients think than what standardized surveys reveal. Patient anecdotes can be very powerful statements about opportunities that organizations have to improve. Take the time to ask patients and their families what is important.

3. Establish a voice of the patient council that meets regularly to keep the "pulse of the consumer" and understand what patients are thinking about. Ensure that it is well represented and attended by senior leadership, and empower patients' activism by implementing some of their suggestions. Patients deserve to have a direct window to the top of the organization.

4. Remember that patients do not want to be our customers. They come to us often at the worst time in their lives. Because

patients are not sophisticated healthcare consumers, they use proxies to rate us. The little things matter to patients, and they will use these details to judge our effectiveness at care delivery.

5. Every patient has a story, and telling these stories to caregivers across the organization is a powerful way to remind people why they work in healthcare. Share patient letters and stories frequently across the organization. Open meetings with a story, and make sure that the information goes all the way up to the board of directors, who work to support the mission and, therefore, are caregivers as well.

Execution Is Everything

S hortly after becoming CXO, I learned a hard lesson in humility and the difference between talking about strategy and having the ability to execute on strategy. I read a hospital trade journal article about the emerging patient experience field—an article that did not mention Cleveland Clinic. I was surprised. We were the first U.S. hospital to have a CXO, with the first department focused on the patient experience. I thought we were well on our way to success. My arrogance led me to believe there must be something newsworthy we could offer the publication. After all, we were Cleveland Clinic—people should want to know what we were doing.

I called the reporter and inquired whether we could participate in another article covering some of our initiatives in progress. She provided a stiff dose of reality: "I know of Cleveland Clinic and your office. So you are the CXO? What have you done that actually improved the patient experience?" I described our strategy and how we were thinking about the patient experience, but it was all anecdotal. She pushed right back, "You have terrible scores! Why would anyone want to read about what you're doing? Call me when things get better!" She was absolutely right, and it taught me a valuable lesson on the importance of having something that was working. Brand recognition, the correct strategy, and good ideas get you nothing if you don't execute successfully.

Setting Patients First as true north and adding the patient experience to an already long list of strategic priorities was easy, but getting down to business and making it happen was another matter entirely. We had a burning platform, passionate people, and agreement on what was important, but I had no idea where or how to start. I had no mentor, no role model, and no coach. There were no textbooks and no real articles about tactics and execution. We had not yet teased out the concept of the three Ps: process, people, and patients.

When I speak to healthcare audiences, they strongly identify with this conundrum. They see the need for adopting a more patient- and family-centric environment but frequently express frustration about getting going. The most frequently asked questions when I speak to other hospital systems are "Where do we begin?" and "How do we start?"

A running joke in medicine is that surgeons are not trained to think but to do. So I felt like I wasn't living up to my training. Successful execution is worshipped in any industry. This was an important lesson instilled by my colleague and friend Ananth Raman, UPS Foundation Professor of Business Logistics at Harvard Business School. I was first introduced to Ananth shortly after becoming chief experience officer. He is a passionate believer in the importance of the patient experience and was studying the Clinic's efforts to improve. He spent his career studying factory operations and how processes are more efficient when you take the human element out of production.

Ananth recognized that healthcare was a business that required humans to make the product—healthcare delivery—more efficient and caring. We had long conversations about what the patient experience meant and its value to the organization. We discussed how important it was for patients and how improving it would be transformative for healthcare. And he always pushed me hard about how we would execute: "Jim, how do you fix it? How do you improve it? What are the tactics? Everyone agrees it's important, but how do you execute?"

It's challenging to answer, in part, because those assigned to lead patient experience initiatives frequently lack operational experience and have little control over operations. They're figureheads, given an important responsibility to transform an organization but few resources to do it. This is a difficult but not impossible task, and effectiveness is largely determined by skill in building coalitions of operational leaders. The ability to begin and move projects forward requires consensus and buy-in. It sounds difficult, and it is. But remember that the purpose is to put patients first. Getting people on the bus to do something is much easier when the goal is to improve the way we take care of people.

This is exactly where I found myself when I took over the patient experience for Cleveland Clinic. I had a handful of employees and a mandate to change an organization of 43,000, including powerful physician, nursing, and human resources stakeholder groups. If I wanted to do something at the bedside, I had to negotiate with nursing. If I wanted to address training or culture, I had to confer with human resources. If something affected a patient operational area, such as food service, parking, or cleaning, that was the purview of operations. Each leader had ideas regarding priorities and how to frame the problem. This is one reason why midlevel operational leaders have difficulty moving a patient experience agenda and why it's critical to select the right leader for the initiative. If a nurse leads the patient experience, a strong physician partner is essential. Similarly, a physician leader needs a nurse partner. Nonclinical operations leaders need both.

When I first became CXO, we could not articulate what a successful execution would look like, let alone discuss tactics to drive it. And just as everyone had a different patient experience definition, there was an equal number of ideas on improvement. Some felt we needed to start a smile campaign. Others believed we needed more nonclinical people visiting patients daily. The ideas came nonstop, multiple, free-flowing, and overwhelming. I was almost paralyzed, not knowing where to start or what to try. And there were conversations about the "low-hanging fruit," a phrase I detest, and queries about "the easy, quick wins" and "gaining some early successes." Everyone looked at me, asking essentially, "What are you doing? What are you trying? And how can we help you?" The expectations to improve were intense.

Cleveland Clinic was also in the midst of a major organizational integration effort. We were essentially a hospital holding company working to integrate various pieces of our organization into a hospital operating company and an integrated health system. It was impossible to suggest ideas without being challenged about how they would impact and be implemented across the "enterprise." If you forgot to use the word *enterprise* in every proposition, people regarded you as failing to grasp what *enterprise* meant. A colleague on the executive committee took a very public shot at me, "Jim, you just don't understand what strategy in an integrated health system is all about."

It was a recipe for disaster: the pressure to try something, coupled with not really controlling anything and having to negotiate with powerful colleagues who had rigid ideas about what was important. The first few months of my new job were exhausting. Fortunately, my boss was the consummate CEO. "I have your back, Jim. Take your time to figure it out," Cosgrove told me. I was grateful for the breathing room.

I thought the best way to start was to go small, to try modest projects without enterprise implications to see whether they worked. If we got something to work in a microenvironment like a single unit or department, we could scale it up to the enterprise. (Enterprise be damned; the patient experience is driven at the local level!) We also needed to better understand what was happening at the unit level before we attempted something enterprise-wide.

So our start was this: We identified one of our worst HCAHPS-performing units and assembled a team consisting of the nurse manager, a representative from the Office of Patient Experience, a physician champion, the supervisor from environmental services, and others involved in care coordination, such as the social worker and case manager. This team met weekly for about an hour to identify problems contributing to patient dissatisfaction. The team reviewed HCAHPS data and talked to patients and staff. The goals were to collect real-time data, identify opportunities, and, when possible, solve identified problems quickly.

The unit team quickly saw several areas for improvement. Many patients needed endoscopy procedures, and fasting is required as prep. More frequently than we thought acceptable, the procedure was delayed, with the patient waiting, unable to eat, and confused about the timing. Or worse, the procedure was rescheduled for the next day, causing significant patient dissatisfaction because it required continued fasting. Sometimes the postponements caused delayed discharges, so this was an opportunity for operational improvement, as well as enhanced patient satisfaction.

Because the unit's population typically had multiple medical problems, significant care coordination was required for successful patient discharge. Cooperation between the social worker and care coordinator was essential, but it quickly became apparent through our weekly meetings that these individuals abhorred working together and did not communicate effectively. Their mutual dislike was so intense that they avoided being on the floor at the same time, which obviously complicated care coordination. Our team also discovered that the nurse manager was often sequestered in her office handling paperwork and other business and did not regularly round on staff or patients. Furthermore, physicians rarely talked with nurses about care plans.

This small team, huddling once a week for about an hour, unearthed a variety of opportunities, some of which could be fixed easily and others that required more time and effort. Getting the nurse manager to spend more time rounding required her manager to set and enforce new expectations. Getting the social worker and case manager to work together simply involved critical conversations about their job responsibilities and holding them accountable for participating in teamwork. Improved schedule coordination between the unit and the endoscopy suite would require a better process, but identifying the problem was an important first step.

This modest unit project was a "quick win" and captured some "low-hanging fruit." A month after we started huddling to address problems, the unit's HCAHPS scores saw the highest rise in the organization—and in the history of the hospital (see Figure 9.1). To say I was thrilled would be a vast understatement. I felt like I had struck gold. This pilot project proved we could actually impact HCAHPS scores with simple solutions driven by frontline caregivers.

When I updated my fellow executive team members about the project and showed these metrics, Steve Glass, our CFO, looked at me and said, "Now, this is really important stuff." Cosgrove agreed! We demonstrated we could change the patient experience in measurable ways.

These small initial projects taught us an important lesson about piloting at the local level. But our next steps demonstrated the challenges of rolling out something enterprise-wide. We had scored a success because we went right to the local level for implementation of the patient experience huddles. When we tried to expand this tactic to other units and hospitals, we found little agreement that this was a best practice, despite our data. The patient experience huddle was considered an option, not a mandate. Every unit required coaxing the unit manager, the physician leader, and others to participate. We did not yet have the ability to force implementation, so it was only a soft win.

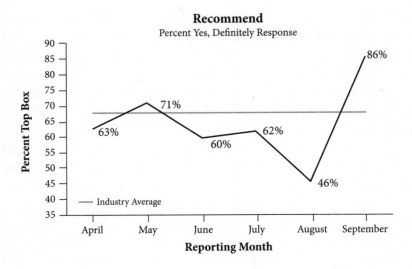

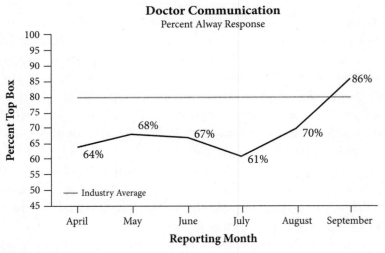

Figure 9.1   A "quick win" in a unit project.

This early project also taught us lessons about hospital processes and tactics. Hospitals are full of processes, literally thousands of interconnected systems and processes that together deliver the complex product we call healthcare. Before we could layer on any patient experience "solution," we had to first ensure that the basic hospital processes were functional. These processes generally work efficiently and achieve what they're designed to do. However, many processes are managed in silos,

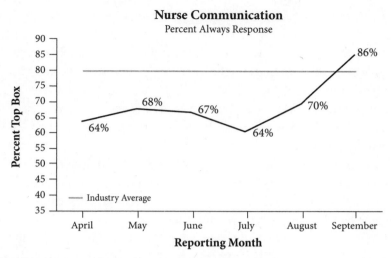

Figure 9.1   A "quick win" in a unit project *(continued)*.

with staff in charge of one process having no idea what other silos deliver. Their systems do not communicate, and they're not engineered to work together.

An endoscopy being delayed or cancelled without informing the nursing team or patient is just one example. Many nurses complained they were powerless over what was happening in endoscopy, and yet they had to break bad news to patients about postponed procedures. Hospitals run on process. System failure results when processes don't function effectively (endoscopy scheduling) or don't interface smoothly with other processes (coordination between the endoscopy suite and the nursing unit). No amount of smiling, or layering service excellence tactics on top of the problem, will improve the experience for the patient. We have to fix broken processes.

It's difficult to identify and repair faulty hospital processes. It also takes leadership courage because broken processes are typically owned by poor managers or managers who lack accountability. If meals delivered to patients do not match their menu selections, that needs to be fixed. If patients receive a continual busy signal when they call for appointments, that's a problem that needs to be fixed. It's a fallacy to believe that more layered service excellence strategies, extra apologies, or work-arounds will mitigate these problems. Fix what's broken, and develop or outplace the bad manager. Don't just put a Band-Aid on something that doesn't work.

If silos are beginning to come down and we're reasonably sure hospital processes are functioning, the question becomes what can be implemented to help make a difference. This brings us to the topic of best practices and another lesson learned from our experiment on the floor. There are good processes or tactics considered to be best practices that should be implemented.

A best practice is defined as "a method or technique that has consistently shown results superior to those achieved with other means and that is used as a benchmark. In addition, a 'best' practice can evolve to become better as improvements are discovered."[1]

To be worthy of consideration, a best practice should be scalable in your environment and help attain your goals. When the practice was implemented in other areas, was improvement sustained, and what was the duration? There are differing opinions regarding how long something must work before it's considered a best practice to be implemented more broadly; I recommend three to six months. Best practices should also have an associated metric so you know whether they actually make a difference.

Winnowing best practices is an important component of a patient experience improvement program. We cannot do everything, and what we choose to do should have broad impact. Nurse hourly rounding, or as some call it, purposeful hourly rounding, is an example of a best practice. This involves a nurse going into a patient's room every hour and running through a checklist. The following are typical questions:

1. Do you have to use the bathroom?

2. Do you have pain?

3. Do you need to be repositioned?

4. Do you need your belongings moved closer?

5. Do you need anything else?

This practice has been demonstrated to improve patient satisfaction scores, reduce call-light usage, decrease falls and pressure ulcers,[2] and reduce medication errors. Clearly, this best practice affects patient safety, quality, and satisfaction; its impact on the organization can be high yield.

At Cleveland Clinic, hourly rounding was practiced sporadically. When we evaluated the HCAHPS scores of floors where it was practiced routinely, performance was better. At one of our community hospitals, a nurse manager whose HCAHPs scores routinely achieved the 90th percentile was convinced it was due to routine hourly rounding.

K. Kelly Hancock, now our executive chief nursing officer but at the time director of nursing for the Heart & Vascular Institute, agreed to conduct a pilot. She picked several units and mandated hourly rounding. We added a new question to the inpatient survey sent after discharge asking patients whether a nurse visited hourly. Using the standard HCAHPS format, we asked whether a nurse always, usually, sometimes, or never came every hour. We collected 4,000 patient responses during the 90-day pilot.

Results were striking. If patients said they "always" saw the nurse, nursing domain HCAHPS scores achieved 90th percentile performance, as shown in Figure 9.2. Scores progressively worsened as the patient responded "usually," "sometimes," or "never." There was little doubt purposeful hourly rounding made a significant change in the scores. Hancock's pilot validated in our organization what was well described in the nursing literature. The improvement was so significant that Cosgrove

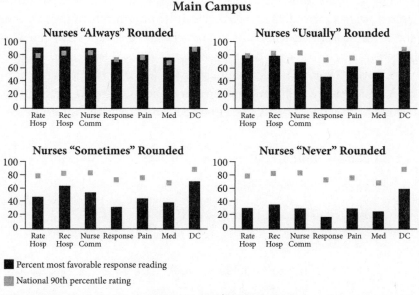

Figure 9.2   Nurse hourly rounding and HCAHPS scores.

mandated nurse hourly rounding for all units, an unprecedented move that has had meaningful impact on the organization and how we care for patients. This is an example of how we took a best practice, tested it in several local environments, and, after confirming effectiveness, implemented it enterprise-wide.

To ensure that rounds are done, we continue to survey patients about them, and we require bedside nurses to complete a tracking sheet in patient rooms. Nurse managers routinely audit the practice in their units. Nurse hourly rounding is a best practice that impacts not only patient satisfaction, but safety and quality, and it should be routinely practiced in every hospital worldwide.

This pilot also taught us an important lesson about partnering with critical stakeholders. Hancock was an early supporter and critical ally in all our efforts to improve the patient experience. While at the time she was responsible for only a small portion of our overall nursing infrastructure, without her leadership and support of this pilot, it would not have been successful. Once HCAHPS scores demonstrated the magnitude of improvement, the rest of the organization could not oppose implementation. Patient experience leaders need critical stakeholder collaborators like Hancock for efforts to succeed.

Our sophistication regarding how to tackle patient experience problems slowly improved. We were successfully piloting small projects, we had identified critical stakeholder partners, and we were slowly achieving success.

HCAHPS survey results would soon be linked to reimbursement in 2013, and we knew this would create a tremendous burning platform for our messaging. HCAHPS questions are neatly organized into different domains:

1. Nurse Communication

2. Doctor Communication

3. Responsiveness of Hospital Staff

4. Pain Management

5. Communication About Medicines

6. Discharge Information

7. Cleanliness and Quietness of Hospital Environment

8. Reputation-Related Measures

These domains allowed us to set HCAHPS scores as the initial primary outcome metrics for improving the patient experience. Anyone involved in hospital operations knows there are literally hundreds of metrics we could have chosen. For the patient experience alone, there are well over a hundred questions in the various surveys we distribute. As leaders, we cannot ask the organization to focus on all of them, but we must establish the most important ones.

We formed HCAHPS improvement teams for each domain, encompassing any projects or activities affecting that particular domain. Each team was led by a project manager and had broad representation from across the enterprise. We made it very clear that the team represented the enterprise; if a domain-related project was not sponsored by the team, it was not official and would not be resourced.

The quiet at night improvement team established the Help Us Sustain Healing (HUSH) protocol, which consists of the following elements:

1. Signs reminding people to be quiet posted on the nursing units

2. An announcement made at 8 p.m. to notify patients and visitors that it was nighttime and they needed to be mindful of patients resting

3. Dimming of lights on the nursing units

4. Closing the doors of some patient rooms

5. Providing education material asking patients and visitors to be mindful of patients' recovery and to keep voices low and the television off after a specified time

The HUSH protocol also assigned team leads at every nursing unit to drive the tactics. In addition, the project leader audited individual floors for compliance and also supplied sound recordings of each floor. This information was fed immediately back to nurse managers and the HUSH champions.

Dividing up the HCAHPS domains also allowed us to distribute responsibility throughout our operational areas. A good example is cleanliness: the environmental services (EVS) team, those responsible for cleaning the hospital, took ownership of the cleanliness scores. Every EVS caregiver is trained on how his or her work impacts HCAHPS scores and the patient experience. Unit HCAHPS scores are regularly distributed to EVS caregivers. Cleveland Clinic's cleanliness scores have made significant improvements and lead our peer group of major health systems, as shown in Figure 9.3.

Led by an innovative leader, Michael Visniesky, Senior Director for Environmental Services, EVS has become an energized and engaged team, adopting slogans and contests to engage caregivers. The team created buttons proclaiming, "Always clean!" But since Medicare banned the word *always* from the lexicon of what we're permitted to say to patients, the EVS team developed a new button slogan, "Our goal: Clean at all times!" Participating in leadership rounds one day, I asked an EVS caregiver assigned to clean a nursing unit exactly what her role was. She responded, "My job is to ensure a great patient experience by helping our patients." That is employee engagement!

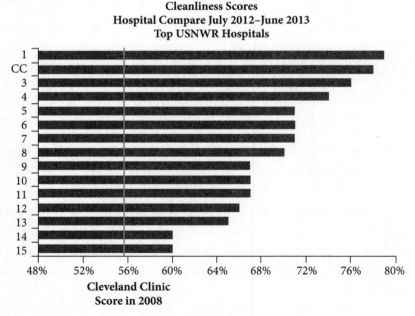

Figure 9.3   Improvement in cleanliness scores.

Sometimes Things Don't Work

Not all ideas are good ones, and while we hope to figure that out before we implement them across the enterprise, sometimes we're fully deployed before we realize that tactics are just not having the desired effect. Making sure your program is adding value is extremely important, and stopping a program that is not having impact, while difficult, is at times necessary.

I inherited a program called *service navigators*. These were 12 non-clinical individuals assigned to specific inpatient floors. They rounded on patients daily to ensure they had everything they needed. For instance, if a navigator rounded on a patient who complained of not seeing the doctor, the navigator would call the doctor. If the patient needed help with preparations for going home, the navigator contacted the social worker or care coordinator. If the patient needed an extra pillow or blanket, the navigator would get it. If the patient was in pain, a nurse was found.

These caregivers were not licensed and were not considered clinical practitioners, so they could participate only in very rudimentary non-clinical activities. But they took care of lots of little details and bridged the gap between other providers.

At first, we believed this extra help was really impacting the patient experience. But we started to notice that floors with navigators were not performing any better than floors without them. The program was started after what appeared to be a very successful pilot on one of the inpatient floors. During the pilot, HCAHPS scores were evaluated before the start of the program and after it was up and running. Inpatient satisfaction scores had improved significantly. The improvement was attributed to the navigator program, so it was adopted in most units across our main campus hospital. After nearly two years of full implementation, we did not realize similarly improved scores in the other units.

More carefully evaluating the navigators, we discovered that while they were still rounding on patients, they had morphed into pseudo project managers and were conducting a variety of other activities for the units. One of the navigators chaperoned the volunteers who brought therapy dogs. This was just busywork; the volunteers didn't need a chaperone. Some navigators had been "captured" by the units as extra caregivers to help out with duties as assigned. Overall, the navigators were spending less time rounding on patients and more time doing things not directly improving the patient experience performance.

We conducted a controlled trial, splitting a unit. One half had a navigator visit every patient daily, and we tracked all patient issues. The second half, which had a similar service line and patients, would not have a navigator. HCAHPS performance would be the ultimate measure. We ran the pilot for two months, reviewed patient feedback every week, and carefully tracked HCAHPS results.

The navigator certainly filled a variety of service gaps. Patients needed more frequent communication with providers, and they had a variety of service needs, like occasionally requiring clean bed linen. The navigator developed good relationships with patients and families. She was a trusted member of the team and generally viewed as someone who could get things done. However, the HCAHPS scores did not change. Intense navigator follow-up made no difference in how patients rated their in-hospital experience.

The program needed to be retired. It was a difficult decision to lay off a dozen people, but it was right for the organization. Throwing in the towel when something isn't working is tough. Managers and leaders tend to become emotionally attached to "good ideas." Once programs are started, they're often hard to stop and even more difficult to relinquish when layoffs are involved. The navigators were a terrific group—committed, hardworking, passionate, and caring. Every unit manager with one thought the navigator was a treasured member of the team, invaluable for care delivery. I would never dispute that; however, the navigators were not having demonstrable impact.

When I communicated the reduction in force to the affected clinical chairs and nursing managers and our key leaders across the enterprise, people were not happy, and some were outraged. There was shock and disbelief that we would eliminate such a "vital service" to patients. Many predicted that HCAHPS scores on the affected floors would take an immediate, significant plunge. Some expressed their displeasure to me directly; others talked behind my back. It was clear the navigators had won the hearts and minds of their leaders, and extracting them from their units was not a pleasant task. Everyone warned me that patient care would suffer without them and, more important, that HCAHPS scores would nose-dive. It would be less than honest to say I wasn't worried they might be right. Only one nursing director supported my decision; in retrospect, this was more likely out of friendship than her actual belief that it was the right thing to do.

It's hard to walk into a room of 12 people and say they're losing their jobs. In January 2011, we shut down the service navigator program. For two months I sat on pins and needles awaiting the first complete set of HCAHPS numbers without the navigator program. I was definitely feeling pressure, but I held fast to the results of our study. Our decision was validated: for three months, we tracked each floor that previously had a navigator, and there was no degradation in scores. In fact, some scores increased. The service navigator program was an expensive one everyone believed had significant impact on the patient experience, but in reality there was no correlation.

The experience taught me three important lessons about patient experience tactical implementation. First, preserve scarce enterprise resources for strategic initiatives. The navigators had taken on a variety of other roles to help drive patient experience improvement in their units. Many of these tasks were not part of the enterprise vision for patient experience improvement but were activities the local units considered important, and the navigator was a resource. This ties back to the elephant description challenge I laid out earlier. I would never tell someone his or her idea to improve the patient experience was bad, but I would not deploy limited enterprise resources to implement a nonstrategic initiative. We used the HCAHPS data as a broad measure for the program, but we did not incorporate a process metric to monitor whether the navigators were effective.

The second important lesson is that practices must be carefully examined before broader rollout. The service navigators pilot had shown tremendous promise; however, when reevaluated under more rigorous circumstances, the program did not perform as thought.

Third, while not proved by data, this experiment validated for me the meaning of the patient experience. Processes and operations must function effectively. Patients may have liked having someone around to fill in the gaps and attend to little things. But the navigators were never an acceptable alternative to effective care delivery. They essentially became a crutch to support a bad or failed process. Patients may have appreciated the navigator calling a physician who failed to round, but this didn't prevent them from giving the physician an unacceptable HCAHPS score for not communicating. Likewise, if the room was dirty and the navigator got EVS to clean the room immediately, this was no substitute for the room being cleaned in the first place. The patients were correctly using the survey to rate their perceived experiences based on what happened before the navigator intervened. In essence, the navigator became a work-around for processes that should have functioned appropriately to begin with.

There are many tactics that impact the patient experience. Every tactic should be a best practice, be easily understood, have clear process metrics that permit managers to monitor adoption and usage, and have sustainable impact on a particular outcome. It's also important to realize that, as the saying goes, the way to boil an ocean is one cup at a time. Not all new programs can immediately be implemented on an enterprise scale. Not only is this challenging to do in large organizations, but the cost of failure can be extraordinary. Test something first on a small, frontline unit, and if it works, establish whether it's transferable to the rest of the organization, and then determine how to scale it.

Finding early partners is critical. Just because you're in charge of the patient experience will not mean you can order people to implement something. The Cleveland Clinic patient experience would not be as successful without the assistance and early partnership of Hancock. She was not in charge of all of nursing then, but she commanded tremendous respect and knew nursing operations better than anyone else I knew.

Improvement isn't always just big structural change; often, it's paying attention to the little things. The pilot with one of our worst-performing units taught us that endoscopy scheduling and basic caregiver communication have significant impact on the patient experience. It's critical to examine the impact of everyday processes.

Effective Execution Requires Metrics

Tactics alone aren't sufficient to compel an institution like Cleveland Clinic to embrace the importance of achieving a consistently great patient experience. We are a data-driven healthcare organization. If something is a strategic priority, metrics need to support and sustain it. In the beginning, few of us were paying any attention to our data about the patient experience. Good execution required that we disseminate the patient experience data we collect to all levels of management.

We had plenty of data along the care continuum, and we needed to make sure that it was driven vertically down through management (Figure 9.4). Data needed to impact strategic decision making, support implementation of tactical best practices, and touch individuals at the front line who were operationalizing the change. Strategic data became the overall enterprise goal that all senior leaders needed to understand and follow. Ultimately, they would be held accountable for their performance. Supporting best practices, such as nurse hourly rounding, is tactical data. This information is disseminated across units throughout the enterprise for managers to follow and share with their frontline nurses. Regularly distributing communication scores to the physicians is an example of sharing operational data. It is used for individual performance improvement.

Driving transformational performance improvement in patient experience requires that an organization establish a strategic priority, set goals, and provide metrics and data to every manager. Because they are accountable for driving patient experience improvement, managers need to understand how their role relates to the organizational goal. Driving

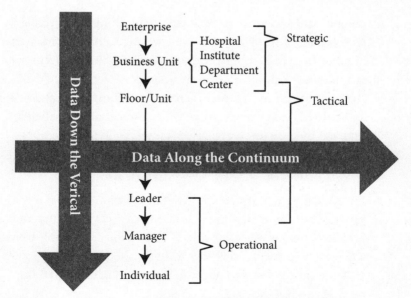

Figure 9.4 Driving data down vertically through management.

data to every manager also ensures that we have a standard to recognize and by which we hold people accountable for their work.

Given that resources for implementing new tactics will continue to contract, we must be smarter about our approach to problems. Cleveland Clinic is mapping high-level patient flow through our system to better understand where to target improvements for maximal impact. We must select projects that impact multiple areas and performance measures. For example, we've used HCAHPS scores as targets for improvement, while many of the programs we've implemented have impact beyond the inpatient environment. Improving physician communication broadly impacts inpatient and outpatient communication, as well as coordination with nurses and other caregivers. If we wander too far into the weeds chasing a single metric, we'll lose the ability to transform care more broadly.

In summary:

1. Talking about improving the patient experience is important, but ultimately success will be defined by the ability to execute. Actually getting something done and showing improvement in a defined outcome measure will demonstrate that the patient experience initiative is more than just a marketing campaign.

2. Operational success requires coalition building with critical stakeholders. The patient experience touches everything in the organization; remember, our goal is organizational alignment around the patient (the customer). Successful execution will require support from leaders across the organization, and your ability to build a strong team of willing stakeholders will help improve the execution of new processes. Gain broad support for new initiatives, but use your proximity to the boss and get leaders to mandate when necessary.

3. Fix broken basic hospital processes first. Creating new processes or implementing new tactics as a work-around for a broken system is wasteful and will not fix the problem. We have a tendency to assume that everything is already working well and that the only way to improve is to implement something new. That is not the case.

4. Whether your system comprises 1 hospital or 100 hospitals, start with small projects that can create early wins. Ignore the pressure to "enterprise" something immediately. There is no company research and development office in the world that doesn't experiment before it rolls something new out. This is no different. Figure out if something is going to work on a small scale, measure its effectiveness by determining if it improved an outcome, see if the process can be sustained for a defined period of time—say, three months—and then determine how to scale it.

5. Identify best practices. Do not waste time and money on programs or tactics until you have investigated and trialed best practices that have been demonstrated to work in other hospital environments. Everyone has his or her own definition of the patient experience and his or her own ideas on how to improve it. Do not let that get in the way of using things that we already know work. There are programs that work and work well, such as nurse hourly rounding. This is a best practice that should be mandated for every hospital in the world.

6. Learn from others. Big, successful organizations like Cleveland Clinic have a tendency to believe that the only good ideas come from within. Wrong! My CEO has a saying: "We need to stop breathing our own exhaust fumes." We have learned a great deal from hospitals much smaller than we are and from businesses in completely different industries. Look around; there are good ideas out there.

7. Have the courage to divest a good idea that doesn't measure up. It is hard to shut down a program: leaders and managers become emotionally attached to their "baby," employees may lose their jobs, and shutting down something is sometimes harder than building it. Some holdout supporters will also manipulate data to demonstrate success when there is nothing but failure. Be objective and critical in your program evaluations, and be steadfast in your need to terminate something when it is clear that it is not effective.

Healthcare Requires Service Excellence

How often have you stood at a service counter in a retail business or patronized a restaurant where it seems everyone ignores you? Recently I was at the checkout of a large electronic consumer products store. Nearly every employee I passed while browsing stopped to ask whether I needed anything. When I got to the cashier, the young woman behind the counter was typing on her smart phone, while I stood right in front of her with my purchase. She finished typing, put the phone down, and rang me up, without acknowledging me or even looking at me. As she was executing my transaction, another employee arrived at work and walked behind me, and she yelled out to him, "Hey, Ron! Where you been? What's up?" She finally looked at me and asked whether I would like to pay with cash or credit.

It's critical that everyone in our organization acknowledge and, when needed, try to help our customers. These interactions create an important first impression, and subsequent positive impressions, that convey we care. I've stated previously that you don't need to be a medical professional to be a caregiver. You also don't have to be a medical professional to be nice to patients or help them find their way around the hospital. Needing healthcare services is stressful enough without that stress being compounded by bad interactions with our people or organization.

Like many major medical centers and large hospital complexes, navigating the halls of Cleveland Clinic can be difficult. In 2008, shortly after we opened the latest addition to our main hospital, the Sydell and Arnold Miller Family Pavilion, we created a program called the Red Coats. These men and woman have a strong predilection for customer service and are stationed throughout the main campus simply to help people navigate. If you are lost or have questions about where to find something, the Red Coats can help you. The program has been immensely popular with patients and our employees, and we frequently receive comments about how the Red Coats have established lasting relationships with some of our patients. It has greatly enhanced way-finding in our organization.

Having a group of specially trained greeters has been effective, but one of our goals is to have *every* caregiver greet and assist every patient and the patient's accompanying friends and family members wherever they are in our facilities. You can station only so many Red Coats throughout the campus, so we need alignment among everyone to help. Each caregiver has the opportunity to create a positive, lasting impression for patients.

Service Excellence Is Not Just Smiling

I hate when people say hospitals need to be like hotels. Hospitals are *not* hotels. I have never stayed at a hotel where people come into your room at three o'clock in the morning and do things to hurt you, like draw your blood. I also generally stay in hotels when I am happy, like on vacation. People are generally not happy to be in a hospital. We also simply cannot add more amenities to make patients happy when often we have to do things they will not like. But as Micah Solomon, a patient experience consultant, points out, healthcare should be "healing with hospitality."[1] Solomon goes on to say that the healthcare industry has an "insular nature, which makes the status quo self-reinforcing . . . in other words, healthcare providers and institutions compare themselves to each other," which makes learning from others more difficult. There is no reason why we cannot learn from other industries such as the hospitality industry to improve what we do.

I enjoy staying at The Ritz-Carlton hotels. They're a bit pricey, but I like how the employees smile and say hello when we pass in the hallway. If I'm standing alone looking lost, someone always stops to ask whether I need assistance. Like most males, I prefer never to admit I'm lost or need help, so it's a tad annoying, but I still find it a nice touch. At a Ritz-Carlton, I'm never lost, I never wonder where the restroom is, and I never want for anything. Because I'm not a billionaire, that kind of service and attention is cool.

The Ritz-Carlton and other great service organizations excel at having every employee acknowledge and help customers. This is called *service excellence*. It's a little hard to define, but a very good start is the opening line of a paper by the late Robert Johnston, professor of operations management at Warwick Business School in the United Kingdom: "Service excellence is both obtrusive and elusive. We know when we have received it and, rather more frequently, we know when we have not."[2]

For healthcare, this service excellence definition better aligns our thinking: "the ability of the provider to consistently meet and manage patient expectations. Clinical excellence must be the number one priority for any healthcare system. However, the best healthcare systems combine professional (clinical) service excellence with outstanding personal service."[3]

Cleveland Clinic has the *clinical* excellence; now we must build and sustain the *service* excellence. Successful service excellence programs don't require perfect delivery of scripted phrases or behaviors at every customer touch point. What *is* required is a framework for everyone in the organization to understand and consistently deliver a basic set of behavioral standards at every touch point. For instance, we don't need every person in the organization asking patients or their families if they're lost and offering directions. But teaching caregivers to pay attention to how our patients and families behave—so if, for instance, they look lost, the caregiver will offer assistance—is part of the framework. We don't want to oblige everyone to walk around smiling and saying hello to all our patients. But we want our caregivers to acknowledge people when they pass in the hallways. A friend introduced me to the concept of the "lizard's brain"—when behavior and actions are reflexive and innate. Service excellence should be that.

A good service excellence strategy is also essential to meet patient expectations. Patients come into the hospital with anxiety, fear, and an expectation that we will be there and take care of them. When a service failure allows the patient to form the impression that we don't care, or the patient forms the impression that we aren't compassionate, we've failed to deliver to the standard the patient is expecting. The interaction can potentially define us. What we delivered as an experience did not meet expectation.

One day on leadership rounds, Cosgrove and two other members of our executive team walked into a patient's room and asked how everything was going. All of the patient's responses to Cosgrove's questions about care were positive. Our chief nurse, part of the team that day, thought the patient was holding back and asked him if something was bothering him. The patient looked at Cosgrove and said, "You know, Dr. Cosgrove, I'm a Vietnam veteran, and I'm dying of cancer. You would think someone in my circumstances would be treated with a little more respect than being called 'sunshine.' And by the way, Dr. Cosgrove, if you hadn't noticed, I'm black, and to me, being called sunshine is a racial slur!"

Needless to say, Cosgrove was shocked and immediately apologized. As a fellow Vietnam veteran, Cosgrove had immediate empathy for the patient and his need for respect. This patient's expectation was that he be referred to by his name or by "sir." Is this too much to ask? His experience was obviously something entirely different.

When we discussed the situation with the offending physical therapist and reviewed her performance with her supervisor, we found that the employee was actually exceptional. "Bubbly" is how one nurse described her. "Someone you would want taking care of your family." We discovered that the word *sunshine* was just part of this employee's regular patter and that she used it frequently. There was no ill intent on the part of the employee, but what this interaction created was a very typical expectation-experience mismatch. The patient wanted one thing, he received another, and it made him quite upset. It also illustrates that care can be going perfectly, but a minor interaction may lead patients to define our organization as a place that makes them feel uncomfortable and disrespected.

Some reading this may consider the patient holding us accountable for the word *sunshine* to be minor and that hospitals and other organizations should not be judged on such interactions. I don't disagree, and certainly delivering high-quality care is more important than remembering how to refer to someone. However, if we accept that a patient's state of mind is important to his or her overall well-being, then we should be concerned about the little things. We should eliminate things that could cause the patient to be upset or more uncomfortable in an environment that is already stressful. It should not be up to us to judge what is or isn't right for the patient. This patient wanted to be treated with dignity, not only because he served our country, but more important, because he expected us to be culturally sensitive to his race. It's the least we can do for a man of distinction (a veteran) and a fellow human being dying of cancer.

Seemingly modest, unintentional words or actions can trigger people to be upset. While I'm very informal, and most of my patients call me Jim instead of Dr. Merlino, I would never want them to address me by some pet name. I find being called "sweetie" or "honey" distasteful. We certainly can't predict how people like to be addressed, and we also can't read minds to understand whether certain words may irritate people. But we don't need to do either, because we can train people to consistently employ a framework that will avoid such triggers. If we don't know the name of the patient or what he or she wishes to be called, the appropriate form of address is "sir" or "ma'am." Using appropriate generic salutations will ensure that we don't get this simple expectation wrong. If we know the patient's name or preferred form of address, that should be our standard. It is also not wrong and very easy to simply ask the patient, "How would you like me to address you?" The interaction between the dying black veteran and our physical therapist illustrates how a service excellence program and behavioral standards can help.

How We Apologize Is Also Important

Service recovery, or how we apologize and make amends, is also an essential component of a service excellence strategy. Recognizing when mistakes are made, apologizing for their occurrence, and doing something to make it better are critical to good customer service. In the hospitality industry, a typical example of service recovery is receiving an apology and a free dessert for a hair in the soup or a round of drinks on the house for waiting too long for a table. However, in reality, the theory and mechanics of service recovery are much more sophisticated. In healthcare, we cannot offer a "service bribe" to make people better. Our only recourse is to try to correct the problem and make people feel like we care by doing so. It's not just about saying you're sorry.

When we experience a service failure, we get angry. The degree of anger is proportional to the event. We will be more angry when we are sitting in the airport waiting for our flight and it is suddenly cancelled and less angry when we order a specific coffee and discover down the street that the barista gave us the wrong one. But in both cases, we experience some level of discontent. That discontent or anger rises abruptly and, as time progresses, starts to level off. It reaches a plateau and eventually subsides. This is not to suggest that we forget the event and just let bygones be bygones, but generally our heightened anger is not sustained. Evidence suggests that if we apologize as that discontent is rising or at its highest point, usually immediately after the inciting event occurs, then there's a tendency for the apology to be dismissed, as the person delivering it gives the impression of not really listening. However, if we do something to acknowledge the mistake—show empathy and apologize— the service recovery is believed to be much more effective and meaningful and tends to be accepted by the customer as sincere. This is referred to as the anger-hostility curve (Figure 10.1).[4]

Having a robust service recovery strategy is not only the right thing to do; it also helps protect the brand. Paige Hall, CEO of AboutFace, actually suggests that when service failures occur, if they are appropriately recovered, customers report a higher level of satisfaction with the organization.[5] A critical component of service recovery is not just apologizing, but taking appropriate action to fix the problem.

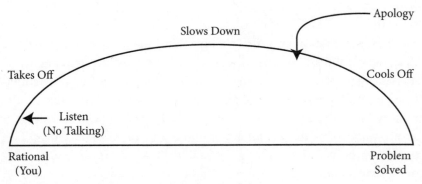

Figure 10.1   The anger-hostility curve (adapted from Timm).

This is especially important in healthcare, because any patient complaint involving medical care is defined as a grievance by Medicare and can affect a hospital's Medicare credentialing. Such complaints must be recorded and available for audit by Medicare. However, there's a caveat: if the problem is fixed immediately, then it does not need to be recorded as a grievance.

For instance, if a patient's intravenous line (IV) is causing pain, the patient reports it to the nurse, and the nurse takes care of the problem, it's not a grievance. However, if the patient complain, the problem is ignored, and it requires supervisor involvement to address the problem, then this is a grievance. Medicare's policy is common sense. The opportunity is nearly unlimited for mistakes and complaints in a hospital. Giving frontline people the opportunity to immediately address them and apologize is common sense. Medicare's policy focuses on monitoring really outrageous problems and those that don't get addressed. There are a few exceptions, where the complaint may fall into specific categories such as abuse, neglect, or fraud. But in general, providing immediate recognition and resolution of a patient complaint eliminates the need for grievance reporting. So having a good service recovery strategy and training every caregiver how to apply it is good for patients and the business.

Communicate with H.E.A.R.T.

The legendary service culture found in organizations such as The Ritz-Carlton hotel company and Walt Disney Company is the product of strategic intent and comprehensive tactics, including a training and development program all employees are required to attend regularly. We knew that Cleveland Clinic needed a service excellence strategy, tactics, and training program, but we faced several challenges and requirements. First, we wanted a program tailored to the healthcare environment and for healthcare workers to accommodate the nuance that the healthcare customer is not always right. Second, there were sporadic efforts to implement similar strategies in the past that failed because there was no program to sustain them, and we wanted to rectify this. Third, we wanted a program "developed by us, for us" to accommodate our culture. Finally, the tactics needed to support a solid approach to service recovery to avoid the escalation of complaints to grievances.

As part of the effort to create the Cleveland Clinic Experience, an employee focus group discussed best-practice behaviors in addressing our patients. The focus group also considered behaviors and actions we should use with each other. The resulting formula reflected important elements of service excellence:

1. Introduce yourself and your role when you meet someone.

2. Use the 10/4 Rule: At 10 feet, make eye contact and smile. At 4 feet, maintain eye contact and greet warmly.

3. Use sir or ma'am when you don't know a patient's name.

4. Use a person's preferred name when known.

5. Clearly communicate expectations: "I am here to . . ."

6. Offer to resolve concerns or forward them to the appropriate person.

7. Use active listening. Pay full attention to the person speaking. Reword the message to ensure understanding.

8. Show empathy. Try to put yourself in the patient's place.

9. Use common courtesy. Say please and thank you and open doors for others.

10. Anticipate needs, and offer to help without being asked.

11. Thank people.

These 11 points are neither unique nor original to Cleveland Clinic, but they summarize what our employees thought was important to display with patients and each other. The items on the list represent commonsense, everyday behaviors for civilized society. Can anyone disagree that we should employ them when interacting with patients or fellow caregivers?

A module of the Cleveland Clinic Experience program introduced our 43,000 caregivers to the expected service excellence behaviors. We subsequently summarized and packaged them into our S.T.A.R.T. with Heart customer service training program:

S   Smile and greet warmly (use sir/ma'am or preferred name).

T   Tell your name, role, and what to expect.

A   Actively listen, show empathy, and assist.

R   Rapport and relationship-build.

T   Thank the person.

The Clinic had already been using a complementary service recovery module, Respond with H.E.A.R.T. that had previously been developed by Cleveland Clinic caregivers:

H   Hear the story.

E   Empathize.

A   Apologize.

R   Respond.

T   Thank the patient.

All employees are trained on the behaviors when they participate in the Cleveland Clinic Experience, and the service excellence program is self-sustaining. You can't put people through training and expect the behaviors to be present forever. Rather than refresher courses, we wanted to create a culture of service excellence in which employees would support and police the actions of each other. The Coach with H.E.A.R.T. program teaches select caregivers to look out for H.E.A.R.T. behaviors and service recovery, compliment people doing a good job, and help those struggling. A coach can be anyone, not necessarily a manager or leader, but merely a coworker with expanded interest in doing the right thing and helping develop a highly performing service culture.

An important element of the Coach with H.E.A.R.T. program is providing developmental support without being negative or degrading. We also did not want to create an environment where failure to use the tactics became punitive. Service excellence requires training and maintenance, and the coaching program was developed to help reinforce doing and saying the right things. We want our people to use their natural enthusiasm and commitment to their jobs and for the entire organization to be wrapped around our framework. Immediately disciplining an employee for not using service standards was not an acceptable course of action. Everyone occasionally has a bad day, may not feel well, or may be provoked by the actions or words of a patient and pushed off a high-performing game. We wanted to create an environment where people can help, support, and learn from each other. The coaching program helps to build that environment.

Collectively, S.T.A.R.T. with Heart, Respond with H.E.A.R.T., and Coach with H.E.A.R.T. make up our Communicate with H.E.A.R.T. service excellence suite of programs. It is a service excellence program developed by healthcare workers for healthcare workers in a healthcare environment. Over 45,000 present and past caregivers at all of our sites throughout the world have been trained on the H.E.A.R.T. program. We have successfully adopted it for use in our Middle Eastern operations and have implemented the program in more than 15 other healthcare organizations, to public employees in a small city, in two Las Vegas casinos, and at a home health agency, and we've begun deploying it successfully with employees of the Cleveland Metropolitan School District. The different perspectives obtained from working with organizations outside healthcare have strengthened the model. It has also helped validate our work by demonstrating that the approach is scalable and works in other environments.

We offer a similar program for our contract workers. Patients and families don't know that food-service workers or parking attendants don't work for Cleveland Clinic. Employees of the companies delivering these services are seen as Cleveland Clinic caregivers just as much as anyone directly receiving a paycheck from our organization. These workers must be aligned around our organizational priorities and trained in service excellence just like anyone else. Each year, William M. Peacock III, our chief of operations, holds a seminar for leaders of our suppliers. Part of the seminar includes discussion of our Patients First philosophy and the expectations we hold for our business partners.

Our service excellence program is not about scripting. Consumers are not fooled by the mechanical mannerisms that scripts create; those interactions are robotic and insincere. Instead, we provide our people with a framework from which to create their interactions. When we introduce employees to H.E.A.R.T., we ask them to imagine how they would want someone to use the framework with them and how they would want to see it delivered. We also believe that the program is not yet complete or comprehensive. Every year, we find new environments in which to use Communicate with H.E.A.R.T. to strengthen the model and improve the program. We are trying to create that "lizard's brain" in every one of our people so that the behaviors become innate and reflexive.

Successful service excellence does not happen in a vacuum. It requires people who are passionate, compassionate, and committed to helping others, including both patients and coworkers. Successful implementation of our service excellence program requires the entire talent management infrastructure I addressed earlier in the book. Finding the right people, screening them for our values, and holding people accountable for actions and behavior are all critical for a service excellence endeavor to be successful.

For cross-training and evaluation, we've created a mystery shopping component to the program, Shop for H.E.A.R.T. In large organizations with many different sites, it's easy to deploy employees who don't know or have never been seen by colleagues in another area. We train managers and other leaders how to conduct mystery shopping and send them to experience frontline staff interaction. The mystery shoppers use a checklist for S.T.A.R.T. with Heart behaviors, immediately score the frontline staff, and offer valuable feedback to their managers. This approach helps managers observe the framework deployed in different environments and offers valuable perspectives on the range of delivery techniques employees use with patients. We also have started an employee mystery shopping program, where our caregivers can provide direct feedback about their experiences. It's hard for anonymous mystery shoppers to penetrate the front desks of healthcare, but employees who are also patients are able to relay their personal experiences. We encourage them to document and report both the good and the bad, and we provide this feedback to managers and the front line.

Service Excellence Requires Accountability

A robust service excellence strategy encompasses not only a tactical framework for caregiver behavior, but coaching and mystery shopping components that are necessary to ensure consistency and reliability. I tend to fly a single major airline and am very familiar with its efforts to try to ensure great customer service. But the employees fail at consistency. If you fly frequently, you notice the variation. Sometimes the flight attendants are friendly, sometimes they aren't. Generally, the pilots make a brief introduction before takeoff and offer a "welcome aboard" once airborne, but sometimes they don't. I'm a rather nervous flyer, so when pilots fail to make these announcements, what else do they fail to do on their checklists? Just training people in service excellence standards isn't enough; there must be tactics to ensure consistency and sustain reliability.

Service failure can have a long-lasting negative impact. Repeated service failures may lead patients to believe that organizations can't or don't want to improve.[6] A robust service excellence strategy is not typically utilized in healthcare settings. However, service excellence is a low-cost, easily implemented program that can have significant impact on how patients view the organization and may also help reduce the number of reportable Medicare grievances.

Patients Are Not Always Right

A healthcare service excellence strategy must also accommodate the times when we cannot make a patient happy. Healthcare is the ultimate service business, but the customer is not always right. Cosgrove was out shopping one day when a person approached him and asked, "Why am I unable to schedule an appointment at Cleveland Clinic?" He was certainly befuddled and apologized to the person and promised to look into it and have someone respond. What this person did not reveal was her diagnosis of Munchausen syndrome by proxy. This is a mental illness and form of child abuse in which a primary caregiver exaggerates or fabricates illness or symptoms in a child to get attention. These are very difficult cases that require careful supervision, and when a minor is involved, there is usually court-ordered supervision. This is the ugly side of the patient experience, the side that doesn't get attention and celebration. But there are many patients who have supervised access to medical care or who have been "fired" from healthcare organizations and are no longer permitted to utilize services there.

Limiting patient access to healthcare or firing patients and preventing access is not something that is done hurriedly or easily. Such actions can be done only by the Ombudsman/Patient Relations Department, and there are strict guidelines to protect the patient and organization. We make every effort to do the right thing for patients and place the burden on the organization to ensure this. These challenging patients often can raise their voices and become threatening. A comprehensive service excellence training program teaches employees how to remain calm under very difficult situations and to always treat the patient with consistent communication, dignity, and respect.

When seeing patients in my clinic one day, my assistant alerted me to a patient in the lobby of the executive offices yelling at the top of his lungs and threatening to remove his clothing, so I needed to get there as soon as possible. At first, I chuckled in disbelief, wondering why there was no one else who could take care of this. Just another day in the patient experience! By the time I arrived, one of my administrative colleagues and five police officers had intercepted him. The patient was screaming that Cleveland Clinic was trying to kill him and demanded to speak with someone "important" immediately. We were able to deescalate the situation and eventually guide him to the office of the ombudsman to determine the best way to help. He said that he had a life-threatening need for surgery, and it had been delayed. He did not understand why and believed his doctors had discriminated against him because he did not have insurance.

In the world of patient complaints, we say there are always three sides to every story. The patient's side, the organization's side, and what really happened. Sorting out the truth can sometimes be a little tricky. In this case, our organization's side of the story was very different from the patient's and likely closer to the truth. His medical record read like a legal brief from caregivers who were trying to protect themselves and the organization. He had a long history of noncompliance, missed appointments, and threats against staff. What he said about his condition was true, but the treatment had been delayed because of him, not us. He was scheduled for surgery but had missed an appointment with his surgeon two days before the lobby incident, and then came in on this particular day and demanded that the surgeon see him immediately. But the surgeon was out. The patient also neglected to tell us that he had threatened the surgeon's team and the anesthesiologist with physical violence if anything happened during surgery. The surgeon called me and said there was no way he could operate on this patient. He was very upset, didn't believe he could think straight, and worried about how this patient would behave in the hospital.

Under these circumstances, with threats of physical violence against caregivers, the hospital is well within its right to fire the patient. It's hard to argue that the members of the surgeon's team would not have been in fear for their safety, as well as preoccupied by the patient's potential behavior. As our team calmed the patient, let everyone cool off, and contemplated our actions, the surgeon called me back and said, "There is no way we can fire this guy. If we do, he will die. He needs surgery, and we are the best people to do it for him. We will get it done." That surgeon's call summed up what we are all about: putting patients first and delivering world-class care. The patient had his surgery at our organization, and he had a successful outcome. There was nothing more important than making sure we helped this person in need, despite the fact that he would likely never perceive that we treated him with dignity and respect and say so on his survey.

People do not realize what a tough business healthcare delivery can be. Healthcare professionals are screamed at, threatened, and occasionally physically abused every day across the world. This tends to happen more frequently in psychiatric units and emergency departments. When I was a resident, I was once kicked in the chest by a drunken trauma patient. My colorectal surgery colleague had a patient throw a cell phone at her head, causing a laceration on her face. A nurse on one of our psychiatric units had her face clawed by a patient. These terrible things happen every day in the process of delivering care to people, so we have to recognize that despite our desire to constantly deliver patient-centered care, at times it is simply not possible.

We Must Talk About Empathy

Teaching service excellence may be easy, but sustaining the behaviors is challenging for any organization. People must be constantly reminded, and given some of the complexities we deal with every day, as illustrated by the previous examples, it can be emotionally challenging for healthcare workers to be consistent. One thing that helps is talking about empathy. We are no different from the people we serve.

From the very beginning of Cleveland Clinic's efforts to improve the patient experience, even those predating me as CXO, we've always endeavored to express empathy more broadly across the organization.

Empathy can be a difficult concept to grasp, but most in healthcare understand that it's important. The term can mean different things to different people, and while there are standard definitions used by people who study it, it is not universally understood. Empathy is an example of a latent construct, meaning it is believed to exist and people can validate it when they encounter it, but they often have difficulty describing exactly what it is or means. There is also a constant debate regarding whether it is innate, can be learned, or is some combination of both.

Empathy is probably one of the most misunderstood terms in the world of healthcare. It's also one of the most overused. As healthcare leaders, we want all of our caregivers to have and express empathy. We're *always* talking about that. But the vast majority of healthcare workers have never been exposed to it. We have placed considerable focus on empathy at Cleveland Clinic since Cosgrove's pivotal interaction with Harvard Business School student Kara Medoff Barnett (see Chapter 3). You could say she kick-started our conversation. Our challenges have been how to better message empathy, how to teach it, and how to get all of our caregivers to be more empathetic.

To be empathetic, you must have insight into your own personality. Cosgrove has long subscribed to the emotional intelligence concept pioneered by Daniel Goleman.[7] He argues that a critical element of leadership success is not intellect or hard work but the ability to understand how one's actions and beliefs impact decision making and interactions. To continue our efforts to extend empathy across the organization, our caregivers need to have an understanding of emotional intelligence and how it applies to their interactions with patients and fellow caregivers.

We decided that the focus of one of our manager training forums would be that emotional intelligence is necessary for empathy, which gives us the ability to drive more compassionate care. Two to three times a year we pull all of our managers—approximately 2,200 people—together for a training session. We open each forum with a video and wanted one that demonstrated empathy to properly kick off the discussion. I've seen a lot of materials that attempt to portray empathy, including many videos. One particularly caught my attention—a Chick-fil-A employee training video shown at an innovation conference I attended in Chicago. Chick-fil-A has a reputation for superior customer satisfaction and a strong commitment to values. It takes tremendous organizational commitment to stay closed on arguably one of the busiest retail days of the week, Sunday, so that employees can spend time with their families. The company produced a video shot in one of its stores highlighting the personal situations of customers and employees. The point, and title of the video, is *Every Life Has a Story*. The video demonstrates to employees that most customers and fellow employees are fighting some kind of battle and "Everyone we interact with is a chance to create a remarkable experience."[8]

The concept grabbed me immediately; the video was essentially demonstrating empathy. I walked away wondering whether we could use a similar approach to capture patient and caregiver stories. Wouldn't the life events of patients and the people taking care of them be that much more powerful? I started showing the Chick-fil-A video to others on my team and across Cleveland Clinic, and at first, many people did not agree with my interpretation or perspective. They couldn't make the connection, and some thought the video was too dark. This was my thought exactly! We're not in a field where it's always about happiness and joy.

I sat down with Sue Andrella, our senior director of media production, and we started a conversation about using video to capture people's stories. Andrella leads a team of talented creatives who produce tremendously powerful patient stories that we use at a variety of leadership events. I showed her the Chick-fil-A video and gave her my thoughts, and interestingly, while she had never seen this video, she had exactly the same thoughts as I had and had already been thinking about ways to use video to demonstrate empathy. Her team went to work. She reviewed several scripts with me, and we haggled over the types of stories and how they would be filmed, and we wrestled with how to link powerful patient stories in a very complex and sprawling hospital system. Should we use real patients or actors? Do we put patients and caregivers together? Do they need to be connected? What score should we use? Should there be a voice-over? Finally, Andrella, a couple of members of her team, and I met for a final script review before filming. I quickly read the script, pushed it back across the table, and said, "Let's just start." There's not a creative bone in my body, and I was having trouble visualizing from the script. I was familiar with her team's work and knew that once Andrella and her team got started, they would put together an amazing piece. After filming and editing for several weeks, Andrella called to say the rough cut was done. I insisted on seeing what they had completed and went to the studio. While some minor technical finishes were still needed, the team had scored. My gut was wrenched, and I sat captivated and silent as the rough cut played. When I saw the little girl pet the therapy dog and the caption came up, "visiting Dad for the last time," I could no longer hold my emotions, and tears came to my eyes. I realized while watching the images that I wasn't feeling sorry for people: I was feeling what they were feeling and felt empathy for most of the situations. It was uncanny! I believed we had developed a tool that could get people to relate.

As we prepared for the January forum, I had a rough cut of the video in my office, and Cosgrove walked in. He knew about the project, and I asked whether he wanted a preview. Clearly moved after seeing it, he sat silent for several seconds, and said, "Wow, that's powerful!" He decided to show it at his annual "State of Cleveland Clinic" address.

Today, our *Empathy: The Human Connection to Patient Care* video sits in the public domain on YouTube and a variety of other social media and Internet sites. We have permitted its use to anyone as long as he or she doesn't alter it or use it for commercial purposes. To date, more than 2 million people have viewed it, and over 500 businesses, including hospitals, have let us know they are using it for onboarding and employee training programs. Nearly every week, I receive notification that another hospital is using it for training. In 2014 I spoke at the Association of Professional Chaplains meeting in Anaheim, California, to a group of about 500 professional chaplains. I showed the video at the beginning of my presentation, and at the end one of the attendees went up to the microphone and said, "Dr. Merlino, we are all familiar with this video, and on behalf of all of us here, I want to thank Cleveland Clinic and thank you for producing it; it will make healthcare better!" I was speechless. What we produced and anticipated to be a simple video for internal training to help our people better empathize has turned into a worldwide healthcare phenomenon, something none of us ever considered. In 2014, Sue, her team, and I received the CEO Award of Excellence for our work on the video. This award is given once a year to a team that demonstrates outstanding work to advance the values of Cleveland Clinic. The video is powerful because its message is simple: There are a lot of things in the lives of our patients and coworkers and in our own lives that impact what we do. Recognizing our personal impact and having empathy for others allows us to be our best in taking care of patients.

We produced a follow-up video that I affectionately call *Empathy II*, officially titled *Patients: Afraid and Vulnerable*. It attempts to take the empathy exposure to a deeper level by examining caregivers from our organization who have had serious encounters with healthcare, caregivers as patients. This video is also posted on YouTube.

Service excellence and empathy have applications to any business with customers. Take time to understand customers' perspectives, and make sure that interactions are professional, respectful, and courteous. This is a "lizard's brain" function that should be second nature to everyone in the organization. The stresses associated with delivering healthcare are unique and require each of us to understand what we bring to our roles every day. Emotional intelligence is a relatively new discipline but a skill essential to truly understanding our intrinsic bias and to putting ourselves aside to empathize with what our patients or customers are going through. Can we teach emotional intelligence and empathy to our caregivers? It's really not an option, but a requirement.

To summarize:

1. All service industries should implement a robust service excellence strategy. It does not matter if you are responsible for delivering products or services to patients, consumers, or other business customers, service excellence will ensure that your customers are treated with courtesy and respect and are well served. Good service excellence is not just about smiling and saying thank you, and it is also not about scripting. It is a robust framework of tactics to ensure your people are consistently delivering the service and building the relationships you need to make your organization successful.

2. Service excellence strategies must include service recovery tactics. There is a science behind saying, "I'm sorry." Service recovery tactics in hospitals are not only good to have; they can also help to reduce the number of hospital complaints

and grievances. Every employee in a hospital should know the appropriate framework to recover service and apologize.

3. Talking about and teaching empathy are important to help employees understand what it means to be on the other side of what we do. Empathy is critically important in healthcare because of the stress and anxiety patients experience, but empathy can apply to any business that has customers. Better understanding what your customers are experiencing will help you deliver better services.

4. Patients are not always right and don't always act appropriately. We have to try to help people as best we can, but sometimes that is never enough. Recognize that what patients complain about may not have occurred exactly the way they believe it did. Investigate patient complaints carefully to get all sides of a story and ensure you have the full picture.

5. Teach emotional intelligence. It is an important concept. Being aware of how you react and respond to situations and understanding how others react and respond not only will help create a better work environment, but is critical for delivering empathetic and compassionate care.

Doctors Need to Communicate Better

Osbourne Bodden lives in the Cayman Islands. For most of his career, he worked in the financial services industry, including two of the top four U.S. accounting firms. He had recently retired and was now running a small business that he had inherited from his mother. The night before I opened the fourth annual Cayman Islands Healthcare Conference, I was invited to a small dinner with a group of business-people to discuss patient experience. I had the pleasure of sitting next to Mr. Bodden and his wife. He shared with me the story of his mother who had recently passed away. He described her as a "tough old bird," some-one who had opinions and "took care of business." He explained how she had raised her child and suffered through hardships. She started and managed a successful small business in 1955, becoming one of the first female business owners in the Cayman Islands, and she had lived to the grand age of 86. He went on to tell me about her healthcare experience. He had been very close to his mother and was responsible for taking care of her. Together, they had discussed her frail health, as well as her wishes and expectations. When she became ill, she feared the diagnosis of cancer and expressed this to her son. He had taken her to see a physician, and he asked the physician to broach the topic gingerly so that his mother could adapt and "warm up to the idea." Unfortunately, the physician did not listen and blurted out to his mother, "You have cancer, and we have to start treatment immediately."[1]

Bodden describes the interaction: "My mother just shut down. She did not want to hear it, and left the hospital and never came back." His mother went to Cuba for care. She felt that she was treated more like a person by her Cuban doctors than the ones she had seen in the United States. She continued her care at Baptist Hospital in Miami, and then came back to the Islands, where she spent her final days.

Mr. Bodden is not just any small businessman in the Cayman Islands; he is also the Honorable Minister Bodden, the Minister of Health, Sports, Youth, and Culture—a leader in a position to change things! As he continued to describe to me at dinner: "We lose sight—in healthcare—that we are dealing with people and families, that we are required to treat the soul as much as we have to treat the disease." This story is unique because it was relayed to me during a random dinner conversation in a foreign country and because the first doctor he described worked for us in our Weston, Florida, facility, but the theme is common, and it plays out every day in healthcare across the globe.

There's an important, significant disconnect between how we as providers think we communicate with patients and how patients rate our ability to communicate. As a profession, we do a poor job of communicating with patients. If you ask physicians to rate themselves on patient communication, they'll say they are excellent and further espouse that they have excellent patient relationships. While true for many, and perhaps even most, this certainly does not extend universally.

We evaluated three months of written patient comments at our main campus. Almost half of the 540 comments about physicians were negative, and nearly three-quarters of the negative comments related to how physicians communicated (see Figure 11.1). Common themes were lack of compassion, inadequate explanations, poor listening, and poor coordination and communication with nurses and other caregivers. Most disturbing was the theme of "bad attitude."

If over a span of three months, half of the comments made by patients were negative, how does this reconcile with physicians' belief that they are great communicators? It's partly because physicians seldom receive direct feedback from patients about their experience with them. Most hospitals and practices don't provide this information directly to

Physician Patient Comments

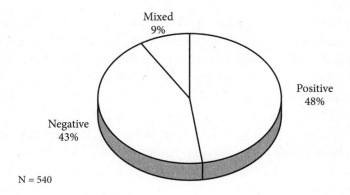

Opportunities for Improvement
Doctor Communication Verbatims

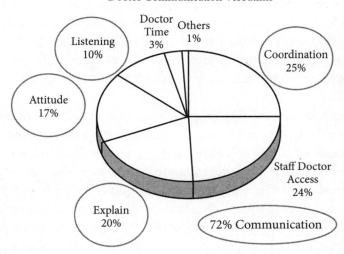

Figure 11.1 Comments and the opportunity for improvement.

doctors. It's also because physicians in general doubt that effective communication skills are a valued part of their responsibility. For a variety of other reasons, including fear of reprisal and concern for hurt feelings, patients often won't provide direct negative feedback to their physicians. However, when patients are in the comfort and, more important, the anonymity of their homes, that reluctance evaporates and patients are forthright.

Observing physicians in the office environment provides insights into these communication challenges. When patients first enter the doctor's office, they are often anxious to describe their condition. When a physician solicits the patient's agenda, or allows patients to open with the "chief complaint," patients feel more empowered and believe the physician is paying greater attention. A study published in the *Journal of the American Medical Association*[2] demonstrates part of the problem. The authors reviewed 264 patient-physician interviews from 29 board-certified primary-care physicians. Physicians solicited the patient's chief complaint in only 75 percent of the interviews, and the patient was allowed to complete an opening answer in only 28 percent of interactions. For patients not allowed to complete an opening answer, the physician interrupted after an average of 23 seconds. The patient would have needed on average only six additional seconds to complete the answer. Soliciting the chief complaint or, as the authors describe it, the patient's agenda, is the first step in the physician-patient communication interaction. In primary care, an area perhaps considered more patient-centric than other specialties, doctors were not meeting the mark.

Putting the entire blame on physicians is unfair. Some of the problem likely rests with patients' interpretations of our interactions, influenced by memory or affected by high anxiety, drugs, or a medical condition. Patients' reluctance to ask questions or desire not to challenge the physician can also affect how much they understand.

I tested this theory anecdotally by sending a medical student into 20 patients' rooms 10 minutes after my visit. The student asked the patient, "Do you remember the plan of care that Dr. Merlino discussed with you?" Fewer than half of the 20 patients could recite the plan for the day. Patients have difficulty with simple things such as remembering physicians' names. David L. Longworth is chair of the Medicine Institute and associate chief of staff for professional staff affairs at Cleveland Clinic. As part of his responsibilities, he precepts medical residents in the ambulatory clinic. Longworth likes to demonstrate to the doctors in training that patients have difficulty remembering and that physicians must communicate clearly. When he walks into a patient room with a resident,

Longworth introduces himself, providing his complete name. At the visit's conclusion, he asks whether the patient remembers his name, and frequently fewer than half do.[3]

For Doctors, the Patient Experience Is About Communication Skills

When I assumed the CXO role in July 2009, our main campus physician communication domain was at the 14th percentile of all U.S. hospitals, among the poorest of all our HCAHPS measures. The performance of private practice physicians in our community hospitals was even worse. Improving physician communication was imperative, and there was nowhere to go but up.

As I mentioned earlier, one of our first tactics was to show our scores to groups of physicians to familiarize them with the measurement process and data. We shared hospital-level performance and talked about the survey process, explaining the way questions were asked, how patients were allowed to respond, and the methodology that Medicare used to score surveys and distribute results. We talked to doctors in departmental, staff, and leadership meetings and held community dinners with private practice groups. We learned that our doctors were essentially clueless regarding their performance metrics. Few knew what the HCAHPS survey was, let alone that it contained questions evaluating how physicians communicated with hospital patients. Before I interviewed for the CXO position, I likewise had no idea physician communication skills were rated by patients.

It was essential to get the data to the physicians. When Cosgrove led the Department of Thoracic and Cardiovascular Surgery before becoming CEO, he was tasked with consolidating Cleveland Clinic's open-heart surgery programs across northeast Ohio. Getting a group of heart surgeons to work together and standardize their practices was certainly no easy task. One of the tactics he employed was data transparency. He released unblinded individual surgeon and program performance data throughout the department so that everyone could see everybody else's data. He perceived that physicians, especially data-driven and inherently competitive heart surgeons, would use the individualized numbers as an improvement tool, and they did.[4]

Cosgrove perceived that getting data to physicians would shorten their learning curve on the HCAHPS rating process and drive communication performance improvement, so we decided to release individual scores to every physician in our group practice. We chose to convert all of the HCAHPS scores to percentile rankings so that physicians would understand how they stood relative to peers across the country. In addition, the Medicare Hospital Value-Based Purchasing (HBVP) Program uses percentiles to judge performance, so this would provide consistency.

I suspected that our release of data would be rather controversial and that our physicians would not necessarily like what was coming. Cosgrove wanted us to release unblinded scores immediately. "Post them in the lounges!" I recall him saying. However, I counseled that we proceed more gradually. Despite the educational meetings, most physicians still had little grasp of what HCAHPS was, let alone that they were individually scored on patient communication. Cosgrove humored me, and we released scores to individual doctors with their partners' scores blinded, which coincided with a major campaign to educate physicians about the measurement process.

Distributing individual data to doctors also taught us a great deal about the process we use to measure communication skills. We wanted to better understand what physicians thought about the HCAHPS survey process, given our reliance on it for our primary patient experience data. As we anticipated, after scores went out, doctors started paying much closer attention to the survey process and data. Physicians are highly trained in data interpretation and very skilled at using data to drive the way they practice. Complaints and criticism of the HCAHPS process started to pour in via phone and e-mail. The most common were:

1. I can't get the data.

2. There is no comparative data.

3. The standard is too high.

4. The sample size is small.

5. I don't have the support I need.

6. Other people impact the score.

7. My scores are low because I work at high volume.

8. No one will help me get better.

Part of me wanted to say, "Look, the data is the data, and we can't change the process. It's the hand we're dealt by the government. There's really nothing we can do, so don't shoot the messenger." But we prepared responses for each of the top complaints because it was very important to address the physicians' issues. We needed buy-in, and you don't get that by ignoring people's concerns.

The first two complaints essentially became moot, as we now were distributing data. We chose the 90th percentile as the standard because it's Medicare's benchmark for comparison against all U.S. hospitals and physicians. The 90th percentile also represents an "A" grade, and this is where we should be as an organization.

The sample size being too small is absolutely a valid criticism. Even the number of surveys Medicare requires from a hospital is not statistically valid. We advise physicians and their leaders to look at trends in the numbers and avoid seeing them as a snapshot. If a physician is in the 10th percentile in a single quarter, the communication scores are possibly invalid. But if the physician is in the 10th percentile over three or four quarters, it's probable that the physician needs to improve his or her communication skills.

The comment that "others impact my score" is an important one. The HCAHPS communication domain is linked to the discharging physician. If there is only one doctor who takes care of the patient while hospitalized, then it's easy to assign accountability. But hospital patients typically are cared for by many physicians. On my service, even if I see my patients daily until discharge, there are still interns, residents, and fellows participating in care. A patient with complicated medical issues may have many staff physicians providing care. So others do impact a physician's score. But achieving a high score on this metric requires teamwork, not just individual performance. I tell physicians the scoring process is determined by the Centers for Medicare & Medicaid Services (CMS), something we can't change. But determining who helps us take care of patients is our choice, so we have an obligation to monitor our consulting physicians and house staff. If a consultant or resident is not communicating well with patients, that negative interaction will likely be reflected in the responsible physician's HCAHPS scores, so perhaps we should choose different consultants.

To prove this point when educating physicians about the process, I unblinded one-quarter of my individual HCAHPS data from 31 inpatients. Seven belonged to my partners, but I either had admitted them while on call or had briefly covered for a partner traveling out of town. For the total 31 patients, I ranked in the 50th percentile for communication performance. If I removed the 7 patients that were not mine, my score jumped to the 99th percentile. I did this not to prove I'm a great communicator but to illuminate reality on the units. Taking care of in-hospital patients is a team sport, and we have a responsibility to work together and police the team.

Many physicians complained they had low communication scores because they took care of a high volume of patients. They legitimately argued that there is a trade-off between productivity and good communication. Our main campus hospital is full of focused, high-volume specialists. Scholarship confirms that high-volume proceduralists tend to have better-quality outcomes.

We probed this argument by closely examining the performance data of a relatively homogeneous practice group. Cleveland Clinic has one of the largest and highest-volume cardiac surgery programs in the world; we are the highest-volume U.S. provider, with the next competitor at just half of our volume. Each of our cardiac surgeons is very productive in relative-value-unit (RVU)[5] performance. Essentially, they are a group of about 10 surgeons who are top in their field, see a comparable profile of patients, have extremely high quality standards, and have similar office and clinical support. Most of these surgeons had excellent communication scores, but a couple did not. While this was a small analysis, it clarified that highly productive physicians can also have excellent communication skills.

The cardiac surgeons and their leadership were early adopters of patient experience initiatives. Bruce Lytle, chair of the Sydell and Arnold Miller Family Heart & Vascular Institute, frequently brings a patient's family into his office after an operation and talks until the family is comfortable and has no more questions. He invited me to speak at a Cardiovascular Surgery Department meeting, and I presented a slide showing blinded physician communication scores. All except two were at or near the 90th percentile. At the end of my talk, Lytle remarked, "Everyone here knows who has the low scores and why. That ends today!" The two surgeons did not regularly round on their patients, and Lytle rightly believed this was reflected in their scores. Subsequently, the two started rounding routinely, and their communication scores went up. This is a great example of physician leadership at the local level and demonstrates how a simple tactic—rounding on patients—can have meaningful impact on patient perceptions of physician communication skills. It also reinforced that institute and department chairs could drive significant improvement in the communication scores by taking responsibility.

The final complaint expressed by physicians about HCAHPS scoring data, the lack of available improvement assistance, was especially important feedback. Since we started discussing the scores, physicians had asked for tactics they could use to improve. While we gathered some tactics previously analyzed in physician communication scholarship, most improvement recommendations came from asking our own high-scoring physicians for their success secrets. Some of these suggestions are common sense and used by many physicians. But consistently using all of them during patient interactions is critical. They include:[6]

1. Introduce yourself. Tell the patient and family who is in charge of their care.

2. Address the patient by "sir" or "ma'am" and use the patient's name if you know it.

3. Partner with nursing on rounds and to discuss plans of care.

4. Ensure that the patient and family understand the care plan.

5. Set and manage patient expectations.

6. Answer patient questions.

7. Engage others who may impact patient perceptions, such as extenders and residents.

8. Respect patient privacy.

9. Recognize that patients judge you by how you look and what you say.

10. When possible, include the patient's family in discussions.

11. Ask patients and visitors how they are being treated and whether they need anything.

12. Discuss pain management.

Our team also produced a comprehensive communication guide, designed by our doctors for our doctors. We balanced information from different practice environments and specialties, with more than 50 private and group practice physicians contributing. An easy-to-use checklist with simple suggestions accompanied extensive material for more in-depth study. Providing information from busy clinicians and keeping it practical and useful gave the guide credibility with frontline practitioners.

Communication Skills Must Be Developed

But releasing HCAHPS data, educating physicians about measurement, and distributing a communication guide were not enough. Physicians are important engines of our organization, critical assets that require continual investment. We had an obligation to help them communicate better. We needed a new program to help improve their skills. And teaching established physicians to communicate better with patients would not be easy.

Over the course of my first year as CXO, chief of staff Joseph Hahn and I had numerous discussions on how to approach this training. Substantial commitment and resources would be required for success. Doctors would have to buy in and perceive it as worthwhile, but there would be pushback and criticism. The program would directly impact the sacred doctor-patient relationship. I suspected it would be one of the hardest things we would do in the patient experience.

Hahn and I finally established a few ground rules. The effort would be led by respected frontline physicians. It could not be physicians in leadership or those at career start or end needing something to do. The planning group also needed to encompass believers and those not yet fully convinced. A healthy dose of realism and skepticism would ensure a much more robust and successful program.

It needed to be practical and interactive to effectively serve and appeal to our high-performing, world-renowned medical staff. The training had to be highly relevant to busy, frontline clinicians, improving not only how they communicated with patients but how they practiced medicine. The training had to be as much about improving physicians' effectiveness, efficiency, and expertise as about enhancing patient perceptions of physician interactions and communication. While we had little idea what the final program would look like, we knew that lecturing to a bunch of experienced doctors in a classroom about improving their communication skills would not work.

We took an important lesson from the nursing education world. Non-nurse experts can teach nurses about any topic except nursing practice, where they have zero credibility. Only nurses can teach nurses about practice standards. Why should it be any different with physicians? The program had to be led and taught by active staff with peer and clinical credibility. Even though there are programs in hospitals across the United States using different professions (nurses, social workers, and so on) to help physicians improve communication skills, we felt we should use only physicians.

I don't believe I could be successfully coached to improve my patient communication skills by a nonphysician peer. He or she might have different perspectives and expertise than I do, yet what I most value is someone who has actually shared the experience of caring for patients, being ultimately responsible for them, and owning the patient experience medically and emotionally, as I have tried to do as a staff physician. We are a physician-led organization, and our leaders must model relationship-centered skills, as all other staff members are watching our behavior. Our team also was sensitive about avoiding a power differential between physicians and other providers in the classes.

We wanted to start the training with our staff physicians for these reasons, and we found our leader in Adrienne Boissy, a neurologist and neuroethicist serving in Cleveland Clinic's Mellen Center for Multiple Sclerosis. As patient experience leader for the Neurological Institute, she had had several highly successful projects, including ones to improve staff and resident communication skills. She had a passion for patient engagement and communication and was a well-respected physician within Cleveland Clinic. In the summer of 2010, Hahn and I asked Boissy to assemble and lead a team of other medical professionals to research, benchmark, design, develop, and pilot a program for improving medical staff communication skills. She agreed, with one condition: that the training outcome would not be an improvement in HCAHPS scores. She argued that the HCAHPS questions did not capture what truly constituted the physician-patient relationship and that healthcare providers aren't automatically inspired to change behavior because of fallible numbers. Rather than an organizational imperative to move a score, Boissy believed the communication curriculum should recognize the extraordinary work done by healthcare providers and capitalize on their experience and insights. She advocated very successfully that this was as much about enhancing physician practice as it was about improving patient perceptions. We agreed.

Communication Training Must Be Practical

Our charge was very specific. The program could be based on theory but had to be practical and taught interactively so that doctors would practice new skills. The program needed to be applicable to every type of physician and patient encounter and relevant to busy clinicians. It had to be useful to physicians who brought effective skills to the table as well as physicians particularly challenged by communication, without being viewed as remediation. Credibility and utility were paramount, given that many physicians might not see need for the training.

In initial discussions, Boissy included Timothy Gilligan, a solid tumor oncologist who also had a passion for improving patient communication; V. J. Velez, a hospital medicine physician; David Taylor, an interventional cardiologist; David Vogt, a liver transplant surgeon; Saul Nurko, a nephrologist; and Amy Windover, a clinical psychologist and director of communication skills training at the Cleveland Clinic Lerner College of Medicine. The team members spanned different specialties, both medical and surgical, and had a range of practice experience from 7 to around 30 years. Each member of the team was a busy clinician, and not everyone believed a program was needed or would be successful. In fact, when Boissy recruited training facilitators, she chose several who were well respected within the organization and their fields, despite being unsure if they were interested in communication skills training.

Their input was critical to understanding how both supporters and skeptics would receive and respond to the program.

The team examined various communication models and programs but eventually focused on the Four Habits Model.[7] Developed by Richard Frankel and Terry Stein, the Four Habits Model is empirically validated and creates a framework for the clinical encounter, particularly in outpatient settings.

We hired a physician-trainer from the American Association for Communication in Healthcare (AACH) to train six clinicians to be facilitators, capable of teaching other physicians. Each clinician went through the equivalent of a full week of training, useful to kick off the effort and bond the core team.

With trained facilitators on board, we evolved from using the Four Habits Model to a model that more closely fit our organization and providers and developed our own custom training program for future facilitators and physician participants.

We designed a one-day course, Foundations of Healthcare Communication (FHC), to teach physicians the relationship-centered communication skills. A team of 2 trains a group of 8 to 10. The FHC course is learner-centered and focuses on one-on-one interactions and skills practice with standardized patients[8] and each other. The complexity of the skills increases throughout the day, and facilitators adjust the training to individual physician needs. Doctors completing the course remark that it's very applicable to clinical practice, and even the most skeptical walk away with new skills.

From beginning to end of the daylong sessions, facilitators actively engage in learning opportunities relevant to their participants. A variety of educational strategies are used, including modeling, small- and large-group facilitation, video review, and skills practice with standardized patients and real-life scenarios. The course also leverages peer feedback and self-reflection for the majority of the learning, rather than a prescriptive approach.

We select new facilitators carefully and deliberately to include an increasing variety of specialties, perspectives, and practice experience. We also consider who might eventually serve as a peer communication skills coach. We learned early that just because someone wants to be a facilitator or people like the person doesn't mean he or she is right for the role. We often ask a leadership team member to meet with potential facilitators, as well as confer with their chairs and sometimes even their peers.

Because the stakes are high, the facilitator pool must look like our physician population and reflect our learners. Some respond to a more authoritarian approach, while others prefer more nurturing. Seasoned physician facilitators command respect, while younger staff members have greater flexibility and enthusiasm. When possible, we pair teachers with like specialists—for example, surgeons teaching surgeons. We would never select a pediatrician just out of residency to coach a 20-year veteran cardiac surgeon on ways to improve communication. We're fairly sure it would be a bad experience for both. Matching peers makes it much more difficult for an experienced clinician to dismiss the training. This was one of the brilliant ideas the team developed and is a critical factor in the program's success.

As we proceeded with the FHC course, our team identified important gaps and, as a result, designed and implemented a new proprietary framework, the Relationship: Establishment, Development, and Engagement (REDE) Model of Communication. It focuses explicitly on relationship building, with key components to drive physician engagement and satisfaction, as well as compliance and malpractice risk mitigation. The model recognizes the healthcare relationship as mutually beneficial to both patients and physicians, and knowing there was attention to their needs was critical to physicians. The REDE model encourages empathy throughout the clinical encounter and is flexible for both inpatient and outpatient settings. Mnemonics are employed to improve recall.

Initially, there was pressure to train every house staff member before tackling the attending staff. Boissy pushed back, contending this was the path of least resistance and would not result in sustained change. She argued that sending trained house staff out with untrained attending staff who didn't communicate effectively would undo the training. The role models had to be trained first, she maintained. Now, all new attending staff physicians and house staff members go through the one-day communication training as part of onboarding.

Scholarship demonstrates that good communication between providers and patients improves patient satisfaction,[9] patient emotional stress,[10] treatment compliance and adherence,[11] patient health outcomes,[12] medical errors and malpractice,[13] and, remarkably, physician satisfaction.[14] The inpatient and outpatient communication scores of physicians who have taken FHC have seen significant and sustained improvement.

Cleveland Clinic is self-insured for malpractice and has a very capable legal defense team, and medical malpractice and risk payout is very low. Physicians with high communication scores have even lower claim and malpractice risk than our overall profile, further supporting the importance of the training.

The team has also been collecting self-reported quality-of-life data from physicians who have taken the program, and there's emerging evidence that these scores are improving as well.

The most validating metric has been anecdotes from physicians who have gone through it. Skeptical and occasionally even hostile physicians have taken the one-day training and emerged as believers. Eric Klein, a seasoned urologist, chair of the Glickman Urological & Kidney Institute, leader in the patient experience, and excellent communicator, called after taking the class and said he had believed going in that there was nothing it could teach him. He was impressed with the depth and thoroughness of the program and immediately sent an e-mail to all institute physicians advising them to complete the course.

At the 2012 Patient Experience: Empathy & Innovation Summit, Boissy moderated a panel including Edward Benzel, a neurosurgeon, and Thomas Rice, a thoracic surgeon, each with more than 25 years' experience, that discussed the REDE model and communication training. They described how it changed the way they structure their encounters with patients and made them more efficient and effective.[15]

The panel illuminated a very important characteristic of our physician communication training. True to Boissy's original insistence, the program is not about improving patient perceptions, but rather about building physician skill. We spend enormous resources every year learning how to practice our skills through extensive continuing medical education (CME) coursework. But we spend no time learning ways to improve *how* we practice medicine. Physicians typically have no formal training in how to interact with patients and generally acquire their personal skills by watching mentors and other physicians. Just like any other medical skill, patient communication and interaction can be taught and learned, and practicing makes us better. We are not just teaching physicians how to communicate better; we are helping them learn better ways to practice. That's an important differentiator that sets this program apart.

We Must Help Private Practice Physicians

In December 2012, we started releasing quarterly HCAHPS physician communication score data to private practice physicians privileged at our community hospitals. All data is unblinded. When we first discussed releasing the data, there was concern that it would anger the physicians. But this is what patients are saying about them, not what we're saying about them. It's really no different than patients airing their gripes on social media. In addition, it's what physician leadership and management teams are seeing. It seemed only fair to share the data with our private practice physicians rather than talk behind closed doors. We pushed this information to physicians in the community because we know what's coming in the environment, and providers should not be blindsided once government mandates it. We have an obligation to help physicians who care for our collective patients improve. Surprisingly, there was barely a murmur of dissatisfaction. Many physicians still had no idea this data was collected and wanted information on how to improve.

We're answering that call and modifying the program to help private practice physicians. Taking care of patients is a partnership, and we all have responsibility to help each other. The messaging we've adopted for our private practice colleagues is that investing in improving communication and relationship skills is right for patients and ourselves and helps us do our jobs more effectively.

Following the same principle of using peer physicians, we trained two private practice physicians to be physician facilitators. Using them and our staff doctors, we trained several groups of private practice physicians. As far as we know, this was the first time a healthcare system offered daylong physician communication training to private practice physicians. When employed physicians take a day off work, they still get paid. When private practice physicians take a day off, they lose income, so we needed to devise incentives for them to enroll. We've offered physicians CME credit and are exploring options such as starting late in the day and running courses in the evening and on weekends. Helping physicians enhance their communication skills will improve patient care, ultimately impacting safety and quality, so we're determined to make the training readily available to as many community physicians as possible. We are just starting to roll the program out to our community hospitals. The medical executive committee of one of our large community hospitals has suggested the course be mandated as part of its credentialing and privileging process. Our team has worked with a group of private practice physicians to ensure that the content is applicable to their practice environment. Recognizing the importance and impact of improving physician communication skills, The Doctors Company, one of the largest malpractice insurers in the United States, had agreed to offer premium rebates to private practice physicians who take the course.

Our communication training has been so overwhelmingly successful that we've established a Center for Excellence in Healthcare Communication (CEHC). The CEHC offers not only the FHC course but an entire interdisciplinary advanced communication curriculum, led by an intensively trained peer facilitator team. Our elite physician trainers are now sought by other healthcare institutions for training their physicians. One of our team's greatest accomplishments is creating the facilitator training program led by Amy Windover, which trains physicians from a variety of different medical and surgical specialties, including neurology, hospital medicine, colorectal surgery, interventional cardiology, urology, general surgery, gynecologic surgery, pediatrics, and cardiothoracic surgery. We've also trained advanced clinical-care-provider facilitators to lead communication training for their peer groups. The training blends skills, theory, evidence-based literature, and group facilitation. Throughout our facilitator training, we treat our participating colleagues the same way we expect them to treat our patients and families. Windover also holds quarterly faculty meetings to further develop the facilitator skill set and ensure consistency of methods. This training and work is perhaps best summarized by a facilitator who wrote, "This is the best thing, by far, I have done in my entire career."

Cosgrove and Hahn, as well as the entire executive team, have gone through the program. Every metric we follow has improved, including HCAHPS, Clinician and Group CAHPS, and patient complaints. But most rewarding are comments from physicians who went into the course unconvinced that it would help and emerged believing that it would make a difference in their practice. Boissy was absolutely right. This is not about improving HCAHPS; this is about creating an experience for our providers that celebrates their expertise, builds their relationships with each other and with patients, and better equips physicians to provide amazing caregiving every time to every patient.

In summary:

1. Effective physician communication is a critical component of the patient experience. It impacts not only satisfaction but patient safety and quality of care as well. Most physicians believe they are excellent at patient communication, but the data suggests otherwise. Like a new medical treatment or surgical skill, effective communication skills can be taught and require practice and maintenance for proficiency.

2. Improving communication skills is not just about improving the patient experience; it is about developing essential physician skills. These are areas of development that physicians do not typically have an opportunity to work on and are skills that are not frequently valued by hospital leaders and healthcare organizations. Physicians are compensated through continuing medical education to drive more efficient, effective, and productive practices. Personal development of critical skills such as relationship building and communication style receives little attention. Recognize that these skills are important for physicians' professional development as well as their medical skills development.

3. Disseminating communication data to physicians is a critical first step in improvement so that they understand how they are measured and where they stand with patients. Many physicians have never seen this data and are quick to point out its deficiencies. Recognizing data limitations is important, but directionally, the data is generally accurate. If physicians repeatedly receive low scores, there is likely a problem with how the physician communicates with patients.

4. The most effective physician communication improvement tactics are those driven by physicians. Improving a physician's communication skills is very personal behavior change. Having critical conversations with physicians who have been in practice for a long time that what they have been doing may not be as effective as they have always believed is a delicate situation and requires care. To be effective, I believe only respected physician peers can initiate this conversation and get doctors to pay attention. Use physicians to drive behavior change among their physician colleagues.

5. To improve communication and relationship skills with physicians, peer-based coaching in small-group learning sessions is a more effective tactic than didactic learning. Group participants can be leveraged to help teach their colleagues as they each participate in exercises.

6. Many physicians have good practices to engage and communicate with patients. Collecting these best practices from physicians in your organization and sharing them with others is a quick way to help others improve their communication abilities and demonstrate that you are benchmarking your own organization to help drive improvement.

Making Patients
Our Partners

f I'm helping to lead the patient experience from the top down, Dave deBronkart is leading it from the bottom up. DeBronkart is a cancer survivor diagnosed with Stage IV renal cell carcinoma in 2007. The disease had metastasized to his lungs and bone, and he was given a median survival time of just 24 weeks. He has an amazing story.[1] Seven years later, deBronkart has gone from patient to crusader, working to drive patient empowerment across the world. DeBronkart believes in patients taking more control of their healthcare and advocates a shift in the balance of power from providers to patients. DeBronkart uses the nickname e-Patient Dave, with the *e* standing for "empowered, equipped, educated, engaged, and expert," characteristics he believes critical for patients to be successful partners in their healthcare journeys.

I first met deBronkart at the TEDMED 2012 event in Washington, D.C., when he and I participated in a joint interview, "What Makes a Doctor-Patient Partnership Flourish?"[2] We were both asked, "Who's really responsible for your healthcare? Is it you, the patient, or the doctor?" DeBronkart observed, "The vast majority of what people do to take care of themselves and their families is themselves, but I run out of skills and information sometimes, and I go to my doctor, so it really is a partnership." I agreed, stating that the responsibility for successful patient care belongs to both doctors and patients.

Only when this partnership is strong can we ensure that providers deliver safe, high-quality care in an environment where patient expectations are fulfilled and patients are satisfied. Patients need to become more involved, ask more questions, and understand what to expect. Patients need to become their own advocates, and if they are incapable or unwilling, family members or friends must step in to help.

To some patient advocates, this idea is controversial; to others, it's downright repugnant. They will argue that caregivers have a responsibility to provide knowledge, protection, communication, and education to patients because they simply are not prepared to be equal participants. I don't completely disagree; the job of healthcare workers, especially doctors and nurses, is to be advocates for their patients, and we are all educators and caregivers. Yet while patients have a distinct disadvantage when it comes to healthcare knowledge, no one knows an individual's history or body better than the patient.

But healthcare delivery customarily has been quite unidirectional, an environment in which it is difficult for patients or families to function as successful advocates. Throughout history, physicians were healers, most likely elders, with almost mystical status. Doctors occupied an exalted, even royal, social position and possessed knowledge that was neither questioned nor challenged. Furthermore, hospitals are intimidating and unfamiliar places. Patients are anxious, worried, and, in some cases, terrified about their condition and whether they will survive. They fall into a pervasive submissiveness and become afraid that challenging their healthcare team will be reflected in the treatment they receive. Cleveland Clinic randomly interviewed 1,000 patients from across the United States and found that less than half ask questions and challenge their physicians, and an astounding third of all patients trust everything their doctors tell them. Eight percent said if they disagreed with the doctor, they would find a new one instead of raising a challenge.

Family Members Are Uncomfortable as Advocates

My father's experience is a good illustration of this behavior. Dad never really liked going to doctors and, fortunately, was healthy most of his life, with only minor ailments. The family eventually convinced him to see an internist annually for a checkup. I remember sitting in my cubicle as a fellow at Cleveland Clinic when Dad called, saying how pleased I'd be of a recent step he took. Naturally, I was curious. He noticed blood in his urine, and instead of calling me, he immediately called his physician, who quickly saw him in the office. The doctor did a urine test, confirmed the blood, and prescribed antibiotics for a suspected bladder infection.

My heart sank. In my surgical training, blood in the urine of a 77-year-old male is considered cancer until proven otherwise. My father immediately could read that I was unimpressed and asked what was wrong. Concealing my suspicion, I urged him to see a urologist to confirm the diagnosis. He was adamant about not doing so and was absolutely convinced there was no need. He trusted his physician and was unwilling to question his diagnosis.

My personal anxiety grew because I also knew and trusted his physician. I wondered why he hadn't made the same presumption and immediately ruled out the more serious diagnosis. I called the physician to express my concern and vividly recall this conversation and how I felt. I didn't want to offend the doctor by questioning his medical judgment or suggesting that he had done something wrong. I ruminated about causing a stir if I were wrong about my suspected diagnosis. Being on the other side for the first time, I almost didn't know how to help my father—whom to call or what type of specialist to consult. Should I push Dad to see someone else immediately, or should I allow this to play out? Maybe it *was* just an infection. My Type A personality and all my years of medical education and surgical training were suddenly reduced to ineffectiveness and garbled thinking as the potential "son of a newly diagnosed cancer patient." I became a submissive victim of healthcare.

While unintentional, the environment that we create—in which patients and their families feel submissive and powerless to challenge us—is dangerous. It's dangerous for patients, and it's dangerous for us, because we're ignoring an important resource that can help us make the right decisions and ensure the delivery of safe, high-quality healthcare. Medicine today is very complicated and involves teams of highly skilled caregivers collaborating to deliver effective medicine and successful outcomes. Patients and families are as much a part of this team as the surgeon or anesthesiologist who performs the procedures.

Patients Must Be Our Partners

The concept of patient involvement has gone through several iterations and definitions in recent years. Healthcare leaders have considered how to better *involve*, *educate*, *empower*, and *engage* patients, and today's buzzword is to *activate* patients. While there are nuances to these terms and how they apply to healthcare delivery, they all foster the same thing: greater participation by patients in their health.

I prefer to characterize patient involvement as a *partnership*. A partner is defined as "a person with whom one shares an intimate relationship."[3] Or my favorite definition of partner is, "one that is united or associated with another or others in an activity or a sphere of common interest."[4] I can think of no better example of where people need to be partners than the working relationship that exists between caregivers and their patients.

As a surgeon, when I examine patients with previous abdominal scars, I inquire about the surgery. I'm often stunned that patients frequently don't remember or will say something like, "My prior surgeon took out a piece of my bowel, but I don't recall exactly why he did." It's inconceivable that someone is admitted to a hospital, undergoes anesthesia, has something cut out of his or her body, and can't remember what was done or why!

While U.S. health literacy varies by education level, ethnicity, and age, it generally is low.[5] As education level rises, a comprehensive understanding of complicated medical care and decisions remains difficult. Even physicians, given the increasing sophistication of medicine and super-subspecialization, cannot be expert in all diseases. As providers, we have a responsibility to help level the playing field by how we deliver information and interact with patients.

Patients can help us and help themselves by being better educated about what's going on in their lives. I'm not advocating that they need to be experts in healthcare or well-read about their particular problems. However, they are and become inherent experts in *themselves*. It can be very helpful for patients to understand the basics of their disease and treatment—keeping a comprehensive inventory of what has occurred, how they were treated, how they responded, and what their bodies "tell them."

Patients and family members can also be helpful in numerous other ways. Imagine if, before coming into the hospital, they all understood the importance of hand washing and were educated on how it decreases potential complications. We could then partner to help reduce these complications. If a caregiver coming into the patient's room did not either wash her hands or "foam-up," the patient, family member, or friend could ask the caregiver to do so before proceeding. Imagine how powerful and helpful this could be to improve compliance with the very important task of washing hands. Many providers would be annoyed at the challenge, but we should welcome it!

The same type of partnered interaction is possible with medication delivery. At Cleveland Clinic, we instituted a program called Ask 3/Teach 3.[6] We ask our patients to pose three simple questions when receiving a medication in the hospital: What is it? What's it for? And what are the side effects? Likewise, we instruct nurses to deliver this information at the distribution of medication, teaching the patient what it is, what it's for, and the possible side effects. We're endeavoring to empower patients to assume a greater role in helping nurses create a safer environment for dispensing medications.

I remember being annoyed as a resident in training when patients and their families asked multiple questions. Residents are often tightly scheduled, exhausted, and very task-oriented. They want to get their work done and go home. As caregivers, we often fail to realize that patients or family members who ask a lot of questions are offering us a gift, which we should gladly accept. They're challenging us to make sure that we're doing everything possible to provide effective care. Additionally, listening to patient and family questions actually validates whether we are communicating effectively. The questions that patients ask help us remember things. We should want all patients to be annoying "question askers." It makes us better and helps them understand their case.

We should encourage patients to be more involved in partnering with us because it is the right thing to do, but we also recognize that the world is different today. Patients are savvier and are leveraging new ways to get our attention and make sure that we involve them in their care. Morgan Gleason was 11 years old when she was diagnosed with juvenile dermatomyositis, an autoimmune disease that causes weak and painful muscles, skin rashes, fatigue, and fever. She was in the hospital, being treated for a complication of her disease, when she finally got fed up with people not involving her in her care. She complained that the medical team would come in really early in the morning when she was too sleepy to interact with them, but what really annoyed her was that too often the doctors and nurses would talk to her parents outside of her room, excluding her from the conversation because she was a child. She took action. She made a video called "I am a patient and I need to be heard" and posted it on YouTube. Overnight, she became a celebrity patient advocate. Morgan helped open the 2014 Patient Experience: Empathy & Innovation Summit. She was interviewed by Dr. Deirdre Mylod, executive director of the Press-Ganey Institute for Innovation, on stage in front of more than 2,000 people.[7] Her comment to doctors: "You go to med school to become a doctor, but we don't go to a patient school to become a patient"—implying that patients want to know what's going on and be partners in their care.

We Must Manage Patient Expectations

Healthcare reform today is putting hospitals and providers at the center of a three-way squeeze, caught in an ever-shrinking triangle of decreasing reimbursement, tightening regulatory requirements, and increasing patient expectations. Heightened patient expectations result from greater consumerism in medicine. Leveraging patient expectations through patient partnerships will help us deal with diminishing resources and increasing regulatory burdens. To successfully leverage rising patient expectations, hospitals and providers must make two critical changes to improve how patients and their families interface with the healthcare system. First, expectations must be brought into line with reality, and second, patients must take greater responsibility for managing their care.

Better aligning patient expectations with reality is critical. One of the most poorly recognized concepts in the patient experience is the idea of an experience-expectation mismatch, shown in Figure 12.1. Patients have preconceived notions of what will occur in the healthcare environment, and they often leave having experienced something very different from what they had expected (think of the patient referred to as "sunshine"). Patients gather these notions from their friends and family, the media, the Internet, and a variety of other sources. Our goal is to match

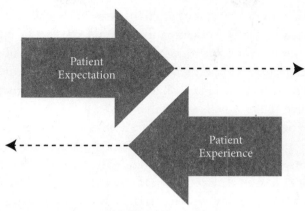

Figure 12.1   Experience-expectation mismatch.

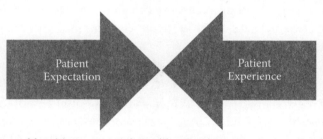

Figure 12.2   Matching expectation with experience.

the expectation with the experience, shown in Figure 12.2. But unless the individual has been a patient before, he or she will have no true under-standing of what it's like to be in the hospital.

What patients expect vis-à-vis what they actually experience plays an important role in how they ultimately define or perceive their care. A longtime Cleveland Clinic leader, Joanne Zeroske,[8] president of one of our community hospitals, was working with her physicians and nurses to improve patient satisfaction with pain control. She spent time observing two orthopedic surgeons who practiced at her hospital. One surgeon always informed patients that there would be severe pain; he would do everything possible to help relieve it, but he made no promises. The other surgeon told patients he was an expert in conducting a particular proce-dure and they would have minimal or no pain. Guess how patients rated each surgeon regarding his ability to effectively treat pain? The one who set level and honest expectations had higher scores, with patients more satisfied regarding the way their pain was managed. There's nothing that truly prepares one for postsurgical pain. When patients are unprepared, or worse, expect not to have pain, they are surprised or disappointed. It's important for caregivers to explain to patients exactly what they're going to experience and how pain will be managed.

The patient bedside nurse call button is another great example that demonstrates the importance of managing expectations. Patients often assume that when they summon the nurse with the call button, someone will respond immediately. I refer to this as the "nurse pop-up response system," an unrealistic understanding and expectation of healthcare delivery on inpatient units. The nurse is likely taking care of four or five other patients in the typical med-surg unit. Despite the best nurse manager intentions regarding coverage and other tactics to mitigate slow response, it's never immediately that someone arrives at the patient's bedside.

We often believe that patients score us low on surveys for response time because they get angry when we don't come immediately. But that's not quite what happens. Imagine you are a patient and push the call button for something relatively simple and nonurgent, like more water. If no one responds quickly to address the request, you don't get angry because of the service failure; you become anxious and concerned, thinking, "If I only need water and no one comes, what will happen if I have an emergency? Maybe no one will come, and I could die." Even if the unit secretary immediately answers the intercom and informs you that someone will be in soon, if it's 20 minutes before the water arrives, you still get anxious because you don't know what's going on. There was an appropriate immediate response from the secretary, but you have no idea that the water request may have been triaged, that the nurse or nurse assistant knows about your request, but it was placed as a lower priority. You become angry, believing you were ignored.

Nowhere is the experience-expectation mismatch potential greater than at hospitals spending tens of millions on amenities to deliver the "Ritz-Carlton experience." At some hospitals, patients have an expectation that they are coming to a five-star hotel suite. This is unrealistic and nearly impossible to deliver, given the environment in which effective healthcare is delivered. Patients believe they come to the hospital for rest and are upset when nurses come in to check vital signs in the middle of the night or when blood draws happen early in the morning so they are available for medical rounds. Hospitals are not hotels, and we must be careful not to set this expectation. We certainly can do a better job of managing when vital signs are checked, medication is delivered, and lab draws occur, possibly allowing patients longer periods of rest during the middle of the night, but we must be careful to balance this with what's right for patient care.

A similar situation exists relative to the hospital quiet-at-night HCAHPS domain. There is a patient expectation that hospitals are quiet places. Some of us remember the *Marcus Welby, M.D.* television series, in which "quiet" was an essential aspect of the hospital experience. Overlay this with the "Ritz-Carlton of hospitals" analogy. I have news for patients: hospitals today are not Marcus Welby quiet, and they are not five-star hotels. Hospitals are noisy; there's a lot going on. Thirty years ago hospitals were low-tech, and patients were much less ill. Today, hospitals have patients with much higher acuity demanding more attention. Care is complex, nursing ratios are stretched, and there is a great deal of activity that takes place on nursing floors. They aren't quiet! We need to inform patients not to expect quiet so they don't judge us as too noisy when they expect something else.

If you review the verbatim patient complaints Cleveland Clinic receives about noise, they mostly relate to having a roommate; caregiver activities such as vital-sign checks, blood draws, and so on happening in the night; and loud conversation at the nursing stations. We may be able to reschedule blood draws until the morning, but patients must understand that under most circumstances, the nurses are supposed to come in at 3 a.m. to check vital signs. It's a hospital, and it's the nurses' job to monitor patients' condition.

Patients and Families Must Also Be Reasonable

Like other hospitals across the country, Cleveland Clinic has essentially eliminated specific visiting hours. This means that family and friends can visit patients at any time without restrictions, a move that is consistent with national nursing recommendations and patient standards as articulated by the Joint Commission and the Centers for Medicare

& Medicaid Services. Eliminating restricted visiting hours is the right thing to do for patients. We want to ensure that patients' families and friends are close by to provide comfort and support. I agree with the statement issued by the Institute for Patient- and Family-Centered Care that the family is "respected as part of the care team—never just visitors—in every area of the hospital, including the emergency department and the intensive care unit."[9]

Now that visiting hour restrictions have been lifted, family and friends have a responsibility, however, to be "professional" partners of the care team and to hold themselves to standards appropriate for a hospital. There are certain behaviors and actions that do not pass the test of reasonableness.

Imagine patients sharing a room:

1. Is it reasonable that a patient have multiple visitors late at night, potentially disturbing the patient in the next bed?

2. Is it reasonable that a young female patient have her boyfriend sleep in the chair next to her bed, compromising privacy for her neighbor?

3. Is it reasonable that family members bring young children and allow them to play in the room?

4. Is it reasonable that one patient allow family members to eat a meal in the room, while the other patient may not be able to eat?

I hope everyone reading this will agree that these actions are unreasonable. While we lack exact statistics on the number of semiprivate rooms in U.S. hospitals, a figure commonly cited is approximately 60 to 70 percent. This means that most hospital rooms are semiprivate and patients must share a room with a neighbor. We cannot rebuild our entire infrastructure to accommodate private hospital rooms, hence the need for guidelines on visitation.

We have a responsibility to protect every patient's privacy. Typically, enforcement of these reasonable visitation standards falls unfairly on bedside nurses. Actions that limit or restrict certain visiting behaviors can lead to a negative patient experience assessment. This is unfair to the hospital. Patients and their families have a responsibility to be considerate. They should apply the same standard we apply: how would they expect to be treated? Consider an analogy from the airlines, which purport to allow each passenger one piece of carry-on luggage and one personal item in the cabin. This standard is rarely enforced; passengers bring multiple items onto the plane, which slows the boarding process and hogs overhead compartment space. Patients, like passengers, need to be reasonable.

We Must Teach People How to Be Patients

We healthcare professionals spend enormous time educating patients about their disease and its treatment. But we spend little or no time talking to patients about what it means to be a patient and what to expect during hospitalization. The anxiety, fear, and confusion inherent in all hospital patients is exacerbated by them not knowing what's going on and being unable to anticipate what will be happening.

To address this healthcare communication loophole, in 2011 Cleveland Clinic worked with an outside technology company to develop an online engagement module about being a better hospital patient. The program helps patients understand key processes and interactions that will define their experience, including how to partner with our healthcare team to make the hospital stay more satisfying. Our hypothesis was that if we discussed with patients what to expect during their hospitalization, we could level-set expectations against the reality of the environment, enhance patients' comfort level with the hospital encounter, and drive improvement in inpatient satisfaction scores.

Structuring information around the HCAHPS domains, we educated patients regarding what to expect during hospitalization and suggested tactics that might improve the healthcare experience. We informed patients that the average inpatient nurse cares for four to five patients and may not be able to answer a call button immediately due to caring for another patient, but the team would respond immediately in an emergency. We informed patients that hospitals are not quiet, and while we work hard to create a healing environment, it may be noisy and there may be interruptions. We informed patients that pain is very difficult to completely eliminate and could be a very real part of their experience. We let them know we would do everything to try to make them comfortable and they should let us know when we were not successful, but it was possible that we could not completely take the pain away.

Regarding the most important part of the hospital environment, communication, we asked patients to be partners with the healthcare team and to write down their questions to be well prepared. We also asked patients to empower their families and friends to serve as surrogate communicators and advocates.

We tested the effectiveness of the program by comparing two groups of patients undergoing similar procedures. When patients were informed that nurses come as soon as they can when the call button is pressed, satisfaction with response rates was higher. When we helped patients ask better questions of their care team, satisfaction with communication was better. When patients were educated about the hospital environment, they were more forgiving of interruptions and their perception of quietness was higher. We found that patients' expectations could be set to a level that was realistic. The group that received the "what to expect education" scored us higher in every HCAHPS domain.

Cleveland Clinic is doing other things as well to address the expectation-experience mismatch. Our service excellence program, Communicate with H.E.A.R.T., has built-in training modules to help caregivers appreciate that everyone has a role in setting expectations for patients. Every patient-provider encounter should be wrapped in a conversation about what to expect, beginning from the patient's point of access and through the clinical areas when care is discussed. What we provide to patients before they even arrive on campus can include information about parking, navigation, their healthcare team, or the philosophy of care delivery.

An old adage in medical training is that discharge planning begins at admission. We often say that, but we typically don't design our processes to support it. Care delivery is a longitudinal journey. In 2013 when we redesigned our hospital admission guide, we worked with our care teams to ensure that we provide patients and families with information to help plan discharge. We provide a patient and family member checklist that includes reminding them to think about things such as who will assist the patient when he or she leaves the hospital, who will schedule follow-up doctor visits, and so on. This helps patients and family members better prepare for transitioning care to the home environment.

Healthcare reform and the emergence of accountable-care organizations and population health-management strategies have brought the concept of patient partnership to prime time. Healthcare organizations will be subject to increased pressure to manage decreasing resources more effectively. One strategy to reduce waste and improve care delivery is to shift payments from volume-based care, or getting paid for doing *things*, to value-based care, or being paid for delivering care *better*. Incumbent upon this strategy is the incorporation of tactics to engage, or *activate*, patients. Healthcare organizations are developing programs to enable patients to do more; however, the focus cannot be unidirectional. The risk and responsibility must not be solely on the provider; patients must play a role as well. We can call patients to remind them to take medications and ensure they have follow-up visits scheduled. We can even go to their homes and check on them and bring them to their visits. But we cannot force them to eat properly, take their medications, or avoid unhealthy habits such as smoking. Promoting wellness, managing health, and curing disease require a 100 percent effort, not only from the provider, but from the patient and family members as well.

Growing consumerism, driven by the increasing availability of information, as well as rising insurance premiums and deductibles, is making the patient a much more important player in healthcare decision making. Patients today have access to incredible amounts of healthcare information. The Internet provides a wealth of information, including access to scientific findings, hospital and provider ratings, marketing content, and, increasingly, cost data. Additionally, the explosion of social media is making the exchange of opinions and ratings much more accessible for patients seeking to understand their various treatment options. Social media is also a great "leveler" for patients, as it is giving them a powerful forum to get the attention of healthcare workers and organizations.

Patients are no longer just patients, consumers, or customers; appropriately, they are our partners. We need them to help us by taking care of themselves and understanding not only their disease but the environment in which they are treated. We need them to be advocates and challenge us. There has never been a better time or more tools to help meet deBronkard's goal of creating empowered, equipped, educated, engaged, and expert patients, or Gleason's goal of making sure patients are heard.

In summary:

1. Patient care is complicated, and patients and families can help ensure safe, high-quality care by becoming our partners, which means taking more responsibility for their care by asking questions, learning about their disease, understanding their behaviors that can negatively impact their health, ensuring compliance with recommended treatments, and knowing what it means to be a patient beyond just their disease.

2. Providers have to remember that patients and their families are relatively unsophisticated consumers of healthcare who fall into a very submissive relationship with healthcare professionals. This combined with the fact that health literacy in the United States is generally very low requires us to actively work on strategies and tactics to help raise the level of patients' participation so that they are better partners in their care. We should embrace patient activism and recognize that it is a powerful tool to help us do our work more effectively.

3. Providers have a responsibility to go beyond educating, engaging, and activating patients and ensure that they understand the treatment environment and set the expectations of what patients will encounter. We spend a great deal of time speaking with patients and families about disease and disease management; we also need to talk to them about what to expect in the hospital and at other points in their healthcare journey. This will help prevent the expectation-experience mismatch that so many patients experience. Imagine the impact on safety if every patient and family member would help watch out for errors and felt empowered to speak up when they suspect something is wrong or just have the courage to question us.

Getting It Done Has Defined Our Success

Our greatest patient experience achievement has been our ability to execute the work, an achievement I owe to my mentor and friend from Harvard Business School, Ananth Raman. He helped me understand the importance of how to operationalize the change.

Execution has taken our patient experience improvement from aspirational goal to operational reality, gained the respect of leaders across Cleveland Clinic, and drawn the attention of healthcare institutions around the world. The success of our execution is palpable. Our organizational metrics are improved, our caregivers live the patient experience, our leaders drive it, and most important, our patients feel it. The challenge going forward is to sustain and improve upon what we've done. It's easy to fix something broken; it's much harder to take something successful and make it better. While our strategy will evolve and tactics will come and go, the navigational focus of patients as our true north and our fundamental alignment around the patient must never waver.

In January 2014, I spoke to a group of physicians from Hillcrest Medical Center in Tulsa, Oklahoma. The Medical Group's CMO, Jeffrey Galles,[1] e-mailed me after the meeting and observed that his senior hospital leadership often says, "We can't all be Cleveland Clinic." My response was, "Yes, you can!" It's about leadership mindset and how the organization aligns around a Patients First philosophy and sets the patient experience as a strategic priority. And while it's true that initially we invested materially in our patient experience initiative, today we know better how to achieve success without spending a lot. Setting a patient experience strategy and developing and executing tactics need not be expensive. Implementing nurse hourly rounding does not require infrastructure or special technology; it requires leadership, training, and accountability. Distributing physician-specific scores to doctors and teaching them communications skills require are efforts that the courage to start, leadership, and accountability. You see the common threads here. Leadership rounding is another great example: it could be started tomorrow by every hospital CEO throughout the world, for low cost and high payoff.

Personal Learnings

I've read many books and articles on organizational transformation and leadership, and they're all very good at describing what and how things were done. Few have addressed the leadership missteps or learning opportunities in the struggle to be successful. I didn't enter medicine to be a healthcare organization leader but fell into the role. The information in this book represents the work of numerous people, many much smarter and more capable than I. The results are neatly organized and presented here, which does not do justice to our trial-and-error process. When I talk about what we've accomplished, I often tease audiences that they're seeing the "sausage," which tastes great, but is the end product of a very bloody factory that we have long since closed down. Even with the many people dedicated to Cleveland Clinic's initiative, it's hard work and takes time. My own experience on this journey has taught me several very important, yet sometimes difficult, lessons:

Don't expect results overnight. Think long term. I remember day one of my new role as CXO being ready to change the world and Cleveland Clinic along with it. However, this doesn't happen fast. Enthusiasm and excitement are important, but thoughtful decision making with a long-term perspective is critical. As I have said multiple times, we also have to be considerate of how our decisions impact the system. One small improvement, when not considered appropriately against the system, can have unintended negative consequences on other areas of the organization. Looking for instant gratification in this work can lead to dangerous mistakes that negatively affect people and the organization. Cosgrove began his patient experience journey in November 2004. My journey started in July 2009. We're both still very much on the ride, with a lot of work to do. Recognize that you're taking on organizational transformation. Healthcare is not used to this type of patient-centered focus or change. If there is anything you take away from reading this book, let it be that patient experience improvement is a multiyear proposition. Be patient, but be persistent.

There are a lot of ways to do something right and a few ways to do something wrong. Be flexible on what you choose as right. From a senior position in enterprise leadership, it's tempting to issue mandates that everyone do something the enterprise way. But healthcare delivery is highly nuanced, and bedside care is not an assembly line or one size fits all. The hospitals in our system range from a world-prominent, 1,200-bed specialty facility focused on high-acuity tertiary care to small community facilities. We have adopted the concept of "One Cleveland Clinic" to ensure that we standardize critical strategies and tactics. But failure to recognize and accept that each facility has its own local culture and individual needs will lead to certain failure. It works best when leaders and managers are permitted to tailor the implementation and delivery. Such local ownership drives more effective adoption, because we're putting faith in local skills to execute. Nurse hourly rounding is a best practice that should be implemented in every unit of every hospital across the world. But as long as there's documentable process performance, how hourly nurse rounding is implemented should be driven by the local environment. Not every patient door must have a checklist to prove compliance. Another good example is plan of care communication between physicians and frontline nurses, also a best practice that everyone should implement. But whether that communication happens at the bedside, after the physician rounds, or via physicians reporting to the nurse manager should be an issue of local control reflecting what works best for the individual practice environment. Assuming that we know how everything should apply to every care environment is wrong, and it's a mistake we tend to make when we do not consider the entire organization.

Recognize that you will make people mad. To this day, I'm sure there are people who would like to see my position, our department, and the effort we've all put into improving the patient experience disappear off the face of the planet. Not everyone is on the bus, and not everyone will appreciate what you're endeavoring to do. Some will be against the concept, some will be against the leader, and some will be both. Our challenge is to transform the halfhearted 10 percent of the organization and get rid of the 5 percent who are employed in healthcare for the wrong reasons. Determination in the patient experience field is important, but resilience is critical. Both chief of staff Joseph F. Hahn and clinical services CAO Cynthia Hundorfean remind me continually to "do what's right, and the rest will take care of itself," which is sage advice. When dealing with resistance, it's important to be respectful and act with integrity, but ultimately, when you take the side of the patient, you'll never lose. I've contended many times with people who dislike me personally, but that's OK as long as we agree that improving the patient experience is the right thing to do.

Committees are important, but don't use them as a substitute for leadership. I have watched hospitals, ours included, get bogged down in committee-think. Sometimes it seems that every major initiative and decision needs to be vetted by a committee, subcommittee, or task force. This is probably a phenomenon more commonly seen in healthcare because of its multiple stakeholder groups and legacy governance structures. But some of our best decisions that have had tremendous impact on the organization were made by command-and-control leadership because someone took responsibility to lead. I have occasionally been criticized for this approach, but I think our results speak volumes about our methods. I am not advocating that we make decisions without consultation and vetting, but sometimes decisions need to be made. We can save people a lot of time and the organization a lot of money by not using a committee for every initiative. Cleveland Clinic does not have a patient experience advisory committee. It has a leader, me, and a strong partner, the executive chief nursing officer, who lead our enterprise efforts. We consult extensively with each other as well as with others across the enterprise, but we are held accountable for the work; therefore we make decisions and we operationalize them.

There are a lot of enthusiastic caregivers who want to be involved in the patient experience, but you need to find qualified talent to help

you. Sometimes organizations tend to hire leaders because of relationships or personality. Look for ability and accomplishments. Similarly, outside ideas, especially those that potentially impact culture, are easily targeted and destroyed. Likewise, bringing in a lot of outside consultants is often met with the same resentment and resistance. Recognizing talent from within and helping employees realize their potential to drive change allows organizations to say, "We did it ourselves." However, we often have an assumption that we can do anything we set our minds to. The patient experience field has evolved, and there are good strategies, tactics, and, more important, people that can help operationalize improvement for hospitals. We need to find and tap these resources to help us drive more effective change, faster. We have to get over the assumption that we have all the answers and only our people can get something accomplished. Learn from others!

We are in the ultimate service business where the customer is not always right. Often there's less science and more emotion when it comes to managing patient perceptions of care. Empathy goes both ways; just as we must take care of patients, we also have a responsibility to protect our people, because taking care of patients is not easy work. As I have said, when patients complain, there are always three sides to the story: what the patient said happened, what our caregivers think happened, and what really happened. It's easy to get carried away with anecdotes and jump to conclusions—something I term "anecdotal assassination." But our responsibility is to ensure we understand the facts before we act, as we have as much responsibility to our caregivers as we do to our patients. Do some patients fabricate information to manipulate the system in their favor? Perhaps their explanation of what happened may not be the accurate interpretation of reality. Be cautious about taking an anecdote as a burning platform for change. We have an obligation to make sure that we understand the context of the anecdote and don't unjustly assume that our caregiver did something wrong. In some organizations, a carefully placed anecdote or collection of anecdotes can successfully kill a career. We have responsibility as leaders to ensure that our judgments about people are based on evidence and trends of actions, not stories or isolated incidents.

You will experience failure; have no regrets. I'm fortunate to have a boss who doesn't dwell on failures but wants to know about the next good idea. This leadership style is important. At Cleveland Clinic, administrative failure is expected, innovation is encouraged, and not trying or giving up is unacceptable. When I was writing a *Harvard Business Review* article about the patient experience, the editor asked me what I'd change if I could go back in time. I replied "nothing" and added that our progress was the net effect of success and failure and that everything we have done has contributed in some way to our accomplishments. Not everything we've tried has worked, but we persist in picking ourselves up off the ground and trying new things. For every couple of failures, there are home runs that ignite and propel us forward, including the Cleveland Clinic Experience Program, the empathy video, our summits, and the physician communication program, among others. Learn from the failures, but celebrate the successes.

Everyone must be on the bus. As our strategic initiative to implement the caregiver label reinforces, everyone is important, and likewise, no one is exempt. I refer specifically to physicians. I once heard a healthcare consulting executive counsel that physicians are busy, they will get it, and just make sure everyone else is leading it. Wrong! Physicians must not only "get it"; they must be involved in leading and managing the patient experience. Without their adoption and participation, we fail.

Take care of your people. Our people—caregivers—are our most important asset. Delivering care for patients is hard work, and we have to make certain that we look out for our caregivers. Hospitals are dangerous places; we kill people every year. We don't intend to, but accidents and errors in healthcare delivery are well documented, and everyone at the front lines understands the risks. Our caregivers must come to what they do every day engaged and in the moment. We must not let them face a dangerous environment, uncertainty, anxiety, harassment, or bullying. We must adopt a zero-tolerance policy against treating people badly. Most of us cannot imagine what it's like to drive to work every day in fear of interacting with a bullying coworker. Or what it's like to be at home on a Sunday, fretful about facing a terrible, unfriendly, toxic, or dangerous work environment. But *I* know what that feels like, and there are people reading this book who also know what that feels like. We must do better, our people deserve better, and our patients require it.

Do things that people say won't work. If I had a nickel for every time someone said, "It won't work," I would be retired and counting waves on a beach somewhere. And if I *had* listened, we would have done nothing. A host of our best successes were at one time in jeopardy because people spoke against them. Instincts in this business are important. Take the time to learn your organization and know your people and leaders. Understand what's important to them and make allies in your efforts. Once you have a solid footing and have identified a group of supporters, engage them to help you and push forward with new ideas. There will be times when a strong personality registers an objection to a new idea. There will be the long-time administrator who has seen and done it all, and there will be the experienced administrator who knows from all previous jobs that something like this simply won't work. Don't be afraid to buck conventional wisdom. It takes courage and the willingness to occasionally make enemies. But the risk is worth it for the potential organizational impact.

Move quickly. While most improvement efforts take time and decisions must be made thoughtfully, sometimes a good idea just needs to be launched. I must drive my team members crazy when I come in at the start of the week and throw out an idea for a new initiative. They look at me like I'm some kind of disorganized nutcase. Please don't misunderstand what I'm saying. Good leadership and operations management require careful planning and execution—most of the time. But don't get mired in the mindset that every good idea and project needs a comprehensive business plan and PERT[2] chart. Some of our strongest successes came from good ideas that we just started implementing. We had C-suite executives from a large East Coast hospital system make two site visits to Cleveland Clinic to hear about our patient experience strategy and leadership rounding. They wanted to visit again, "To see one more time how you do it." I refused and advised the hospital to just start the rounding and work out the kinks as they went along.

As long as you're mindful of scale, not going too fast with something too big—not going to enterprise scale immediately—there's something to be said about just starting a project to see where it leads. In today's healthcare environment, where change is rapid and the future uncertain, speed to adopt can be critical.

Take risks, be vulnerable, and have a little courage. I think one of the best compliments any of my colleagues ever paid me was when I asked him to describe my leadership style; he said, "courageous." I wasn't sure what that meant at the time, but he told me: "You took on something you knew nothing about, improving the patient experience. You challenged the conventional thinking and were not afraid to offer something disruptive: the Cleveland Clinic Experience Program. You never give up!" In retrospect, I understand today much better what that meant. Healthcare delivery and hospital operations are locked in legacy and tradition. They needs to be shaken up a little—executing on improving the patient experience required courage to do just that. It also requires relentless effort to keep trying and working at improving even when things don't seem to be going your way. Beth E. Mooney, chairman and CEO of KeyCorp, and the chairperson of our safety, quality, and patient experience board of directors committee, describes it as "relentless incrementalism."[3]

It also requires vulnerability, a willingness to be uncomfortable. I believe we become too entrenched in the status quo. We worry more about job preservation, colleague happiness, and decorum. If you are not willing to take risks—and that includes your own job security—you will never truly push the envelope on transformational change. Taking a risk requires courage and a willingness to embrace vulnerability.

Never forget where you came from or who helped get you there. I don't think this one needs a lot of explaining. It is something my father told me. I have seen people quickly excel into leadership positions and then tend to lose sight of their team who helped get them there.

Our Passion Is What Sustains Our Charge

We're all part of a healthcare ecosystem. What binds us together—whether you serve in healthcare, are employed by an organization that supports healthcare, or work in any other industry—is that someday, everyone will be a patient, even you. Healthcare providers consider themselves among an elite group; someday, everyone will need what we deliver.

When Pat Ryan took over as CEO of Press Ganey in 2012, he came to Cleveland Clinic to talk about his goals for the company and how he believed *he* could help improve healthcare delivery. I was struck by his word choice; his emphasis was less on his company and more on his personal passion to better a system he felt had terrible flaws that adversely affected patients. In an early conversation, he described coordinating care for a sister who lived out of state because she could not get through to her provider. He discussed his aggravation while trying to help his sister navigate care. He shared her anxiety of not being able to connect with her caregivers. Over the years, he's peppered many of our business conversations with personal and family stories that impact his thinking on ways his company could improve healthcare. He recently announced that the responsibility, the very purpose of Press Ganey, is to help healthcare organizations work to reduce patient suffering, a far cry from an organization that collects and distributes data. His experiences and insights drive his business acumen to improve an organization that impacts healthcare for many.

Robert H. Bazemore, former president of Janssen BioTech, Inc., now president of strategic marketing for Johnson & Johnson, spoke at the 2012 annual patient experience summit about how the pharmaceutical industry could partner with healthcare providers to take better care of patients. He stunned the audience when he admitted to being a cancer survivor whose life was saved by a drug his company produces. You could have heard a pin drop in the auditorium. He talked about "living on the other side of healthcare" as a patient and how his experience, his empathy, drives the way he leads his company every day.

Larry Ruvo, senior managing director of Southern Wines & Spirits of Nevada, is a passionate supporter of the patient experience and advocate for the important role of nonmedical family caregivers in managing chronic disease. Ruvo was the primary caregiver for his father, Louis, who suffered from Alzheimer's disease. Larry invested millions in brain disease research through his Keep Memory Alive Foundation and support of the Cleveland Clinic Lou Ruvo Center for Brain Health in Las Vegas.

Ruvo conducted a touching interview with Siegfried Fischbacher, the lifelong partner and current caregiver of Roy Horn, who was tragically injured during their *Siegfried & Roy* show at the Mirage Hotel and Casino in Las Vegas in 2003.[4] On video link from the Lou Ruvo Center for Brain Health, Ruvo interviewed Fischbacher about his experience as a caregiver. The interview was intense, poignant, and revealing. Fischbacher was candid and vulnerable about his love for Horn and the challenges of helping him through a long and very difficult recovery. The rock-star-famous entertainer, emotionally sharing the challenges of caring for a loved one, demonstrated the other side of the patient experience, the caregiver experience.

Three people, three very different stories, all in a position to impact healthcare. Their stories also help you quickly understand how the patient experience touches all of us in a very personal way.

Like Ryan, Bazemore, Ruvo, and many others mentioned in this book with whom I've had the pleasure to work, my passion to improve is rooted in personal experience, from being on the other side and working on the frontline to care for patients. This is empathy at its very core: understanding what patients go through and appreciating what caregivers experience in delivering great care. It's extremely helpful when leaders in important places have been on the other side and know what it's like. Take time to understand what this means. Whether putting yourself in the place of patients in healthcare or customers in another industry, you'll gain great insights, more finely honed senses, and a keener understanding of what you and your organization need to do to deliver a great experience.

Cleveland Clinic *Is* an Amazing Place

The organization is what it is today because of its long history of innovation, leadership, vision, and the hard work of a lot of people. You may read parts of my story here and think that Cleveland Clinic before Cosgrove was a driven, unfriendly machine that cared only about clinical work and not patients. Nothing could be further from the truth. Patients not only were provided high-quality care, but were, for the most part, treated with respect, compassion, and dignity. I'm confident that for every terrible story like mine, there were dozens of remarkable examples that paint a very different picture.

However, Cleveland Clinic was inconsistent. The organization did not have a singular patient-centered focus, and that needed to change. Cosgrove pointed the ship in the direction of patients, and we haven't looked back since. This book tells you how we sailed, smooth waters and otherwise.

Some might contend that it's acceptable for customer experiences to follow a typical bell-shaped distribution, with some terrible, most good, and a few extraordinary. In healthcare, however, the way we treat our customers—patients—should not be arrayed on a bell curve. We cannot accept anything less than the consistent delivery of safe, high-quality, compassionate, and empathetic care. Who would want to be the patient or family at the bottom of a bell-shaped experience curve? As I can tell you from personal experience, no one. And if my family was at the bottom, so were many others.

When we started our work, most of our frontline workforce, nurses and especially physicians, had no idea that our patient satisfaction was quantifiably inconsistent or even being measured. Many had never heard of the HCAHPS survey. Our inpatient satisfaction scores were among the lowest in the country. We were in the 5th percentile for the cleanliness of our hospital rooms. For how quiet our rooms were at night, we weren't much better, in the 5th percentile. Probably most disturbing of all, we were in the 14th and 16th percentile, respectively, for how well our physicians and nurses communicated with patients. Aggregating our scores, Cleveland Clinic was in the 16th percentile for all of the nearly 5,000 U.S. hospitals reporting data. In another external evaluation, the University HealthSystem Consortium (UHC) benchmark for patient-centeredness, we ranked 51 out of the 98 hospitals reporting at the time. For an organization perceived as a top medical center in the world and deemed a top hospital by *U.S. News & World Report*, having scores this low was bad for our patients and incompatible with our brand. Something had to be done.

Today, as a result of our patient experience initiative and other efforts, we have virtually transformed our organization, as shown in Figures 13.1 through 13.6. Our collective HCAHPS scores have moved from 16th to approximately the 66th percentile. Our individual domain scores in nurse and physician communication are at the 79th and 67th percentiles, respectively. Our reputation scores (overall rating) are above the 92nd percentile. We lead most HCAHPS domains against chief competitive peer groups, including the top five *U.S. News & World Report* hospitals and the largest academic health centers with 1,000 or more beds at a single site. Out of more than 400 participating hospitals, we now rank third in the UHC benchmark for patient-centeredness.

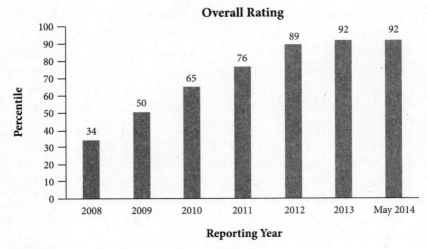

Figure 13.1   HCAHPS overall rating—main campus.

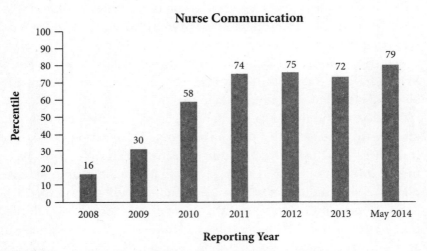

Figure 13.2   HCAHPS nurse communication rating—main campus.

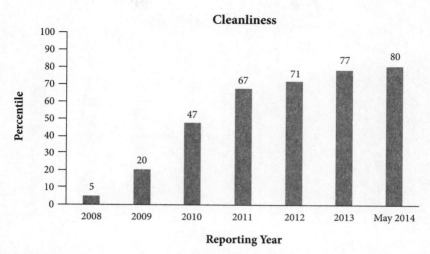

Figure 13.3 HCAHPS cleanliness rating—main campus.

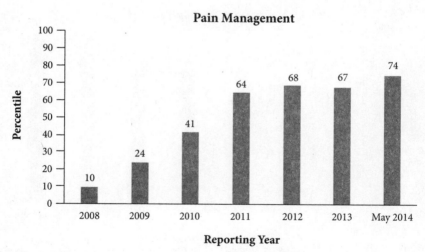

Figure 13.4 HCAHPS pain management rating—main campus.

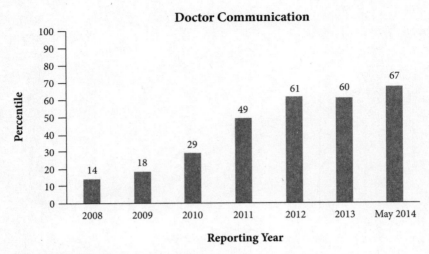

Figure 13.5   HCAHPS doctor communication rating—main campus.

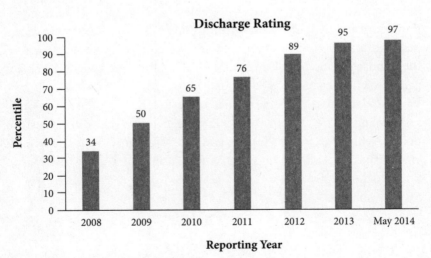

Figure 13.6   HCAHPS discharge rating—main campus.

Beyond the data, the improvement is palpable. Daily, we hear stories from patients or family members about how Cleveland Clinic has changed. Cosgrove often says that when he became CEO, more people complained than complimented him about Cleveland Clinic. Today, that's reversed. While improving the patient experience is a journey that never ends, with no final destination, we clearly have done much more than many believed possible to transform a major, tradition-steeped academic medical center into a patient- and family-centered environment.

At the beginning of the book, I asked you to think about medicine a hundred years ago. Now envision what medicine will be like a hundred years from today. There may be machines that can scan patients and instantly eradicate disease! But will the emotional and spiritual needs of humans change? Will patients seek treatment and cure irrespective of compassion, caring, and empathy, wanting only that their problems be fixed? I hope that the role of compassion, humanism, and empathy will still be strong.

The 360 continuum of patient experience must receive our constant attention. Processes and tactics require continual measurement and adjustment. We must strive to remind all those in our business that they count and that a high-performing culture with patients at the center requires us to be attentive to developing our caregivers. One slip back to the mindset of doing a job and not driving a passion can engender a dangerous event in safety, a lapse in quality, or a failure in service.

We also must make sure that we're listening to customers and responding to their needs. We tend to believe we know what's best for people, which frequently leads us to talk more and listen less. We must ensure that we understand patients as people and address their emotional and spiritual needs as well as their medical needs. Reciprocal to making sure we understand our patients is ensuring that our patients understand us. We're in the ultimate service business where the customer is not always right. We have an obligation to help patients and their families understand what's going to happen to them every step along the journey, but patients and their families must be good partners to us as well.

Twenty years ago, if you had talked to me about the patient experience, I would have wondered what you were talking about. Ten years ago, if you had said I would be leading efforts to improve the patient experience at Cleveland Clinic, I'd have laughed. Five years ago, a reporter challenged me to prove we were making a difference. Today, we have transformed an organization and are helping to lead an industry. In 2013 that reporter's company, HealthLeaders Media, picked me as one of 20 people who make healthcare better,[5] an amazing turn of events.

I know that an absolute focus on the patient and the family is the right thing to do, and it should be the default setting for everyone in this business. I'm fortunate to work in one of the world's best healthcare organizations, but even we can do better. The work is hard, and sustaining it requires constant attention. The letters I receive from patients, family members, and caregivers continue to fuel me to improve the patient experience. They remind me why we're here, and I challenge everyone reading this book who works in or around healthcare to use affecting patient stories to drive you as well.

Improving the experience for our patients is not a destination, but a journey. Success comes in incremental steps achieved by paying attention to the little things, holding people accountable, and pushing the strategy forward. The patient experience is not about making patients happy; it's about how we deliver care. Someday I hope that the patient experience is not a process or strategy that needs to be led by an executive, but simply a state of being for healthcare delivery across the world. This may be unrealistic or idealistic. But our focus must always be on improving care and how we deliver it, providing the safest and highest-quality medicine possible!

We're in an industry where our brand is defined by how well we care for people, and every little thing counts. A pilot once told me that everything on a flight checklist is there because it cost someone's life. Just achieving Six Sigma quality is not enough to ensure a successful experience. When considering enterprise-wide hospital metrics, one bad event out of 1,000 doesn't seem like a big deal to us as leaders, but that one event could have had dramatic consequences for an individual patient and his or her family, friends, and everyone around them. Minor errors lead to catastrophic events, and bad judgment or behaviors create experiences for individuals that they will never forget and from which they may never recover.

Our collective goal is simple: deliver the best possible experience to our patients—or as Ryan points out, reduce patient suffering. It's the right thing to do, it's how we would want to be taken care of, and it's how we would want our families to be treated. Success will not come quickly or easily, but will be achieved with leadership, strategy, focus, and determination. We must strive to do right—all of the time. We would accept nothing less for ourselves or our families; therefore, we should offer nothing less to the people we serve.

We Have a Responsibility to Lead

Many of Cleveland Clinic's best ideas come from studying the best practices of others, so one of our early goals was to help shape the emerging field of patient experience by sharing what we were learning and doing. We're both active listeners and sharers of information. We believe in bringing people together to network, exchange ideas, and learn, helping all to improve what we're doing for patients. But this is more than that. This is a movement.

In 2010 we established an annual Patient Experience: Empathy & Innovation Summit. When I convene it every year, I remind attendees that I'm just like them, someone working hard on the front lines to improve the experience for patients. I commit to helping them, and I ask them to help me by sharing information, exchanging ideas, and networking to advance our collective goal of improving the patient experience together. Attendance since our first year has grown to over 2,100 people representing 49 states and 39 countries, making this the largest independent summit of its kind in the world. We have attracted partners to help drive this very important change, including the American Hospital Association, the American Medical Group Association, the Association of Academic Health Centers, the Society of Hospital Medicine, and the University Health Systems Consortium. We're bringing together our collective thought leadership to drive more dialogue, and we're sharing what we know to help our colleagues improve.

The agendas reflect a diverse set of topics. Andrew C. Taylor, executive chairman of Enterprise Holdings, Inc., parent company of Alamo Rent-A-Car, Enterprise Rent-A-Car, and National Car Rental, opened the first summit with a passionate speech about the importance of customer service and the need to keep customers at the center of everything in business. Son of legendary founder Jack Taylor, our speaker credited Enterprise's customer-centric strategy as key to the company's enduring success. Coming from a well-regarded business leader in a very successful consumer organization, Taylor's remarks were tremendous reinforcement of the principles we believe important and transferable in healthcare.

Every year a sentinel event is the CEO panel composed of top hospital leaders from across the United States. Participants, in addition to Cosgrove, have included Kurt Newman of Children's National Health System, Marc Boom of Houston Methodist Hospital, David Feinberg of UCLA Health System, Michael Dowling of North Shore–Long Island Jewish Health System, Charles Sorenson of Intermountain Healthcare, and Robert Pryor of Baylor Scott & White Health. It's a robust, hour-long discussion about leadership, culture, and the patient experience. They share their insights, challenge each other, and take questions from the audience.

We've had an impressive array of speakers from a variety of different fields in and around healthcare delivery. Gerard van Grinsven, president and CEO of Cancer Treatment Centers of America, who came from The Ritz-Carlton Hotel Company, shared how management is helping to improve the emotional connectivity of patients with the organization. David Schlanger, CEO of WebMD, discussed enhancing the patient experience by helping consumers become more educated, better engaged, and more tightly connected to their health.

General Electric, an early sponsor, twice set up a *kiva*, a giant round room with whiteboards for walls. GE Healthcare's global design team, led by Bob Schwartz, invited attendees to illustrate their ideas on the walls. The kiva became a think tank on ways to improve the patient experience and impact care. GE also sponsored a speaker who shared innovative efforts to redesign the appearance of CT scanners at Children's Hospital of Pittsburgh to make them more kid-friendly. Each CT suite features a theme, such as pirate island adventure, in which the scanner is painted like a pirate ship and the room made to resemble a tropical island. Technicians and nurses play their roles using themed scripts to enhance the experience. Some may believe this is merely window dressing, but data collected by the medical center reveals that children's pain and anxiety levels decrease when they are imaged in these suites.

Every summit has speakers with amazing stories and vital impact, and it has become a success beyond anything we imagined. The hunger for knowledge and sharing shown at the summits demonstrated to us early on the need to keep people engaged in the topic year-round. We also believed that patients needed to be included in the conversation. As such, we founded the Association for Patient Experience (AfPE), www.patient-experience.org/Home.aspx, in 2010. This is an independent, nonprofit 501(c)(3) organization whose mission is "to improve the patient experience by providing healthcare providers; patients and their families; and others with information, education, networking opportunities, and related resources focused on best practices." We wanted the association to be free of commercial bias and not aligned with any business interests so that people would feel comfortable exchanging ideas and information. Membership is free, and thousands receive its newsletter, representing healthcare-aligned organizations worldwide.

If AfPE is the link to frontline caregivers and patients, the Institute for Innovation is the patient experience link back to large healthcare organizations. There is a huge knowledge gap in healthcare delivery. Currently, we simply don't have the ability to bring together large amounts of hospital data from a wide variety of sources to understand complicated patient problems and improve hospital processes. When Pat Ryan took over Press Ganey, he wanted to start a nonprofit research institute to benefit the greater healthcare community. The new institute's purpose would be to bring together health systems to share information, fill in the research gaps, and solve common problems. I was excited by the prospect, as no one except the government was trying to do this. Could we look at millions of patient data points from multiple systems and answer questions, such as what drives readmission, how do you increase patient treatment compliance, and how do you manage a patient's experience? Such information could substantially impact the way we deliver healthcare worldwide.

I agreed to participate as a founding board member but wanted to make certain that information the institute discovered would be available to frontline caregivers from any organization seeking to improve patient care. Ryan agreed, and we determined that the AfPE would be an important distribution channel for the findings and best practices. The association would manage dissemination to any hospital or caregiver needing the information to help improve patient care. It is an exciting collaboration that promises to drive research and push results to the people who need it most.

At the 4th Annual Patient Experience Summit, the AfPE was the first to introduce a peer-reviewed journal exclusively dedicated to improving how we deliver care to patients, the *Journal of Patient Experience*. The cover story in the inaugural issue recounts a physician's harrowing emergency department experience with her dying teenage daughter and highlights the interconnectedness between patients, providers, and healthcare organizations. A feature article by Micah Solomon, "Finding the Heart of [Hospital]ity: Patient Satisfaction and the Healthcare Experience," discusses parallels between delivering hospitality and a great patient experience. With its expanding editorial board of leading academicians, this journal will help advance patient experience scholarship.

There will be a new health education center on the grounds of Cleveland Clinic. It is a wonderful new partnership with Case Western Reserve University (CWRU), my medical school alma mater. It's the first center in the world where nursing, dental, social work, and medical students learn together. When I was in medical school, we never attended classes or worked with nursing students. Imagine the possibilities! If we're to promote the culture we need for developing high-performing teams and high reliability in the delivery of healthcare, this is the place to do it.

CWRU is a pioneer in the field of interprofessionalism for improving care delivery. Cleveland Clinic is a leader in the patient experience, with programs like its physician communication training; a separate program was designed and developed for midlevel providers and nurses. Imagine a scenario in which the basics of interprofessionalism are taught in undergraduate academic programs, with that same model carried through postgraduate medical education and early nursing career development and then becoming the operational standard for delivery of care in the hospital setting and the maintenance of health. The opportunity to transform the delivery of care and the patient experience will be incredible!

President Obama has previously referred to Cleveland Clinic as "one of the best healthcare systems in the world." He honored the Clinic and Dr. Cosgrove by asking him to consider becoming Secretary of Veterans Affairs in hopes that he would transform the VA health system in a similar way to how he has transformed Cleveland Clinic. The VA health system is not unlike any other healthcare system in the United States. Everyday, caregivers walk into the doors of VA facilities around the country determined to work hard and do what is right for our veterans—we must never lose sight of that. Are they perfect at what they do? Of course not, and no one is! Are there processes that can be improved? Can the culture be better aligned around the patient? Absolutely! It is an organization that delivers high-quality care to our nation's heroes, but it needs to realign its focus on wrapping that care around more patient-centeredness. Imagine if the Veterans Administration adopted a "Veterans First" initiative; aligned its work force around serving its most important customer, veterans; defined its focus as safety, quality, and satisfaction; and attacked other things we know are important to delivering on an exceptional patient experience such as patient access. The Veterans system would achieve a patient-centered care delivery model like any other model healthcare system in the world.

Patient Experience Is Global

Just as the Hippocratic oath binds physicians worldwide in commitment to ethical and moral treatment of the patient, a focus on the patient experience—the obligation to keep the patient at the center of everything we do—similarly binds global healthcare organizations and leaders. Healthcare providers around the world experience the same joys and possess the same challenges and opportunities that we do. Not surprisingly, they want to provide safe, high-quality care for their citizens, and they want it delivered with compassion, empathy, and humanity.

Cleveland Clinic's "Empathy: The Human Connection to Patient Care" video has been viewed in more than 200 countries, and I have personally shown it to healthcare professionals from Canada, China, Ghana, Mexico, the Netherlands, Nigeria, Saudi Arabia, South Korea, Turkey, United Arab Emirates, the United Kingdom, and the West Indies. I study people's faces while they watch the video, and reactions are startlingly similar: silence and visible emotion, including the shedding of tears. These universal reactions are not coincidental. The video has real meaning; it makes a tangible connection to their professional calling.

Cleveland Clinic, in partnership with Mubadala Healthcare, is establishing Cleveland Clinic Abu Dhabi. The 23-acre facility, the largest healthcare build in the world, is designed to bring world-class, Western-style medicine to the Middle East. Marc Harrison, my friend and colleague, is the CEO. He will tell you that the entire facility is designed with the patient and family at the center of operations. Harrison grew up in Cleveland Clinic's culture and is transporting every piece of this culture some 8,000 miles away to deliver a similar experience. It will become a model for global healthcare delivery and the patient and family experience.

A few years ago, I chaired a patient experience track for the Arab Health Congress Leaders in Healthcare Conference. Arab Health Congress is the world's largest healthcare conference organizer, and its Leaders series highlights important industry topics. Thomas J. Miller, CEO of customer solutions for Siemens AG Healthcare Sector, delivered the opening address on the critical role technology will play in patient-centered care advances. Newman of Children's National Health System in Washington, D.C., and Harrison of Cleveland Clinic Abu Dhabi traded discussion points about aligning doctors with the idea of putting patients first and fostering the right culture to deliver effective, safe, and high-quality healthcare. This was one of the first international sessions exclusively dedicated to the patient experience and was one of the best attended of the conference.

The former Saudi Arabia minister of health, Abdullah bin Abdulaziz Al-Rabeeah, adopted the Patients First motto for his organization. In his words, "'Patients First' is essentially meant to convey a message to all health practitioners in the kingdom . . . on the crucial importance of pursuing . . . this course of action."[1] His successor, the interim minister of health, Adel Fakieh, has made improving the patient experience a top strategic priority. The brand of patient experience is slightly different, as the kingdom uses the phrase "patient rights and relations." But the goals are collective—ensuring that patients and their families have respectful, dignified, and empathetic healthcare—and our challenges are similar: getting everyone in healthcare to understand and align around that.

Cleveland Clinic also partnered with the Ministry of Health to hold a patient rights and relations conference in Yanbu, Saudi Arabia, attended by some 400 ministry officials. Assisting with the conference was Wael Kaawach, a Harvard University–trained orthopedic surgeon and CEO of Healthcare Development Holding Co., a large healthcare operations consortium in Saudi Arabia. His commitment to patient-centered-ness is fueled by the desire to improve the care of people in his country. Kaawach reminds me that culture is a critical element in illness and must be factored into the experience. "Muslims receive illness and death with patience and prayers. They consider an illness as atonement for their sins," he says.[2] In addition to compassion and empathy, he stressed that in his culture caregivers must demonstrate mercy. Kaawach's passion for the topic and his desire to lead change are driven by more than just a commitment to his people. He is a cancer survivor who has experienced the other side of the healthcare system he is endeavoring to fix. Kaawach represents a common worldwide thread. Efforts to improve the patient experience are typically driven by the individual passion of people on the front lines that have experienced the challenges of patient-centeredness firsthand.

At an Abu Dhabi Health Services Company (SEHA) leadership retreat, chairman and managing director Saif Bader Al Qubaisi stood on stage, recognizing and thanking various leaders for their dedication and organizational commitment. He acknowledged to the roomful of caregivers, "What you do is very hard work." The leadership at SEHA is currently leading a transformation effort to center the entire organization around the patient and drive employee engagement.

Wang-Jun Lee, chairman and CEO of Myongji Hospital and publisher of the *Korean Doctors' Weekly* in South Korea, has invested heavily in the patient experience. Myongji Hospital's new cancer center has infusion suites that overlook manicured gardens. Leveraging technology, cancer patients receiving linear accelerator therapy employ a card that activates preselected treatment room music, aromatherapy, light therapy, and images supplied by the patient. All of this investment and technology is for one purpose: to improve the patient experience. Similar interest in the patient experience is thriving at Seoul's Samsung Medical Center and Severance Hospital of Yonsei University Medical Center.

David L. Longworth, chairman of Cleveland Clinic's Medicine Institute, and I opened a leadership development conference sponsored by General Electric Corporation in Istanbul, Turkey, attended by government and hospital leaders throughout the Middle East and Africa. We challenged participants to think about the patient experience in their countries, asking them to discuss barriers and ways to improve. At the report-out, the energy was electric. Every group agreed with the core tenets: patients first, strategic priority, and leadership. Attendees never before exposed to patient experience concepts became converts. After our session, one of the leaders from an African healthcare facility collared me and said, "You have described who we are and our problems. We have not connected our people—our employees—to the patients, and we need to do this." Months after the talk, every government and hospital represented in the audience is seeking Cleveland Clinic's guidance on transforming its organization to improve the patient experience.

At the opening of one of the annual Hong Kong Hospital Authority conventions, CEO P. Y. Leung discussed that when delivering healthcare in the future, "care, not cure," is what will be important.[3] He reviewed one of the authority's strategic pillars, person-centered care. Throughout the conference, there were discussions of teamwork, safety, and culture.

At the Canadian Conference on Physician Leadership, hosted in conjunction with the Canadian Medical Association and the Canadian Society of Physician Executives, I gave a keynote on the importance of patient experience for the delivery of high-value care. Canada is a model for integrated healthcare delivery, home to some of the best physicians and medical care in the world. At the conference many physicians came up to me and said it is absolutely time that we also become the model for patient-centered care. Louis Hugo Francescutti, president of the Canadian Medical Association, himself a renowned international speaker on culture, agreed that Canadian Healthcare's challenge, like everyone else's, is to get every caregiver aligned around the patient.

I have the honor of knowing some of the most important leaders in healthcare, and I've had the privilege of addressing hospitals, medical societies, physician groups, and boards across the world. Even when I am with leaders from businesses unrelated to healthcare, the themes are the same: the need for customer centricity is paramount. It's remarkable for me to see and hear about other people's work. I have a requirement: when I travel on patient experience business, I must bring back at least one idea to help us; otherwise the trip was a failure. We must learn from each other, share information, and, together, improve what we do for patients.

The need to drive toward more patient-centeredness and implement patient experience strategies is not unique to my organization, your organization, or the United States. It resonates around the world because it's the right thing to do, and it impacts organizational effectiveness across a variety of areas, including safety and quality.

An incident that now reminds me every day why this is important occurred at the patient experience summit held just shy of my fifth anniversary in the CXO role. Johnson & Johnson, our presenting sponsor, erected a "caring wall." It was a place where patients and caregivers shared stories and insights about what's important, and a professional illustrator sketched out visual representations of their thoughts. There were many images that represented empathy, storytelling, love, and care. But the one that resonated most, the one that speaks to the "why," was the illustration that it "could be my mother, father, child, me" (Figure E.1). Do we really need any other visual?

Cosgrove recently remarked to me, "One of the most important things I've done in my career is to define why we're here—for patients."[4] He introduced Patients First to begin the journey of aligning Cleveland Clinic. We were fortunate to start our journey before the patient experience became a national healthcare priority, which is garnering increasing attention not just from regulatory agencies but from employers, payers, and patients around the world.

This is your opportunity to lead. This movement is critical to how you deliver care. Join us!

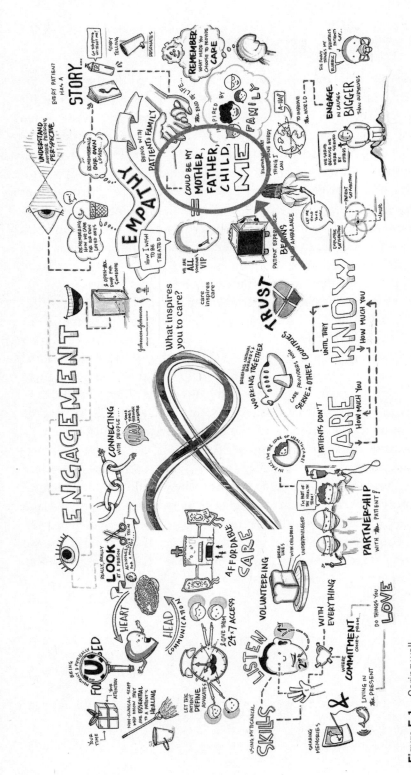

Figure E.1 Caring wall.

238

Notes

Preface

1. Bruce G. Wolff, James W. Fleshman, David E. Beck, John H. Pemberton, and Steven D. Wexner, eds., *The ASCRS Textbook of Colon and Rectal Surgery*, 1st ed. (New York: Springer Science + Business Media, LLC, 2007), 584–600.
2. "Inflammatory Bowel Disease (IBD)," The Centers for Disease Control and Prevention, accessed March 24, 2014, www.cdc.gov/ibd/.
3. Dana Bernstein and Feza Remzi (Chair, Department of Colorectal Surgery, Cleveland Clinic), in multiple discussions with the author over the period January–April 2014.

Chapter 2

1. Sherwin B. Nuland, *Doctors: The Biography of Medicine* (New York: Alfred P. Knopf, 1988), xv.
2. Toby Cosgrove (Chairman and CEO, Cleveland Clinic), in discussion with the author, October 21, 2013.
3. Delos "Toby" Cosgrove, *The Cleveland Clinic Way* (New York: McGraw-Hill, 2013), 116.
4. Cosgrove, in discussion with the author, October 21, 2013.
5. Jon Picoult, "The Watermark Consulting 2013 Customer Experience ROI Study," *WaterRemarks* (blog), April 2, 2013, www.watermarkconsult.net/blog/2013/04/02/the-watermark-consulting-2013-customer-experience-roi-study/.
6. Megan Burns, Harley Manning, Allison Stone, and Jason Knott, *The Customer Experience Index, 2013* (Cambridge, MA: Forrester Research, 2013).
7. "Culture & Diversity," Disney Careers, accessed June 24, 2014, http://disney careers.com/en/working-here/culture-diversity/.
8. Alan Siegel (CEO of Siegelvision), in discussion with the author, July 7, 2014.
9. John T. Chambers (Chairman and CEO, Cisco Systems), in discussion with Cleveland Clinic executive leadership team, March 8, 2012.
10. Harley Manning, "Outside In" (lecture, 3rd Annual Patient Experience: Empathy & Innovation Summit, Cleveland, OH, May 20–22, 2012).
11. The metaphor dates back to a 1988 quote from a crew member on a burning oil-drilling platform in the North Sea and has been adopted by organizational change experts for decades in discussing motivation for change. Daryl Conner,

"The Real Story of the Burning Platform," *Change Thinking* (blog), August 15, 2012, www.connerpartners.com/frameworks-and-processes/the-real-story-of-the-burning-platform.

12. "The 8-Step Process for Leading Change," Kotter International, accessed January 21, 2013, http://www.kotterinternational.com/our-principles/changesteps.

13. Melvin Samsom (Chairman of the Executive Board, Radboud University Nijmegen Medical Center) and Lucien Engelen (Director, REshape & Innovation Center, Radboud University Nijmegen Medical Center), in discussion with the author, November 2013.

Chapter 3

1. "CEO Report: Optimism on the Upswing," 12, HealthLeaders Media, January 2013.

2. "Patient Experience Beyond HCAHPS: Care Coordination and Cultural Transformation," HealthLeaders Media Council Special Report, August 2013.

3. Delos "Toby" Cosgrove, *The Cleveland Clinic Way* (New York: McGraw-Hill, 2013), 109.

4. A story recounted by Cosgrove and Medoff Barnett at the 1st Annual Patient Experience: Empathy & Innovation Summit. May 25, 2010.

5. Paul Hagen, "The Rise of the Chief Customer Officer," Paul Hagen's Blog, Forrester Research Inc., January 24, 2011, http://blogs.forrester.com/paul_hagen/11-01-24-the_rise_of_the_chief_customer_officer.

6. John Commins, "Experience the Patient," *HealthLeaders* magazine, June 2012, accessed online February 1, 2014, www.healthleadersmedia.com/content/MAG-281208/Experience-the-Patient.

7. Anthony Cirillo, "The New CEO—Chief Experience Officer," *HealthLeaders News*, March 28, 2007, accessed online February 2, 2014, www.healthleadersmedia.com/content/88259/topic/WS_HLM2_HOM/The-New-CEO Chief-Experience-Officer.html##.

8. Marc Boom (President and CEO, Methodist Houston), in discussion with the author, September 2013.

9. David T. Feinberg, CEO panel discussion, 4th Annual Patient Experience: Empathy & Innovation Summit, May 20, 2013.

10. Steven Glass (Chief Financial Officer, Cleveland Clinic), in discussion with the author, March 27, 2012

11. J. Michael Henderson (Chief Quality Officer, Cleveland Clinic), in discussion with the author, April 1, 2014.

Chapter 4

1. "Blind Men and an Elephant," *Wikipedia*, last modified January 15, 2014, accessed January 22, 2014, http://en.wikipedia.org/wiki/Blind_men_and_an_elephant.

2. Jacqueline Fellows, "New Approaches to Patient Experience," *HealthLeaders* magazine, August 13, 2013, www.healthleadersmedia.com/content/MAG-295064/New-Approaches-to-Patient-Experience.

3. Jennifer Robison, "What Is the Patient Experience?," *Gallup Business Journal*, September 30, 2010, accessed January 22, 2013, http://businessjournal.gallup.com/content/143258/patient-experience.aspx.

4. Kai Falkenberg, "Why Rating Your Doctor Is Bad for Your Health," *Forbes*, January 2, 2014, accessed January 22, 2014, www.forbes.com/sites/kaifalkenberg/2013/01/02/why-rating-your-doctor-is-bad-for-your-health/.

5. Harley Manning (Vice President and Research Director Serving Customer Experience Professionals, Forrester Research), presentation at the 3rd Annual Patient Experience Summit, Cleveland, OH, May 21, 2012.

6. *Merriam-Webster's Collegiate Dictionary*, accessed January 23, 2014, www.merriam-webster.com/dictionary/experience.

7. Amy Fiern, David Betts, and Toni Tribble, "The Patient Experience: Strategies and Approaches for Providers to Achieve and Maintain a Competitive Advantage," accessed January 23, 2014, www.deloitte.com/assets/Dcom-UnitedStates/Local%20Assets/Documents/us_lshc_ThePatientExperience_072809.pdf.

8. Robison, "What Is the Patient Experience?"

9. "Defining Patient Experience," The Beryl Institute, accessed January 23, 2014, www.berylinstitute.org/?page=definingpatientexp.

10. D. A. Redelmeier, J. Katz, and D. Kahneman, "Memories of Colonoscopy: A Randomized Trial," *Pain* 104 (July 2003): 187–194.

11. Jennifer Woodward. "Effects of Rounding on Patient Satisfaction and Patient Safety on a Medical-Surgical Unit," *Clinical Nurse Specialist*, 23, no. 4 (2009): 200-206.

12. Leah Binder, "The Courage and Triumph of the Patient," *Forbes Pharma and Healthcare* (blog), December 11, 2013, www.forbes.com/sites/leahbinder/2013/12/11/the-courage-and-triumph-of-the-patient/.

Chapter 5

1. John D. Clough, *To Act as a Unit: The Story of the Cleveland Clinic* (Cleveland, OH: Cleveland Clinic Press, 2005), 1-47.

2. A. Marc Harrison (Chief Executive Officer of Cleveland Clinic Abu Dhabi), in discussion with the author, August 2, 2014.

3. Joseph Scaminace (CEO OM Group, Inc.), in conversation with the author, August 2009.

4. Michael Watkins, "Organizational Immunology," *Harvard Business Review* (blog), June 11, 2007, http://blogs.hbr.org/2007/06/organizational-immunology-part-1/.

5. Melvin Samsom (Chairman of the Executive Board, Radboud University Nijmegen Medical Center), in discussion with the author, November 2013.

6. Paul Hagen, Harley Manning, and Jennifer Peterson, *How to Build a Customer-Centric Culture* (Cambridge, MA: Forrester Research, 2010), 4.

7. Edgar H. Schein, *Organizational Culture and Leadership*, 4th ed. (San Francisco: Jossey-Bass, 2010).

8. Elizabeth G. Chambers, Mark Foulon, Helen Handfield-Jones, Steven M. Hankin, and Edward G. Michaels III, "The War for Talent," *McKinsey Quarterly* 3 (1998): 44–57.

9. *Wikipedia*, s.v. "talent management," last modified October 2, 2013, http://en.wikipedia.org/wiki/talent_management#cite_note-war-2.

10. Jenn Lim, keynote at 5th Annual Patient Experience: Empathy & Innovation Summit, May 19, 2014.

11. "Careers at The Ritz-Carlton," The Ritz-Carlton, accessed February 12, 2014, www.marriott.com/ritz-carlton-careers/default.mi.

12. The Joint Commission, *National Patient Safety Goals* (2010), accessed February 12, 2014, www.jointcommission.org/assets/1/18/hap_2010_npsg.pdf.

Chapter 6

1. James I. Merlino, "Conversations with the CEO: Dr. Marc Boom of Houston Methodist," Association for Patient Experience, September 30, 2013, www.patient-experience.org/Education-Research/Articles/Conversations-with-the-CEO-Dr-Marc-Boom-of-Houston.aspx.

2. The I CARE concept was developed in 2004 in an emergency medical services Ethics and Values course taught by educator Chris Le Baudour, who challenged students to identify personal core values. In a brainstorming session, the people in the class distilled their individual lists to the now-famous five. Le Baudour subsequently collaborated with colleague Chris Nollette, PhD, to sort the values into the recognized I CARE acronym, a framework widely used in healthcare and other settings. "The I CARE Story," I CARE, accessed February 15, 2014, www.icarevalues.org/story.

3. Adapted from Dr. William Glasser's work on retention rates.

4. Lead reviewer, Joint Commission, debrief with Clinic executive team, October 21, 2010.

Chapter 7

1. Association of American Medical Colleges, *Medical Student Education: Debt, Costs, and Loan Repayment Fact Card*, October 2013, accessed March 19, 2014, www.aamc.org/download/152968/data/debtfactcard.pdf.

2. Althea Chang, "The Most and Least Trusted Occupations," *Yahoo Finance* (blog), August 9, 2013, http://finance.yahoo.com/blogs/big-data-download/most-least-trusted-occupations-160721749.html.

3. "Honesty/Ethics in Professions," Gallup, Inc., December 5–8, 2013, accessed March 19, 2014, www.gallup.com/poll/1654/honesty-ethics-professions.aspx.

4. "Doctor Contests Revocation of Hospital Privileges," Associated Press, January 22, 2014.

5. Zack Budryk, "Hospital Bullies Pose a Danger to Patient Safety," *Fierce Healthcare* (blog), February 3, 2014, www.fiercehealthcare.com/story/hospital-bullies-pose-danger-patient-safety/2014-02-03.

6. Ibid.

7. Thomas H. Lee, "Turning Doctors into Leaders," *Harvard Business Review*, April 2010, 50–58.

8. Thomas H. Lee and Toby Cosgrove, "Engaging Doctors in the Health Care Revolution," *Harvard Business Review*, June 2014, 3–9.

9. Ibid.

10. "How Does Your Doctor Compare?," *Consumer Reports Health: Special Report for Massachusetts Residents*, May 31, 2012.

Chapter 8

1. Institute of Medicine, *Crossing the Quality Chasm: A New Health System for the 21st Century* (Washington, DC: National Academies Press, 2001).

2. "The CAHPS Program," Agency for Healthcare Research and Quality, accessed July 9, 2014, https://cahps.ahrq.gov/about-cahps/cahps-program/index.html.

3. "HCAHPS: Patients' Perspectives of Care Survey," Centers for Medicare & Medicaid Services, accessed February 4, 2014, www.cms.gov/Medicare/Quality-Initiatives-Patient-Assessment-Instruments/HospitalQualityInits/HospitalHCAHPS.html.

4. Ibid.

5. J. A. O'Malley, A. M. Zaslavsky, R. D. Hays, K. A. Hepner, et al., "Exploratory Factor Analysis of the CAHPS Hospital Pilot Survey Responses Across and Within Medical, Surgical, and Obstetric Services," *Health Services Research 40*, no. 6 (2005): 2078–2088.

6. M. N. Elliot, D. E. Kanouse, C. A. Edwards, and L. H. Hibourne, "Components of Care Vary in Importance for Overall Patient-Reported Experience by Type of Hospitalization." *Medical Care 47*, no. 8 (2009): 842–848.

7. "Patient-Mix Coefficients for July 2014 Publicly Reported HCAHPS Results," www.hcahpsonline.org/files/Coefficients_for_July_2014_Public_Reporting_03-18-2014.pdf.

8. D. M. Clarke, I. H. Minas, and G.W. Stuart, "The Prevalence of Psychiatric Morbidity in General Hospital Patients.," *Aust NZJ Psychiatry* 25 (1991): 322–329.

Chapter 9

1. *Wikipedia*, s.v. "best practices," last modified January 21, 2014, http://en .wikipedia.org/wiki/Best_practice.
2. Margo A. Halm, "Hourly Rounds: What Does the Evidence Indicate?," *American Journal of Critical Care* (November 2009): 5814, doi:10.4037/ajcc2009350.

Chapter 10

1. Micah Solomon, "Improving the Patient Experience: Why Hospitals Consulting Other Hospitals Won't Fix Healthcare," *Forbes*, June 20, 2014.
2. Robert Johnston, "Towards a Better Understanding of Service Excellence," *Managing Service Quality* 14, no. 2/3 (2004): 129–133.
3. *Wikipedia*, s.v. "service excellence—healthcare," last modified January 27, 2014, http://en.wikipedia.org/wiki/Service_Excellence_%E2%80%93_Health_Care.
4. Adapted from Paul R. Timm, *Customer Service: Career Success Through Customer Satisfaction* (Upper Saddle River, NJ: Prentice-Hall, 2001), 59.
5. AboutFace, http://aboutfacecorp.com/services/customer-experience-serivces/ cx-products/service-recovery-index/.
6. Myron D. Fottler, Robert C. Ford, and Cherrill P. Heaton, *Achieving Service Excellence: Strategies for Healthcare* (Chicago: Health Administration Press, 2009), 359–382.
7. Daniel Goleman, *Emotional Intelligence* (New York: Bantam, 1995).
8. *Every Life Has a Story . . . If We Only Bother to Read It*, CFA Properties, Inc., accessed February 19, 2014, www.cathyfamily.com/resources/videos/every -life-has-a-story.aspx.

Chapter 11

1. Osbourne Bodden (Minister of Health, Cayman Islands), in discussion with the author, October 16, 2013.
2. M. K. Marvel, R. M. Epstein, K. Flowers, and H. B. Beckman, "Soliciting the Patient's Agenda: Have We Improved?," *Journal of the American Medical Association* 281, no. 3 (January 20, 1999): 283–287, www.ncbi.nlm.nih.gov/ pubmed/9918487.
3. David L. Longworth, MD (Associate Chief of Staff for Professional Staff Affairs, Cleveland Clinic), in discussion with the author.
4. The State of New York pioneered a similar approach when developing its Cardiac Surgery Reporting System. Since 1989, the state has collected and pub- licly released cardiac surgery outcome data. Open-heart surgeons and surgery

programs with poor outcomes were forced to improve or cease operations, to the ultimate benefit of patients. See "Adult Cardiac Surgery in New York State," New York State Department of Health, accessed February 9, 2014, www.health .ny.gov/statistics/diseases/cardiovascular/.

5. A relative value unit (RVU) is a measure of value used in the Medicare reimbursement formula for physician services. See "The Medicare Physician Payment Schedule," *American Medical Association*, accessed February 9, 2014, www.ama-assn.org/ama/pub/physician-resources/solutions-managing -your-practice/coding-billing-insurance/medicare/the-medicare-physician -payment-schedule.page.

6. James I. Merlino and Robert W. Coulton, "Enhancing Physician Communication with Patients at Cleveland Clinic," *Group Practice Journal* 61, no. 2 (February 2012): 24–32.

7. Richard M. Frankel and Terry Stein, "Getting the Most out of the Clinical Encounter: The Four Habits Model," *The Permanente Journal* 3, no. 3 (Fall 1999): 79–88, http://xnet.kp.org/permanentejournal/fall99pj/habits.html.

8. A standardized patient is an individual trained to act as a patient for the purposes of medical instruction.

9. L. M. L. Ong, J. C. J. M. DeHaes, A. M. Hoos, and F. B. Lammes, "Doctor-Patient Communication: A Review of the Literature," *Social Science & Medicine* 40 (1995): 903-918.

10. Debra L. Roter, Judith A. Hall, David E. Kern, Randol Barker, Karan A. Cole, and Robert P Roca, "Improving Physicians Interviewing Skills and Reducing Patients Emotional Distress: A Randomized Clinical Trial," *Archives of Internal Medicine* 155, no. 17 (1995): 1877-1884.

11. Kelly B. Haskard Zolnierrek, and M. Robin DiMatteo, "Physician Communication and Patient Adherence to Treatment: A Meta-analysis," *Medical Care* 47, no. 8 (August 2009): 826–834.

12. M. A. Stewart, "Effective Physician-Patient Communication and Health Outcomes: A Review," *CMAJ* 152, no. 9 (May 1995): 1423–1433.

13. Wendy Levinson, Rita Gorawara-Bhat, and Jennifer Lamb, "A Study of Patient Clues and Physician Responses in Primary Care and Surgical Settings," *Journal of the American Medical Association* 284, no. 8 (2000): 1021–1027.

14. A. L. Suchman, D. Roter, M. Lipkin Jr., and the Collaborative Study Group of the Task Force on Medical Interviewing, "Physician Satisfaction with Primary Care Office Visits," *Medical Care* 31, no. 12 (1993): 1083–92.

15. Evelyn Theiss, "Art of Patient Satisfaction Meets the Science of Medicine," *Cleveland Plain Dealer*, June 11, 2012, www.cleveland.com/healthfit/index. ssf/2012/06/the_art_of_patient_satisfaction.html.

Chapter 12

1. "About Dave," e-Patient Dave, accessed March 9, 2014, www.epatientdave.com/about-dave/.
2. Stacy Lu, "What Makes a Doctor-Patient Partnership Flourish?," *TEDMED 2012* (blog), October 22, 2012, http://blog.tedmed.com/?p=2178.
3. *Merriam-Webster's Collegiate Dictionary*, accessed March 9, 2014, www.merriam-webster.com/dictionary/partner.
4. *The Free Dictionary*, accessed March 9, 2014, www.thefreedictionary.com/partner.
5. Michael K. Paasche-Orlow, Ruth M. Parker, Julie A. Gazmararian, Lynn T. Nielsen-Bohlman, and Rima R. Rudd, "The Prevalence of Limited Health Literacy," *Journal of General Internal Medicine* 20, no. 2 (February 2005): 175–184.
6. L. Woicehovich, M.L. Rivera, J.I. Merlino, "Ask 3/Teach 3: Improving Medication Communication Scores and Patient Safety," *Group Practice Journal* (February 2013): 20–28.
7. Morgan Gleason interview by Deirdre Mylod, 5th Annual Patient Experience: Empathy & Innovation Summit, May 19, 2014.
8. Joanne Zeroske (President, Marymount Hospital, Cleveland Clinic Community Hospitals), in discussion with the author, July 8, 2014.
9. Institute for Patient- and Family-Centered Care, *Changing Hospital "Visiting" Policies and Practices: Supporting Family Presence and Participation* (Bethesda, MD, October 2010), accessed March 9, 2014, www.ipfcc.org/visiting.pdf.

Chapter 13

1. Jeffrey Galles, MD, e-mail conversation, February 2, 2014.
2. Program Evaluation and Review Technique (PERT), a tool used in project management.
3. Beth E. Mooney (Chairman and CEO, KeyCorp), in discussion with the author, May 2010.
4. Larry Ruvo conversation with Siegfried Fischbacker, 1st annual Patient Experience: Empathy & Innovation Summit, May 25, 2010.
5. "20 People Who Make Healthcare Better—2013," HealthLeaders Media, December 16, 2013.

Epilogue

1. "Minister of Health Inaugurates the First Patient Relations Symposium," Ministry of Health, Kingdom of Saudi Arabia, November 23, 2011, accessed March 14, 2014, www.moh.gov.sa/en/Ministry/MediaCenter/News/Pages/NEWS-2011-11-23-003.aspx.

2. Wael Fayez Kaawach, MD, MBA (CEO, Healthcare Development Holding Co., Saudi Arabia), in discussion with the author, March 3, 2013.
3. P. Y. Leung, MD, "Creating a Systemic Vision for Future Health," keynote address, Hong Kong Hospital Authority Convention, Hong Kong, May 7, 2014.
4. Delos M. Cosgrove, MD (President and CEO, Cleveland Clinic), in discussion with the author, May 2014.

Index

About the Author

James Merlino, MD, is the Chief Experience Officer of Cleveland Clinic Health System and is a practicing staff colorectal surgeon. He is the founder and current president of the Association for Patient Experience. He leads initiatives to improve the patient experience, physician-patient communication, patient access, and referring physician relations across the Cleveland Clinic Health System. He speaks to boards, physicians, and other healthcare leaders throughout the world on the importance of aligning healthcare culture around the patient and delivering on strategies to improve the patient experience. He has authored several articles and is widely quoted in publications. His work and comments have appeared in *Harvard Business Review*, *Forbes*, the *Wall Street Journal*, and Yahoo Finance, among many other outlets. In 2013, *HealthLeaders* magazine named him one of "20 People Who Make Healthcare Better."

Dr. Merlino received his undergraduate degree in business administration at Baldwin-Wallace College and his medical degree from Case Western Reserve University School of Medicine. He completed his residency training in general surgery at University Hospitals of Cleveland, and his fellowship in colorectal surgery at Cleveland Clinic. During his residency, he took a two-year research sabbatical to complete an AHRQ-funded research fellowship in health services research. Dr. Merlino is certified by the American Board of Colon and Rectal Surgery and the American Board of General Surgery. His wife, Amy, is a maternal-fetal medicine specialist at Cleveland Clinic.

American healthcare is in crisis. It doesn't have to be.

Learn how Cleveland Clinic works so well —and why it should be the model for the nation.

"A brilliant doctor and leader lays out practical and thought-provoking prescriptions for America's healthcare future. A must-read."
—Jack Welch, former Chairman and CEO of General Electric Company